ALSO BY MARTIN MARTY

# THE
# CHRISTIAN WORLD

# Martin Marty

# THE
# CHRISTIAN WORLD

## A Global History

A MODERN LIBRARY CHRONICLES BOOK

THE MODERN LIBRARY

NEW YORK

2009 Modern Library Paperback Edition

Copyright © 2007 by Martin E. Marty

Published in the United States by Modern Library, an imprint of
The Random House Publishing Group, a division of
Random House, Inc., New York.

MODERN LIBRARY and the TORCHBEARER Design are registered
trademarks of Random House, Inc.

Originally published in hardcover in the United States by
Modern Library, an imprint of The Random House
Publishing Group, a division of Random House, Inc., in 2008.

LIBRARY OF CONGRESS CATALOGING-IN-PUBLICATION DATA
Marty, Martin
The Christian world: a global history/by Martin Marty.
p. cm.
Includes index.
ISBN 978-0-8129-7677-9
1. Church history. I. Title.
BR145.3.M38 2007
270—dc22      2007019599

Printed in the United States of America

www.modernlibrary.com

246897531

To my grandchildren and great-grandchildren
Global citizens in the making

# CONTENTS

# INTRODUCTION

## LOOKING DOWN, LOOKING BACK

Two millennia after the birth of Jesus Christ the faith of two billion people around the globe is named after him. Telling their story in two hundred pages or two hundred volumes forces tellers to choose proper distances and appropriate perspectives for the task. Constant turbulences mark that story, so it is appropriate to view global Christianity as one might a tropical storm. Typically observers look at such storms, especially hurricanes, from four viewpoints. Studying a grand disturbance of winds and rain from satellite camera distance provides one important kind of knowledge. Closer in, flying safely within the very eye of the hurricane, those aboard weather-monitoring airplanes make available a second kind of information. Next, informed experts who carry responsibilities on the ground—weather-forecasters, medics, mass-communicators, clergy, and rescuers—offer still closer-up pictures. Fourth, surviving victims caught in the path of the hurricane have most at stake and most to tell about their innumerable and diverse experiences.

My perspective here combines information and reporting chiefly from the second and third of these viewpoints. The first we would leave to those philosophers and theologians who work with vast theories, not intimate narratives. As for the fourth approach, local reporters and historians of the Christian third of the human race and their millions of ancestors have to deal with far too many particulars to fit these into two hundred or two billion pages.

Briskly, then, I approach the subject, tempted to say more about methods and scope but aware that doing so would cut into space for the story itself.

A provocative theme, one which is so obvious that it is easy to overlook, provides the thread or the core of this version of the story. Christianity, like its parent, Judaism, and its kin, Islam, is fiercely devoted to One God. Unlike the other two major monotheistic, or One God, faiths, however, this one uniquely witnesses to and advocates belief in the human figure after which it is named. Jews and Muslims do not accord divine status to primal figures such as Moses or Muhammad, but for Christians, Jesus Christ is different. Witnessing to, seeking to serve, placing hopes in, and globally propagating a vision of this God-Man, or Man-God, gives Christianity its distinctive character and force.

The claim that Jesus was divine *and* human has always put off skeptical onlookers and inspired enemies, but it was attractive to believers who saw him thus poised to be the mediator between God and humans. Such humans were seen to have been naturally alienated from God but able to be redeemed in identification with him. In one of the earliest documents of the faith a letter-writer named Paul agreed that Jesus Christ was "a stumbling block [=scandal] to the Jews and foolishness to the Gentiles" (I Corinthians 1:23), which meant that he was a problem to just about everyone.

Publics today, even in nations with Christian majorities, still often find the claims about him to be scandalous. Thus to pray to God in the name of Jesus Christ is offensive to many in civic environments, such as the one created by legislation directed to French public schools or to American public schools in ever more pluralistic America. Some offended Christians then turn aggressive and try to force his name on citizens of many faiths and no faiths on such occasions and at such places. Historians tell how through the centuries Christians in many settings negotiated their way in the face of both external attacks and division within their ranks. Both what are seen as potentials for human good and temptations to do evil relate to the interplay of the divine and the human in Jesus Christ, as interpreted by his followers.

The good resulted from the devotion of believers to the divine-human love of God in Jesus Christ. The evil has ordinarily been evidenced when the devotees accompanied their faith with exclusive claims. These often led them to undertake arrogant, threatening, and evil actions against those who did not share their faith. In the name of Jesus Christ, believers have told simple parables and devised complex dogmas, waged wars and made peace, engaged in acts of mercy or justice and acted unmercifully or unjustly. Though their story can be told with almost innumerable variations, monitoring the scene from our chosen distance and keeping an eye on this thread of belief make it possible for a historian to select significant features of the story in efforts to satisfy curiosities.

"Going global," which means trying to keep a broad focus on Christianity all over the world, as the narrative in this book does, has meant slighting some conventional emphases. Most writing of Christian history in the Western world placed accounts of Europe and North America at the center, but here they have to share space. Such jostling does not issue from any ideological bias against Europe or North America. Rather, viewing Christian experiences in an intercontinental environment will help inform understandings of the past and approaches to the future of believers anywhere and everywhere.

# CHRONOLOGY

*Does not include key figures; their dates accompany their names in the text.*

| | |
|---|---|
| **to 14 C.E.** | Caesar "Augustus" emperor of Rome |
| **29?–33?** | Crucifixion of Jesus |
| **c. 49** | First Council, at Jerusalem |
| **c. 50? 57?** | Paul writes letters, first to Galatians |
| **60?–100?** | Gospels of Mark, Matthew, Luke |
| **64** | Fire at Rome, Nero persecutes Christians, Peter killed? |
| **c. 67** | Paul executed at Rome |
| **81–96** | Domitian emperor, Great Persecution |
| **84** | Christians put out of synagogue |
| **c. 120** | Gnosticism in its prime |
| **144** | Excommunication of Marcion |
| **c. 155** | Justin Martyr writes first Apology |
| **c. 156?** | Montanus preaches, gathers followers |
| **c. 178–200** | Irenaeus Bishop of Lyons |
| **200** | Tertullian converted to Montanism |
| **201** | Abgar, king of Edessa, converted |

416 Council of Carthage condemns Pelagianism

431 Council of Ephesus condemns Nestorius

451 Council of Chalcedon on "two natures of Christ"

455 Pope Leo deals with Vandals, who conquer Rome

460 Patrick, missionary in Ireland, dies

496 Clovis, king of Franks, baptized

527–565 Justinian emperor, reconqueror in Africa and Italy

532 Hagia Sophia rebuilt by Justinian in Constantinople

c. 540 Benedict of Nursia offers "Rule" at Monte Cassino

c. 542–575 Founding of Monophysite churches east of Edessa

c. 563 Columba and Irish followers found Iona monastery

590–604 Gregory I pope

597 Augustine of Canterbury sent by pope to Kent

622 First year of Muslim calendar, Hegira to Mecca

632 Muhammad dies

638 Arab Muslims conquer Jerusalem

643–656 Arab conquests, Egypt, Iraq, Syria, and so on

664 Synod of Whitby in England, Rome over Celts

711–716 Arabs continue conquest, now in Spain

716 Boniface (Winfred) begins Friesian mission

726 Iconoclasm controversy in Eastern Church begins

732 Arabs thwarted by Charles Martel at Poitiers

768 Charlemagne becomes ruler of Frankish kingdom

800 Charlemagne crowned Holy Roman Emperor

843 Icons restored to churches where they'd been removed

863 Cyril and Methodius begin Slavic mission

909 Cluny reform monastery founded

988 Vladimir of Kiev baptized, conversion of Russia

1054 Schism between East and West, condemnations

1073 Gregory VII becomes decisive pope

1076–77 Gregory excommunicates Holy Roman Emperor Henry IV, who does penance

1095 Anselm, theologian and Bishop of Canterbury

1099 Crusader victory, "reconquest" of Jerusalem

1123 First Lateran Council

1130 Two popes elected in dispute

1159 Schism at Rome, two popes, conflict with emperor

1187 Saladin captures Jerusalem

1198 Innocent III, another major pope, enthroned

1209 Francis of Assisi gives rule to his friars

1215 Fourth Lateran Council, defines Eucharist

1216 Dominicans founded

1244 Muslims achieve final victory at Jerusalem

1252 Papal Inquisition established, Gregory IX

c. 1253 Thomas Aquinas teaches at Paris

1281–1924 Ottoman Empire founded, lasts over 800 years

1302 Boniface VIII *Unam Sanctam,* pope over the secular

1327 Meister Eckhart, German mystic, dies

1348–49 The Black Death devastates Europe

1375 John Wycliffe begins reform in England

1378 Great Schism, Urban VI, Clement VII

1415 Council of Constance, council over pope, burns Jan Hus

1431–49 Council of Basel

1453 Constantinople falls to Ottoman Turks

1479 Pope approves "Spanish Inquisition"

1492 Isabella and Ferdinand drive Muslims out of Spain

1493–94 Alexander VI divides "new lands" between Spain and Portugal

1498 Savonarola, reformer, burned in Florence

1506 Pope Julius begins building Saint Peter's in Rome

1509 Erasmus begins to criticize Roman institutions

1517 Luther posts 95 reformist theses

1519 Cortés attacks Aztecs in Mexico

1519 Huldreich Zwingli reforms in Zurich

1521 Luther excommunicated, debates at Worms

1522–23 Ignatius Loyola fashions *Spiritual Exercises*

1524 Franciscans begin work in Mexico

1525 Execution of Anabaptist leader Thomas Muentzer

1529 Protestants get their name at Diet of Speyer

1534 Act of Supremacy in English reform

1536 John Calvin arrives in Geneva to reform

1537 Pope Paul III defends rights of Indians in Americas

1542 Francis Xavier begins work in India

1545–63 Council of Trent

1552 Bartolomé de Las Casas prints his attack on treatment of Indians

1553 "Unitarian" Michael Servetus burned in Geneva

1555 Peace of Augsburg: rulers determine religion

1560 John Knox founds Presbyterian Church in Scotland

1.

# The Jewish
# Beginnings

BLACK SEA

GREECE

*AEGEAN SEA*

Corinth

Ephesus

ASIA MINOR

Tarsus

Antioch

SYRIA

*MEDITERRANEAN SEA*

Tyre

*GALILEE*

*SAMARIA*

Nazareth

*JUDEA*

**PALESTINE**

Jerusalem

*DEAD SEA*

EGYPT

THE JEWISH BEGINNINGS

*Cities of Palestine mentioned in the Gospels, and four cities associated with the apostle Paul.*

*Present-day boundaries (and some names) of states and nations are shown, though in the periods covered in this chapter they had not been formed.*

0    100    200 miles

0    100    200 kilometers

Yeshuanity" or "Jesusanity" would be a natural name for a global community and culture devoted to Yeshua, or Jesus of Nazareth, depending on whether the namers favored his Hebrew or his Latinized name. "Christianity" is instead the designation, and its communal form is not the Jesus Church but the Christian Church. Nor is Christ the last name of this Jesus, but a translation of the Hebrew or Aramaic word *messias,* which means "anointed," and refers to someone appointed to a specific role. To neglect or to obscure the meaning of the title Christ when applied to Jesus, the rabbi from Nazareth, is to miss the point of the earliest writings about him and to skew the story line ever after.

## ANOTHER WORLD TO LIVE IN, AND ITS STORIES

*The Christian World* is an invitation for readers to enter and appraise a global scene, "the world," through twenty centuries. At the same time the Christian "world" also means all the contexts to which Christian believers related and relate. "Christianity" may imply institutions and can be expressed through doctrines and ways of life, but at its core it is a story. Philosopher George Santayana connected "world" and "story" precisely, as will we. In *Reason in Religion* he remarked that "every living and healthy religion has a marked idiosyncrasy." Ask atheists, Buddhists, Hindus, Muslims, Jews, or others to listen to Christians and they will soon discern the main "marked idiosyncrasy": the devotion to Jesus Christ.

As these listeners observe the effects of what they have heard they will note what Santayana told readers to look for, in this case it would mean that Christianity's "power consists in its special and surprising message," rooted in the story of Jesus Christ, "and in the bias which that revelation gives to life." Billions of people have let that revelation "bias" them, so that they could experience joy and peace or, conversely and often at the same time, face persecution, hardship, or even death in its light. Santayana spoke of "the vistas" a religion like Christianity opens, "and the mysteries it propounds," and these will be obvious to all who follow the story. Now: taken together they make up "another world to live in, and another world to live in—whether we expect ever to pass wholly over into it or no—is what we mean by having a religion."

## BEGINNING WITH THE STORY OF JESUS CHRIST

The "special and surprising message" of Christianity begins with Jesus Christ, so if we wish to go back to beginnings, we begin with his story. The earliest Christians were, like Jesus, Jews. This means that they were schooled in Hebrew Scriptures, which Christians later called "the Old Testament." They reread those Scriptures and gave them a "special and surprising" twist. Believers took words of the prophets and claimed that they foretold Jesus, or they told stories of scriptural figures like Moses and Elijah, Noah and Jonah, and saw them as "types" of Jesus Christ and his story.

Jesus was a Jew: that theme needs reinforcing, especially because so much of Christian history is a wrestling with the meanings of Jews and Judaism. The two faiths should have been supportive of each other, as spiritual next of kin. Anthropologists stress what is obvious about kin: "aggression, like charity, begins at home." As the upstart believers in Jesus Christ as the long-promised deliverer of Israel, the Messiah, the Christ, expressed that startling claim, some Jews who did not see him that way and who thought his claims blasphemous ejected the believers in Jesus Christ from their synagogues and persecuted them. For twenty centuries the once ejected Christians exacted revenge or, on any number of grounds, set out on their own to be separate, to define themselves over against those in their parent faith community, as they turned murderous in patterns for which there was little formal and corporate repentance until the late twentieth century.

Getting the story of Jesus right is difficult, and no single interpretation can be satisfying to all 2.2 billion Christians, since they are divided into 38,000 denominations, many of them fashioned to protect and project separate tellings of the story. Yet certain elements of the story stand out. To begin with, the narratives about

Jesus Christ were all written by followers, called disciples or evangelists, which means spreaders of the evangel, the "good news." In these stories, he chose twelve followers to stand out, no doubt to mirror the twelve tribes of Israel. Four books in the Christian New Testament called gospels were named after three authors or editors who pursued parallel tracks, Matthew, Mark, and Luke, while a fourth, identified with John, displays different nuances and intentions. Not exactly biographies or histories, the gospels are narrative testimonies to what the early communities cherished and wanted preserved. Luke tells how he went about his work interviewing eyewitnesses, reading documentary collections, and giving them coherence in his own edited narrative. These gospels stress different aspects of the life and work of Jesus. Luke, for instance, was especially attentive to the marginalized, among them women and children. His Jesus was always at table with outcasts, and he showed special favor to lepers and the physically handicapped—and thus despised—people around him.

In recent times some of the texts which had not been incorporated into what became the shared collection or canon have been discovered as far from Jerusalem as Egypt, where some communities which identified themselves with Jesus long struggled. Other such writings, long known but neglected, receive new attention. To overstate the case slightly, most of these gospels display difficulty with either the human Jesus the Jew or Jesus the exalted being they called Lord. Some pose the whole questions of God and Jesus in arcane, hard to interpret terms. No matter what the claims any of these made and whatever appeal they have now to scholars and seekers especially in the affluent West, for most Christians around the globe it is the four gospel accounts that have provided the focus for their faith, the enchantment of their stories, and the impulse for their ministries and service.

From these gospels the later believing communities have learned how Christians, originally all of them Jews, related to Judaism itself. In the period in which the gospels were being written, the Romans put down a revolt by oppressed Jews. They besieged the city and destroyed the Second Temple, the center of Jewish worship. Most scholars see these traumatic events as elements in the shaping of the gospels. They are reflected in words of Jesus about persecution, death, destruction, and the foreseen end-time. Mainly, however, the gospels have been revered because they provided the story of Jesus' birth, the account of what is called his Passion or suffering and dying, and most of all his Resurrection. Framed by those events is the story of his life

Since Christians make so much of the figure of Jesus, it is impressive and, to many, confounding, that there is so much that they can never know. Archaeology may turn up artifacts that can be studied to color the understandings of the time, but "the historical Jesus," as some scholars call him while pursuing his trail, will always remain a subject of controversy and confusion, always finally elusive. If he was "the exalted Lord," did he claim to be the Son of God or even, clearly, the Anointed of God, the Messiah? Why did the gospels report that he on occasion called himself the Son of Man, a figure vivid in the imagination of some apocalyptic Jews who thrived before his time? How did he become such a cherished figure among those who value the family, while his own family had trouble believing in him and while he so often dismissed and rejected family ties for the sake of the "Kingdom of God" that he was announcing? What did he do from age twelve to approximately age thirty, years about which the gospels are silent and pseudo-gospels tell fanciful tales?

Some gospel narratives tell of his birth to Mary of Nazareth, who was betrothed and presumably later married to a carpenter named Joseph, a man who quickly disappears after a last appearance in a story about the twelve-year-old Jesus. The Gospel of Luke uniquely says that Mary conceived and gave birth while remaining a virgin. Even nonliteralist Christians, who do not believe or need that version of Jesus' story, regard his origins and appearance as somehow shrouded in mystery. He grew up in Nazareth, a place that contemporaries belittled.

The gospels tell us little about Jesus' childhood, or how he participated in family life in the carpentry shop of Joseph. Stop right there, historians tell themselves: Mary, mentioned here so briskly, is the second most referred to and revered figure in Christian history, regarded in the words of one church council as "the Mother of God," and approached as such by Catholic believers. As the exemplary person of trust who was responsive to the divine call, she became an object of adoration or an example of faith and trust among millions and is prominent in Christian art and iconography in all times, on all continents. Probably around age thirty Jesus was baptized in the Jordan River by a major if idiosyncratic prophet, John the Baptist, who drew crowds to the river and the Judean desert. Perhaps John reflected in part the outlook of movements such as the Essenes, whose spiritual kin preserved what were discovered in our time and named the Dead Sea Scrolls. These provided glimpses into the religious complex of the day.

John, quoting the Hebrew Scriptures, pointed the way to Jesus as the greater prophet. Soon Jesus' own ministry of healing, his wonder-working, and his preaching attracted the crowds and the jealousy of those he threatened by his preaching. The texts show him urging people of his time to "search the Scriptures," the stories of the Creation, and of how God covenanted with their forefathers, who often strayed from that covenant. Prophets among them called for a turning, repentance, and now John did the same.

## JESUS AS TEACHER

In his maturity for about three years Jesus preached and healed. He could be calm and reflective, but gospel stories also picture him in a hurry, treating his own message with urgency. When this message focused on what was both the present *and* forthcoming Kingdom of God which he announced, he had to make clear that he was not in such words intending to replace oppressive Rome with royal rule from Jerusalem. Instead, this realm was the sphere of the saving activity of God. For entrance to it people had to do a turnaround, repenting of their errant ways and becoming just and merciful, as he was and as he enabled them to be. Soon—he did not specify and hardly speculated as to exactly when—the world that they knew would be destroyed, and they must be prepared.

Even many who reject all exalted claims for Jesus respect him as a teacher. On some levels this respect seems strangely placed. Few aspects of his teaching were original; parallels to them could be found in authors before his time. Some regard his command to love the enemies to be innovative, but it is anticipated in the Hebrew Scriptures. So many of his followers like to have everything nailed down, all the meanings of the stories made clear and secure, yet he taught in ways that favored loose ends, paradoxes, and even puzzles. The gospels, made up of what some have called "memory-impressions," a literary genre of their own, reflect what his followers remembered and thought were most important of his words and ways. The sometimes contradictory images they circulate portray a humble leader who could weep over a city as well as denounce it. He could console a hungry soul or demolish the pretensions of the arrogant, including religious leaders. As teacher, healer, and wonder-worker he created scandal by the company he kept. All the parables that he told turned everything upside down. What sense should listeners make of it as he spoke of how in the face of the kingdom the small became great and the great small, that the outsiders were turned into insiders and vice versa; the strong were seen as weak and the weak strong, and that all must change and become like little children. He favored children, exemplars for him of life in the kingdom. Modern French novelist Georges Bernanos, through the voice of a fictional priest, said that Jesus' reported word that unless one changed and became like a little child he would have no part in the Kingdom of God was the most terrifying ever heard by human ears. Jesus also showed special regard for women, who were regularly overlooked or even despised in the cultures of the day. His own beloved mother, Mary, and his brothers possessed no privileged rights in the kingdom, while the smelly poor and the ethnically marginal were treated as insiders.

## JESUS THE JEW AND THE KINGDOM OF GOD

Such actions and messages as we have just distilled from the gospels suggest that Jesus had to be disturbing to keepers of good order, including those within the religious establishments. One party of people called the Pharisees, well thought of, especially by themselves, for their scrupulosity in keeping the law, but ill thought of when they were judgmental, appear in Christian imaginations as carpers and eventually as enemies of Jesus that some, knowing how family quarrels are often the most vehement and even vicious, have wondered whether Jesus himself was a Pharisee or had been Pharisee-trained. If so, he was also a Pharisee with a difference, because in the sayings preserved in the gospels he saw Pharisees near him caring less about persons than about principles and policies. He personally violated some of these when on the Sabbath he healed people, since healing was work and work was forbidden among keepers of the inherited Divine Law.

Jesus, who taught as rabbis taught by asking questions, was first of all a rabbi to the gospel writers and some characters in their books. Jewish scholars centuries later gained an early picture of ritual in the synagogue from a story about how Jesus preached in one. His main ministry, however, was in the profane world, the word "profane" (*pro-fano*) having meant that which was outside across the threshold, in this case that of the temple. He spent much energy training a band of people called the Twelve—a number chosen to reflect the twelve tribes of Israel to which his ministry was to relate. He taught them to pray, simplifying worship along the way to the point that financially it cost nothing. No one needed to invest in animals for temple offerings or in incense. They could close their bedchamber doors and pray effectively, better than could the Pharisees who called attention to their praying. Followers must serve the poor and hungry, the unclothed and imprisoned, and in doing so they would be found serving Jesus.

The gospels include three chapters usually called the Sermon on the Mount in which Jesus preached a radical message. Killing had always been wrong; but now even to hate was to violate God's law. Adulterous acts had always been wrong. Now lustful glances, even if not acted upon, or simply coveting, were violations of what God wanted of people. Jesus could thunder judgment and then teach an intimate prayer in which those who followed him were to address God as "Abba," Father, Papa, Daddy. And he preached a way of nonviolence, of not-killing, of turning the other cheek to those who hit them, of loving enemies and of seeking the Kingdom of Heaven while letting worries cease and expecting tomorrow to take care of itself. Some readers have associated a few of Jesus' disciples with Zealots, members of a revolutionary movement, but the weight of the gospels is on Jesus, who is both righteous and reconciling.

One element in his ways that especially offended many was his keeping company with people who should have been kept at a distance. He was caught too often publicly welcoming hated and cheating tax-collectors, prostitutes, outcasts at the table. He sided with outsiders such as a Syrian or a Samaritan woman or a Roman military officer, and not with King Herod of the Jews, whom he dismissed as "that fox." Consistently he announced the Kingdom of God, pointing to the sovereign activity of the powerful God and the saving activity of a condescending God. All this preaching, teaching, healing, and setting of examples was subversive in the eyes of the respectable. The story of how and why he offended religious leaders so much that they wanted him killed admits of many explanations. Their dealing with the occupying Roman authorities was always a delicate proposition, and his ambiguity about dealing with Caesar might upset the delicacy of balance— or the accent on upset could be cited as a threat by inimical Jews.

This man from Nazareth preached radical justice and peace, showing confidence in the purposes of God. At least three gospels, however, show him to be curious about the future, when he asked, "When the Son of Man comes, will he find faith on the earth?" All this occurred in the face of rule by oppressors. A family of kings named Herod, who figure prominently in the early Christian story, ruled under the sufferance and as agents of the Romans. The spiritual focus of Judaism was the Temple in Jerusalem, but in most locales the synagogue, a house of prayer and study, compelled devotion. The sacred laws of the Hebrew Scriptures and many interpretations by rabbis governed the daily life of the people among whom Jesus ministered. Jewish sects and interests competed in Judea, the southern sphere of Jesus' ministry, and Galilee, in the north, where he lived. We read of members in parties or movements, scrupulous Pharisees, "modernist" Sadducees, even the revolutionary Zealots, whose influences were powerful in the surrounding culture.

That culture was quite mixed. For example, the early documents about the Aramaic-speaking Jesus were written in Greek. Roman governors and their tax-collecting agents oppressed the people, for whom revolt was always tempting but usually futile. Expectation that the Messiah, the Anointed of God, would come to rescue Israel was high. Still, the people had lives to live, fish to catch, fields to farm, children to nurture, death to fear, and laws to follow.

Jesus addressed their world by turning everything topsy-turvy, indicating that the reversal of ordinary expectations was God's way. A song attributed to Mary when she heard a message from an angel that she would give birth to one who would "save his people from their sins" was such a turning: the rich would be sent away empty and the poor and hungry filled with good things. God would now scatter the proud and cast down the mighty from their thrones. Jesus was consistent. The stories about him show him to be conversant with people of means, but he chose to be at table with despised and corrupt tax collectors, prostitutes, and other unrespectable sorts. In the Gospel of Luke he especially favored women, the disabled, and the marginal. Crowds, we are told, took to him, and recognized his "special" character. Exactly what that was was debated then and is now: was he the Messiah, the Anointed of Israel? The King of the Jews? The Son of God? God? A wonder-worker? A gentle teacher? A subversive? He often evaded direct answers to questions like those, but it is clear that in the gospel narratives he saw himself to be the hope of Israel.

Someone has spoken of the "memory-impressions" Jesus left, voiced and circulated in stories by eyewitnesses and passed on through the next two generations in the gospels. For all the ways he could chasten, denounce, and judge authorities as well as his own laggard and compromising followers, his overall message was one of love, which they saw as divine, embodied in him. Further, according to these gospels, he reduced all the Commandments to two: the love of God and the love of neighbor. He could jostle listeners, but they were drawn to him as one who invited those who labored and were burdened to find rest in him. He promised never to abandon them, always to be with them. That was what the Kingdom of God now portended and exemplified.

For all the crowd appeal and the miracles of healing reported on in the gospels, he inevitably ran into trouble with authorities. He did not aspire to rule: "My kingdom is not of this world." In the volatile world of the remote outpost called Israel, the local representatives of Roman authority were rendered secondary, though despised. Various parties among Jews—unfortunately pejoratively labeled "*the* Jews" in John's gospel—saw him as a challenger to their authority and considered some of the claims he made to be blasphemous. At a significant move in the gospel stories he turned toward Jerusalem to face popular acclaim by crowds and, in a sudden turn, abandonment by most of them as he faced a trial under governor Pontius Pilate. This representative of Rome delivered him to the people to be crucified. Crucifixion, which meant that the condemned was bound or nailed to a cross and exposed to taunting crowds and the elements, was a common form of capital punishment among the Romans. They saved it chiefly for Zealots or revolutionaries and criminals of the worst sort.

The Jesus of the gospels had foretold this death, and seemed to approach it willingly, though two chilling stories near his end bring a note of realism to it all. In the Garden of Gethsemane the night before he died, he prayed that his cup of suffering be taken away—it wasn't—and when he was near death on the cross he was heard to utter a line from Psalm 22, "My God, my God, why have you forsaken me?" Christians have never found it necessary to come to a formal agreement—the kind of thing a dogma sets out to express—about the meaning of the crucifixion event. All of them identified it with themes from the Hebrew Scriptures. Some saw and see his death as the paying of penalty for the sins of all. Others believed him to be their substitute, since they deserved divine punishment for their evils. Still others picked up on scriptural themes showing that by this death he was actually triumphing as the victor over death, the devil, and sin. Without always being specific, Christians agreed that this death was "for them," and "to save them." Since their faith identifies his sinful believers as his killers, it was a savage irony that found so many through the years twisting this to blame someone else, especially "the Jews," a blaming that was one of the roots of Christian anti-Judaism, the biggest blot on their story.

In any case, the gospels had found him prophesying that he would be killed, an offering for others, sacrificed for the sake of their lives. He had a last supper with disciples, as three gospels match Paul in telling, and then, betrayed by Judas, one of his disciples, he was arrested, taken to priestly and then Roman authorities, in this case represented by Pontius Pilate, who had him crucified. Jews could not execute anyone, so Pilate and thus Rome cooperated. The gospel stories in vivid detail describe his trial, the desertion by his disciples beginning with Peter, his being scourged, his march to a hill where they nailed him on a cross, thus making sure that according to the Scriptures he would be divinely cursed. He died and was buried, and all but some women family members and a few other followers abandoned him, while one of his questioning cries from the cross reflected his own sense of agony and mysterious abandonment—by God.

In the gospel narratives it was these women followers who, having waited a day because the Sabbath did not permit such work, came to the tomb to finish dealing ceremonially with his body. In the same stories, they found the tomb empty.

The special and surprising and, yes, truly idiosyncratic story continued with the accounts that "on the third day," the Sunday after the Friday of his death, he was "resurrected," and appeared to them bodily, but now in different forms. He showed up "in the breaking of the bread" at an inn with two followers who had not recognized him on a long walk. He appeared among disciples when the doors were closed. At the same time, in John's gospel, he showed his wounds to a doubting disciple named Thomas. He ate with some witnesses to the Resurrection, and then left them after forty days in an event called the Ascension, still celebrated forty days after the Festival of the Resurrection (Easter). Ten days later the Holy Spirit, according to Jesus' promise, appeared among them at Pentecost—another day still observed annually by Christians—and in response the disciples became part of the enduring community that was eventually called "the Christian church," the core of the Christianity that prompts our story.

The disciples who had cowered, fled, and said they lived without hope, now regathered, convinced as they were by the witness of those who had "seen the Lord." A sacred meal of the sort he had shared the night before he died was to be a locale where he said he would be present, just as he would be when they baptized newcomers to the faith. He had promised to be with them when two or three gathered in his name. While the adult Jesus never left Palestine, they soon were traveling through Asia Minor and Syria, attracting new followers, evidently of varied social classes. One reads of slaves who were converted and who then won over their masters and owners to the faith. There are also accounts of wealthy and prominent newcomers to the faith. Being persecuted, which meant suffering for the faith in Jesus Christ, far from being a deterrent to conversions, became a lure to prospects for baptism. In Jerusalem, while they suffered from Roman and Jewish attacks, believers endured until 70 C.E., when the city was destroyed. Allusions to some events and often cryptic sayings in the gospels reflect this situation of a destroyed city and of what was becoming two separating faiths.

The line of demarcation left believers in Jesus Christ as the Messiah on one side and those who rejected him as such on the other. Similarly, those who followed Jesus claimed to be free of the strictures of many Jewish laws. From those decisive years, stories about Jesus, sayings by him, and reflections by followers survive in a collection of writings that his followers call the New Testament. These texts appeared chiefly in the first or second generation after he lived among them. A century and more later, followers collected them and named them parts of a "canon," or standard account of the beginnings. Globally, Christians still cherish these Scriptures along with Jesus' only "Bible," the Hebrew Scriptures, which they have translated into well over one thousand languages and dialects. Believers study and preach on the bases of these. They have used them to judge, inspire, or console each other and still argue about their meanings.

## WHAT CHRISTIANS HELD AND HOLD IN COMMON

What, scholars ask, did and do believers and followers on at first three continents and then on all continents have in common? Their studies reveal startling differences and violent debates, wherever Christian communities rose. These places included Asian Palestine, the place of beginnings; Asian Antioch, where their movement got its name; and northern Africa, to where it had spread early on across the Mediterranean. What they held in common could be reduced to a minimalist formula which admits numberless variations: "*The human Jesus is the exalted Lord.*"

Such faith in Jesus Christ left believers with two profound problems which have always inspired arguments and led to factions and schisms. Christians, with their Jewish heritage, could never conceive of being anything other than monotheists. Nothing they would say about Jesus dared detract from their faith in One God. Yet they also spoke of Jesus as divine. To complicate everything, they heard him promise a Divine Presence whom they experienced as the Holy Spirit. Did not the most succinct statement of their focus leave them with not one, but three gods? A modern Asian inquirer once asked, did this not mean that they were being ruled by a Three-Person committee? Equally as troubling to early Christian minds though not to their hearts was a problem that issued from their belief that humans were utterly "other" than God. So if Jesus was somehow God, they pondered, how could he also be somehow human? It took almost six centuries for followers in their councils to come up with never fully satisfying creeds. Their details never met universal agreement nor could they be easily communicated to all publics.

We find Christians through the next two millennia pondering the features of Jesus Christ's life and meaning. Some have had trouble agreeing with the creedal statement that he was truly and fully human. Their majority had to condemn an ancient split-off group of Docetists (*dokein* = to seem), for whom Jesus Christ only *seemed* to be human. Docetists and their spiritual successors were scandalized to think that God-among-them would be ignorant of the future end-time and, worse, would have armpit odor and the need to blow his nose, or that he could cry in sympathy or could cry out in agony. He was divine, and divinity does not "do" such things. The majority, however, assented along with the creed-writers and on the basis of the gospel stories that he was truly "the human Jesus, the Jew." For others the exact opposite affirmation, that rabbi Jesus was and is "the exalted Lord," raised the problems. This claim became the great divider that also separated Christians from all others.

One of the oldest hymns in the New Testament, perhaps issuing from a circle of Hellenistic Jewish believers or written by the apostle Paul, brings the two concepts together: "Christ Jesus . . .

> *being born in human likeness . . . humbled himself*
> *and became obedient to the point of death—even death on a cross.*
> *Therefore God also highly exalted him . . .*
> *[so that] every tongue should confess that Jesus Christ is Lord*
> *To the glory of God the Father (Philippians 2: 7–11)*

Of course, not "every tongue" *does* confess anything like this, but the believers who do are actors in the drama of Christianity. Believing in "the exalted Lord," as Christians do, has created more confusion than did talk of "the human Jesus." Believers would insist that they would not, they *could* not, speak of him as they do if they did not believe that death did not have the last claim on him, as it had on all other humans. Their critics said that believers only *wanted* to believe, or believed that they believed that he was risen. Maybe they were connivers or deluded fools, perhaps traumatized simpletons who underwent a psychological experience that featured the reappearing figure, after his death, of someone whose renewed presence they craved.

More extravagantly, some believers considered that Jesus' having been raised meant that the rotting corpuscles of a dead body had to have been revivified. Paul, that earliest and most influential writer, did not claim this, but spoke of Jesus having been raised as "a spiritual body." Nor did other witnesses speak of the biology and physics of revivification. Paul preached that whatever happened, God had worked an unprecedented and unique "new" thing. The God who had produced the original creation now had brought forth a New Creation. Such a startling belief led Paul and others to begin taking their message to the ends of their known world while their successors eventually carried it to the whole globe, often at great risk among hostile populations.

Christianity, like other faiths, produced double-sided effects, its community often having been made up of healers who killed and killers who healed. In the name of Jesus, believers have engaged in humble acts of mercy and justice. Also in the name of their exalted Lord, Christians have engaged in often violent acts of power and dominion. The story which follows here holds that tension and contradiction in constant view as it traces Christian paths globally. In Jesus' day no one spoke or could have spoken intelligibly of anything global. The first practical modern use of globes would wait until after 1492. Yet if the disciples in Jesus' time had no global concept, some of them reached out to confront the whole inhabited world known to them. These believers had to make a living, and some of them were evidently adept at commerce and familiar with the busy trade routes. They could often combine the quest for gain with the goal of gaining converts.

## PAUL'S LETTERS, THE FIRST SOURCE

Historians like to trace the missionary journeys through the earliest texts. In this case they study the letters of Paul, Jesus' fellow Jew, originally named Saul of Tarsus. He heard a call to declare that the story of the Anointed One of God who belonged to the Jews belonged not only to them. Paul traveled with that message, at least figuratively toting in his luggage and having in memory the same Scriptures that the Jews followed. Along with this Scripture he may have drawn on scraps of written and certainly snaps of oral reminiscences about Jesus. These bits were making their way into the gospels, the reflective narratives about the human Jesus the Jew who was the believers' exalted Lord.

It is bracing and, for many, startling, to begin the global narrative not with the gospels but by relying on letters which Paul wrote to gatherings of Jews and non-Jews. Those who later assembled the sequence of books in the New Testament canon placed the four gospels first and followed them with the letters of Paul and others. Therefore it has been natural for people to think of those narratives as being the oldest texts. Some critics have taken swings at Paul because his writings differ in style and intent from these gospels. They accuse him of having complicated and even betrayed the stories of "the simple Jesus," the mild healer and spiritual figure of Galilee. Such attackers like to isolate Jesus in that simple world, and then revere his teachings as being applicable everywhere.

While Paul traveled almost recklessly, we have seen that Jesus never stepped out of Palestine, later called "the Holy Land," an area hardly larger than Greater Los Angeles or other world metropolitan areas. Only one evidently late inclusion in a gospel offers some lines in which Jesus Christ is heard showing an intention for his message to be brought to "all nations." One wit condensed his mission and manner: "Jesus of Nazareth spent his whole ministry on twelve Jews in order to save all the [fill in here, for example: the Americans or Africans]." The man from Nazareth stayed close to home.

Never was it so with Paul. After he was called to be an apostle—others named the event his conversion—the whole logic of his life led him to transport the faith. Now, he proclaimed, the Creator who had called and covenanted with a particular people, the Jews of Israel, in Jesus Christ wanted to make it possible for all peoples to enter that covenant through faith in the human Jesus. Paul argued emphatically—he did everything emphatically—that God, being God, could never revoke a covenant, so the covenant with Israel remained. After Jesus Christ and somehow "through" him, "all Israel will be saved," the apostle proclaimed. Now the fresh company of believers was part of a new particular people, but what made them peculiar was not that they had to be Jews, but that they were believers in Jesus Christ.

Paul, a self-identified Jew from Tarsus in Syria, was well trained in Jewish law and lore. He wrote about how at first he had been so radically offended by claims for Jesus that he set out to harass and assist in killing those who regathered after their dead Jesus, they said, was raised from the dead. Then against all expectations, he experienced the call which he left mainly to others to detail. He was to be an apostle in this faith, first to the Jews but also among the Gentiles. Paul had never viewed Jesus with physical eyes as had the disciples, yet he claimed that somehow he *really* saw Jesus, who called him to represent him everywhere as the exalted Lord. His climactic goal was to reach Spain, symbolically at the end of the earth, and he made many stops along the way through about eight thousand chartable miles of travel.

## JEWS, CHRISTIANS, AND PAGANS

Most of the first-generation Christians were Jews who kept thinking of themselves as Jews and who often frequented synagogues. The Judaism of their time was portable, and, as they migrated, Jews took their faith to many parts of the Roman Empire. Still, for all of them, though it was announced as "a light to the nations," it had been a particular faith for a particular chosen people. Jerusalem may have remained the physical focus of their worship life until the year 70, and they may have made pilgrimages to it, but many were also culturally at home among ancient peoples elsewhere.

Paul made much of his ties to Judaism as he reached out to these Jews who were "dispersed," hence, they were "the diaspora." This linking was fortunate for Paul because he could go to their synagogues and there find audiences who could appraise his teaching. It was further fortunate because Judaism was named a licit religion in the empire. This designation gave Christians who were mistakenly identified with it a temporary measure of protective coloration from attackers within the Roman Empire. Third, most Jews in this diaspora also wrote and spoke Greek, a cosmopolitan language which provided Christians a means of communication with others that Hebrew or Aramaic tongues would not have made possible.

The situation was at the same time *un*fortunate for Paul, because most of the Jews he encountered took up the debate over Judaism with him and other apostles, but were not persuaded by his claims and commitment. At issue for them was Paul's critique in which he saw them using the Law of God to define their life and serve as the instrument which could win God's favor. The last thing most Jews wanted to hear was that their males, all circumcised, were to accept the uncircumcised, those who did not bear the physical mark of accepting the covenant. Most Jews were repulsed at the new claim of Paul and other followers that Jesus had fulfilled the Law for them. Henceforth, they were told, people could become part of the New Creation and the covenant, thanks to the grace-inspired activity of a loving God. This God, who by raising him from the dead had exalted the crucified Jesus, would now deal with people through him and in his name. Understandably disgusted and infuriated elements at many synagogues reacted in rage. On occasion they chased Paul and his company out of town, sometimes having set out to stone him or to ask the Roman authorities to clear him out of their way. To hear Christians calling themselves "the New Israel," as some did, was understandably enraging to "the Old Israel," which was now being considered unfulfilled by many messengers of Jesus and thus was portrayed as being obstructive of the ways of God with humans.

When in 70 a general, later emperor, named Titus (39–81) conquered rebelling Jews and burned the Temple, they were devastated. As most Christians thereafter went their own way, many developed a tradition of hostility to Jews, an attitude that seemed contradictory among believers who followed and worshipped a Jew. As in most such contentions, there was reciprocity. The first conflicts erupted when Jews forced followers of Jesus Christ out of the synagogues because they could not share belief that he was the Messiah. Thrown out, believers were exposed to Roman law and, unprotected, became subject to harassment and persecution. Problems also appeared on another front. Not all believers were always in conflict with the oppressive Roman government and its rulers, and some even served in the military. Paul himself called for believers to be obedient to higher authority, which meant seeing Caesar as God's representative. Despite this appeal, tragic collisions occurred. Some followers wanted to be loyal to Jesus Christ *and* Caesar. Others found themselves called to engage in imperial rituals which exalted Caesar and thus compromised their allegiance to Christ. For Christians to accept civil authority was one thing, but it was another when they rejected the gods and rites of

Rome. Other sects, sometimes Jewish and usually not, could accept civil authority as the final word in the ordering of life, but Christians could never do so. Persecution often followed because in the eyes of Romans, Christians had no gods so they were therefore considered atheists and subversives.

Christians in turn were divided among themselves over how they should deal with pagans, plenty of whom surrounded them in a society we would call pluralistic. A century before Christian times, one Maximus of Tyre guessed that about thirty thousand gods were being revered. In the face of such worship practices, Christian thinker Theophilus of Antioch in the second century insisted on a complete breach with the adorers of gods. No single policy could claim a monopoly or represent a final solution. After 130, an apologist or intellectual defender, the well-traveled Justin Martyr (c. 100–165), built all the bridges to the larger culture that he could. He saw Christianity to be a fulfillment of what the best pagan philosophers had been seeking. In his *Dialogue with Trypho* he broke totally with Jews, and may have been the first to accuse them of being Christ-killers. Meanwhile his bridge-building work collapsed in 165 when Justin, despite all his efforts to get along, alienated authorities and was put to death.

## From Jerusalem into the Larger World

Jerusalem, where members of the family of Jesus were evidently among the leaders, remained a Christian base until its fall to Titus in 70. The biblical texts tell us that James, called Jesus' brother, and Peter, another follower to whom Jesus had sometimes turned, evidently led a faction which wanted to retain many ways of the old covenant. Paul's letters reveal him going out of his way to neutralize and flatter Jerusalemites as he took up an offering for their poor, of whom there were many within that suffering city. Finally, according to the biblical Book of Acts, also written by Luke, he had to debate them face-to-face, as he later liked to remind them he had done. New Testament accounts of events that happened in his visit to Jerusalem or in encounters with their adherents on the road differ, but, however uneasy the truces and nuanced the agreements, Paul and his partisans chose to become free to carry on their mission among uncircumcised Gentiles. He hoped to do this without alienating Jews who believed in Jesus, as he set out to go everywhere.

"Everywhere" was where Paul did try to travel, first to the chief cities of what was called Asia Minor. His own accounts reveal an almost wholly urban trail. Believers gathered in centers like Ephesus, far from the villages and farms in Judea or in the Galilean hills of Jesus. Ephesus was crowded with altars and cluttered with images of gods. Scholars who argue about how exactly the faith spread to such places so rapidly often focus on the issue of social classes, trying to determine which were most open to the efforts of the Christian emissaries. Romanticists point out that Paul's letters refer both to acquaintances who were slave-converts and to the orphans and widows among the followers who were in need. These evidently also mingled among women and men of means and prominence. Paul himself was a craftsman and business person, a maker of tents for elites, it is believed, and wherever he had worked he sent greetings to hosts or co-workers, significantly, women being among them. Civil authorities seemed most nettled by conversions of merchants and well-off people.

Traveler Paul and various associates seldom settled down very long, but their movements also did not always appear to be frantic. The letters of the apostle suggest that in some places he spent several seasons, and fondly and in gratitude he greeted his hosts along with other converts when writing from far away. Given what is known about the marginal place of women in many of these cultures, it is almost astonishing to see how many women's names appear in the letters. Some of them were teamed with those of husbands, but others were named alone. They clearly engaged in work along the lines that Paul called apostolic, a word that signaled that they had been "sent forth." Paul in a letter to believers at Corinth did insist that women ought to cover their heads while prophesying. In that same letter in which he told women to wear coverings while they prophesied, he also fatefully asked them to keep silent in the public gatherings with men and provided some theological rationales on the basis of which women, he thought, were excluded from prophesying and holding office.

Paul was ambiguous in his attitudes toward the spiritual inheritances from Judaism. While his main message had to do with how God dealt with peoples, he also spelled out what this meant for persons. Staggered and driven to guilt and near despair as he said he had been "under the Law," he wrote that, thanks to God's love, the self-giving of God's humbled human servant Jesus Christ, he now lived by faith in the one he called the Son of God. Such faith became a major theme of the message Paul preached among the growing company of messengers of Jesus Christ and new believers. Entrance to that company was by water baptism, a rite taken over from some Jewish practices and now effected in the name of "the Father, the Son, and the Holy Spirit," the Son being Jesus.

Paul does not detail the act, but he did write that by being baptized, plunged underwater, the new believer had been "buried" with the dead Christ. Then coming out of the water in faith, the same person was a new creature in the risen Christ, a member of the people of God. This ritual, later called a sacrament, continues in almost all Christian bodies and is one of the few elements of Christian prescription that, though practiced in diverse forms and argued over in sometimes imaginative, often wearying, ways, is accepted across the boundaries of Christian communities.

Paul also provided the oldest account of a common sacred meal. Since his explicit references to events in Jesus' life are otherwise extremely sparse, it is appropriate to reproduce his words:

> For I received from the Lord what I also handed on to you, that the Lord Jesus on the night when he was betrayed took a loaf of bread, and when he had given thanks, he broke it and said, "This is my body that is for you. Do this in remembrance of me." In the same way he took the cup also, after supper, saying, "This cup is the new covenant in my blood. Do this, as often as you drink it, in remembrance of me." For as often as you eat this bread and drink the cup, you proclaim the Lord's death until he comes. (I Corinthians 11:23–26)

That passage of text is of extraordinary importance, since it points to the other rite practiced by virtually all Christians everywhere. We cannot here go into the controverted details, but we can observe that most communicants said they experienced at that meal the living presence of the human Jesus as the exalted Lord.

Quoting Paul's final line also points to a stress among early believers, not least of all Paul among them. This Jesus would return. The earliest texts are not all consistent in detail with each other, and Paul himself looked for a variety of ways to point to the expectation of such a return. Belief that it would happen soon impelled him to work with zeal and to ask others also to spread the message. Like so many of his readers and followers, he was able to live with the expectation that history would soon end *and* at the same time he lived with the need to engage in practical activity in God's world, however long that meantime might be.

In that interim, some believers were acquiring a good name because they were generous to each other and to others beyond their own circle. One letter writer converted to a virtual slogan one observation of outsiders: "See how they love one another!" As we follow the story of the agents who believed that the human Jesus was their exalted Lord, we will see that there will be many times when that love is obscured by views of spite and hatred among believers or by their hatred of others. At moments the face of God as proclaimed by them will look fierce and judgmental. The Jesus who humbled himself will be invoked by those who seek and gain power, among them some crusaders, inquisitors, imperialists, the selfish rich and often high-level leaders of Christian communities. At the same time, frequently enough, the message, experience, and effects of love were sufficiently vivid to render the circle of believers and their exalted Lord attractive, and stories of them still charming.

The trail of Paul ends in silence. We know from his letters that he offended authority, was imprisoned, and had to depend upon aides to write for him and to circulate his letters. He did make it to Rome, then the capital of the empire and a future power base for Christians. Since he obviously could not write about his own death and no colleagues left texts on the subject, we are left with traditions and legends which suggest that most likely he was swept up in operations under Nero (37–68), as was the disciple Peter. The corrupt emperor could tolerate the many sects, Jewish or otherwise, so long as their adherents would also leave a proverbial and symbolic pinch of incense at his civil shrines, but Jews, still under special protection, and Christians, who were not, would not do this, regarding such acts as idolatrous. Stories went out that Nero wanted to cover up his responsibility for details of a fire in Rome and, seeking scapegoats, fingered and cruelly executed Christians.

## THE DISCIPLES OF JESUS AND THE WORLD

Rarely, so rarely, had Jesus shown specific interest in the whole world or in carrying the covenant message and word of his exaltation to other parts of it. Yet Matthew's gospel ends with a few lines that some critics say have to be a late addition but most believers in all ages have received as an authentic command and promise, one that matched the ministry of Paul and the traveling apostles before these lines were preserved and made scripturally public as a charter for the global reach:

> All authority in heaven and on earth has been given to me. Go therefore and make disciples of all nations, baptizing them in the name of the Father and of the Son and of the Holy Spirit, and teaching them to obey everything that I have commanded you. And remember, I am with you always, to the end of the age. (Matthew 28:18b–20)

Beginnings of the working out of that commission, "going global," appear in a second document by Luke, a book usually called the "Acts of the Apostles." Its account of Paul's call differs at many points from his own references to it, and reflects the tradition of stories that grew up among followers who heard of Paul's adventures. The first twelve chapters, however, deal with the disciples in Jerusalem, most notably Peter, who becomes a spokesperson for the others. Acts in one place tells the story of how a Hellenist follower named Philip set out to convert the despised neighbors, Samaritans, whom "real" Jews considered half-breed, half-saved. In another story a eunuch, treasurer of a court in Africa who was in Jerusalem for a feast that he as a eunuch was forbidden to attend, was reading a scroll of the prophets. Philip applied its word to Jesus Christ. The story of Christian witness in Africa had begun.

Peter is pictured as a leader of the Jerusalem church, but is seen in Acts as the recipient of a vision which taught him that no one is "unclean" and that he too should be part of an effort to take the gospel to the Gentiles. He and Paul on occasion engaged in conflict, but Acts shows them wearing each other down into a sort of concord over whether Gentiles needed to be circumcised to be part of the covenant, and later writings in his name, presumably written by people of his school or circle, are somewhat dismissive of Paul even when they congratulate him.

Though most of the Jerusalem followers and apostles were Jews, they had much difficulty reaching other Jews. Tragically, as we have seen, the two sets of believers almost from the beginning came to a parting of the ways. James, the brother of Jesus, was martyred in the year 62. As Jewish leaders fought back against Roman authority, followers of Jesus Christ were caught between and were hated by both. Jewish leaders dug in for the sake of survival, but the boundaries they set excluded Christians. The Christians who wanted to blend contemporary Judaism with their new version of faith were caught in the crossfire, demoralized, or wearied—and they faded. The fact that Christians saw so much in the Old Testament that they called a "type," or a foreshadowing of Christ, alienated Jews, who were content with their interpretations and would still wait for their Messiah, the Anointed One who Christians claimed Jesus to be. For those who saw the difference between Jews and Christians as being so radical that here was the constituting of two religions, we have a curious case of one religion taking over the whole canon of another, and interpreting it in such a way that the "other" did not recognize itself in the portrait, or was alienated by it. An interminable and tragic conflict had begun, ironically in the name of one whom Christians came to call the Prince of Peace.

2.

# THE FIRST
# ASIAN EPISODE

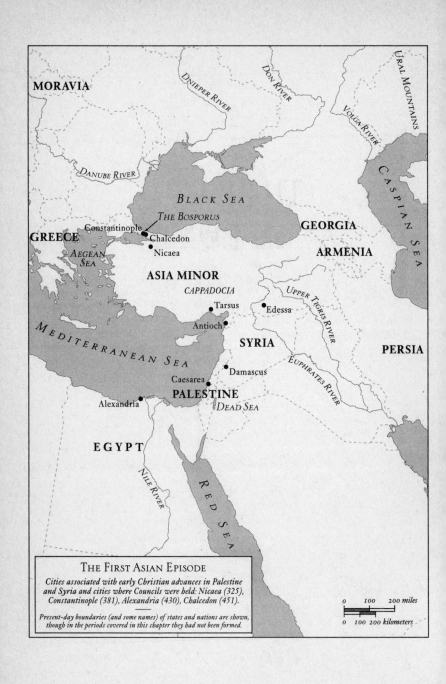

MORAVIA

*DNIEPER RIVER*

*DON RIVER*

*URAL MOUNTAINS*

*VOLGA RIVER*

*DANUBE RIVER*

*BLACK SEA*

*THE BOSPORUS*

GEORGIA

Constantinople

GREECE

Chalcedon

*CASPIAN SEA*

Nicaea

*AEGEAN SEA*

ARMENIA

ASIA MINOR

*CAPPADOCIA*

*UPPER TIGRIS RIVER*

Tarsus

Edessa

Antioch

PERSIA

*M E D I T E R R A N E A N   S E A*

SYRIA

*EUPHRATES RIVER*

Damascus

Caesarea

PALESTINE

*DEAD SEA*

Alexandria

E G Y P T

*NILE RIVER*

*R E D   S E A*

THE FIRST ASIAN EPISODE

*Cities associated with early Christian advances in Palestine
and Syria and cities where Councils were held: Nicaea (325),
Constantinople (381), Alexandria (430), Chalcedon (451).*

*Present-day boundaries (and some names) of states and nations are shown,
though in the periods covered in this chapter they had not been formed.*

| 0 | 100 | 200 *miles* |

| 0 | 100 | 200 *kilometers* |

Hinduism, Jainism, Buddhism, Sikhism, Confucianism, Taoism, and Shinto are Asian religions in all the catalogues and atlases. Scholars of global faiths now find reason to reexplore one more, Christianity. To call Christianity an Asian religion will evoke blank gazes from many in the West who favor "Eastern spirituality" while dismissing or disdaining Christianity. Surprisingly, that faith centered in Jesus Christ, who was a dweller on the eastern side of the Mediterranean in a place that was, in modern conceptions of continents, Asian. The first episode of Christian presence began with Jesus and Paul and company in Asia, where for hundreds of years the believing community was extensive and vital. Asian Christians like to remind others that Jesus was born in Asia, though ancient Asia may have had different connotations than does the modern. The followers of "The Way" were first named "Christian" at Antioch in Syria, which meant in Asia.

The story of this first Asian episode anticipates the later global presence since it helps people recognize that Christianity was situated on three continents through the earlier centuries. Believers within each of these geographical spheres brought special gifts and presented particular problems during interactions within their *oikoumene,* the Greek word for "the whole inhabited world." And, despite the ardors of travel and the difficulty of communicating rapidly over distances, many of them were trekkers and traders who worked their way east from Antioch along the Silk Road through today's Central Asian republics, past Mongolia, and across China. Some of them stayed and established themselves in oasis cities, where their stories became integral to the narratives about Asian empires, dynasties, warriors, and cultures. Second, forgotten in many accounts of early Christianity, is the fact that decisive episodes occurred in Asia Minor where, yes, even that proper noun is a reminder that the sites are Asian. Among spiritual inventions which prospered there and elsewhere in Asia were

Christian doctrines and creeds, modes of government and church architecture, plus refinements of monasticism and mysticism.

## THE CHRISTIANS IN THE ASIAN WORLDS

Exiled or fleeing from Jerusalem around the year 70, many followers of Jesus moved up into Syria. The biblical Book of Acts provides a glance at how the early chronicles reported on the spread of the faith. Barnabas, a renamed Jew ("son of encouragement"), was sent from Jerusalem to the prominent city of Antioch to help bring Jews and Hellenists together. Among them, witness mattered more than reasoning. "A great many people were brought to the Lord" after this "good man, full of the Holy Spirit and of faith" exhorted them (Acts 11:20–24). Barnabas looked up Paul in Syrian Tarsus and brought him to Antioch, where "for an entire year they met with the church and taught a great many people," now named "Christians."

Syria was a strategic locale. The Gospel of Matthew may well have been disseminated from there. The Hebrew and Aramaic speech of Palestine gave way to Syriac there and east of there. Soon after 150 an Assyrian-born convert named Tatian (d. c. 185) cobbled together and harmonized stories and sayings from the four gospels into a single package, the Diatessaron. He was a severe vegetarian, so in his translation John the Baptist was not allowed to eat meaty locusts, as the original had it, but only the side dish, honey. The Diatessaron was the scroll often used by spreaders of the faith who for two centuries moved also from Edessa into other parts of Asia. Scholars can trace the Syriac influence all the way into India, China, Mongolia, as well as at stops along the way in Persia and Mesopotamia.

Antioch, the third largest city in the Roman Empire, made a good headquarters, being near enough to Jerusalem whence migrant believers set out to exert their influence. Local pride and an abundance of talent, however, soon led the Syrians to declare cultural independence. That move forced them to devise or select means of governance, so they borrowed and refined a task and title for overseers, in Greek, *episkopoi*, bishops. They also had to make a case for themselves in a high culture that was largely Greek, so men like Theophilus of Antioch, also around 170, set out to show how the heritage of the Hebrew Scriptures, Jesus' Bible, bore more truth than did Greek philosophy or poetry.

## CAESAR OR CHRIST IN ASIA

Notwithstanding the eloquent arguments of Theophilus and others which were directed toward elites plus the reputations for generosity to others on the part of ordinary Christian women and men, "Caesar" soon moved against "Christ," as Nero had done in Rome. The government set out to extinguish the family of believers. Seven letters dating from around 110, written by Ignatius of Antioch (c. 35–107), mention that others had "preceded him in martyrdom . . . from Syria to Rome for the glory of God." Ignatius, who claimed the prophetic gifts of the Holy Spirit for his office, also helped define doctrine. He attacked the Docetists, that party of believers who contended that Jesus had only *seemed* to be a human. The Antiochians in his train later got typecast for placing their accent on Jesus as fully human. The case for episcopacy and doctrine that was made by Ignatius did not affect the world of Domitian (51–96), who sat in the emperor's chair which Nero earlier had drenched in blood. To him Christians looked subversive, not seeming Roman enough in their religion. The emperor Trajan's (53–117) people pulled Ignatius to Rome, and executed him, thus providing the martyrdom he sought. Deaths like his added to the lure of Christianity and, though Antioch was far from Rome, stories like his helped assemblies in Asia prosper.

A third Asian stop along the way, north of Damascus and east of Antioch, was Edessa, second in regional importance to Antioch and a gateway city to much of Asia. Cosmopolitan Christians who were at home in this trade center claimed the apostle Thaddeus as their founder, but mentally they had moved as far from Jerusalem as they were independent of Rome. For a time they escaped persecution under the regime of an Arabian monarch. Edessa, which was absorbed into the empire in 241 when the Sassanids were victorious, was therefore squeezed between two empires. Elites there spoke Greek but many looked to Persia for philosophy and to the astrologers and the stars for signs, while ordinary folk kept bowing to the deities of Babylon, Greece, and the Arab world. The message of Christians about Jesus Christ had to be adapted to ever more cultures.

## THE CHRISTIAN MOVE FURTHER EAST

While most early Christians, needing a roof over their heads, gathered and worshipped in homes and borrowed public spaces, Edessan Christians may have erected the first public church building. Many believe that from among them issued the churches in Armenia and Georgia to the north, Persia to the east, and then in India and China, further to the east. Most agents of the gospel from there transported Antioch's accent on the fully human character of the divine Jesus. A sign of their cosmopolitanism was the fact that Christians there, when prospering during what was called a "Parthian Peace," did joint Bible study with Jews, keeping on generally good terms with them. A strangely key figure near the end of this rule was philosopher-poet-astrologer Bardesanes, or Bar-Daisan (154–222), who encouraged King Abgar IX (195–214) to be friendly to Christians. Born to Persian exiles and converted around age twenty, he set out to persuade others to accept the faith. Not having everything sorted out spiritually and still absorbing the local religious mix of Edessa, including the astrology which he had favored, he granted more to fate as a weaker equivalent of God than the orthodox allowed. When later bishops found him too friendly to other faiths, some even forbade the reading of his works, so he all but disappeared from Christian histories. Yet he had exemplified friendliness to Jewish, Chinese, Indian, Persian, Greek, Arab, and the beliefs and communities of others. He connected with them through the concept of the Logos. This meant that Jesus, whose body was a phantom, still was the unique thought and word of God, whose way could incorporate all the faiths without demanding that meaningful traditions had to be scorned by the faithful. Excommunicated, he fled to Armenia.

Ardeshir I (ruled 226–241), who founded the Sassanid Dynasty, revived the then moribund religion of Zoroastrianism, ordering that the sacred fires, the special mark of that religion, be ritually relighted. Traditions of tolerance were then replaced by fanatic efforts to fuse crown and Zoroastrian faith. Persecution of Christians followed. On Good Friday in 344, according to tradition, believers had to watch the beheading by Shapur II (ruled 309–379) of one hundred Christian leaders before they were then themselves killed. A historian named Sozomen (c. 400–c. 450) reckoned that the "Great Persecution" between 339 and 348 alone took hundreds of thousands of lives, though modern historians regard such figures as far too high. Most historians also consider to be legendary a typical account from the end of the third century, chronicled in a Syrian Acts of the Martyrs. It was told that a beautiful woman, forcibly wed to a shah, rebuffed her husband and ruler because of her faith, so she paid the ultimate price. The Acts claimed that her face at the end was radiant and "her mouth filled with laughter" as she was ordered stripped, flogged, tortured, and paraded naked. Legendary the details may have been, but treatments of this sort were all too common.

Christians fared better farther north in Armenia, where churches thrived between the Black and Caspian seas. So successful were the first missionaries among the rulers that Armenia, some said, was the first officially Christian state. Origins there are lost in legend but embroidered in rich tradition. Armenian Christians trace their memories back to Gregory the Illuminator (c. 240–332), a Parthian whose parents moved to Armenia, which he left for a while, during which time he became a convert. In this story, upon returning around 300, Gregory was thrown into a pit for thirteen years because he refused to sacrifice to pagan gods. As such stories must, this one turned on a miracle: Gregory was brought from the pit to heal an ailing King Tiridates III (238–314), whom he converted. Whatever grains of truth are part of such stories, they reflect the depth and extent of the conversions of many Armenians, who soon produced their own translation of the Bible, one which helped them shape the community and, eventually, Armenia itself. Gregory is remembered as "the Apostle to the Armenians."

## THE FAR EAST

Then there is what for Westerners is the Far East, more conventionally thought of as Asia than were the Asian places nearer the Mediterranean sphere. Most curiosity centers on the Christian entry into China. Old stories of Christian presence there, long rendered suspect, received some confirmation in archaeological remains. Most notable was the finding in 1625 of a large monument from 781. It told of a Christian agent named Alopen, who visited T'ang Dynasty China in 635. Remnants of that civilization indicated that an emperor's library almost matched what was then the world's greatest collection of books, in Alexandria in Egypt. Emperor T'ai-tsung (to 649), who had Alopen translate Christian writings, promoted tolerance for this faith, and even helped Christians build a place of worship. According to an edict in 638, he declared that Christians should be tolerated along with Taoist and Buddhist adherents.

Two main Christian parties were present by the time that monument was readied, one group called the Nestorians. They held that in the Incarnate Christ there were two distinct Persons, one divine and the other human. Nestorians were favored by the T'ang Dynasty and represented by a priest, while the other party was called Orthodox, led by a monument-builder and scholar. The Nestorian influence declined when that dynasty faded but some adherents long held on in Central Asia. In references from a thousand years after Christ we can read of Christian sites in fifteen urban centers. Against all odds, numbers, and enemies, Nestorian Christians long remained active.

As the Nestorians met frustration along the Silk Road routes, they found a new chance to make their way in northern China, when various peoples were converted. The numbers may not be reliable, but the claim that 200,000 Keraits sought baptism by Nestorians after 1009 gives some sense of the Christian influence among them. Many who may not be familiar with Keraits and other Mongol peoples can pick up the plot when made aware that a youth patronized by one of these baptized Christians, Temujin, grew up to be Genghis Khan (c. 1162–1227). While never a Christian, he did not make it a point to persecute believers. His conquests, from Beijing across Iran (Persia), and Russia, are as well known as the story of his tolerance of Christianity is unfamiliar. His son Kublai Khan (1215–94) also remained relatively tolerant of Christians. Both Genghis Khan and Kublai Khan remained devoted to shamanism, but the two were not the sworn enemies of Christianity that many of the Sassanids had been.

If the story to this point suggested too strongly that congeniality existed among the Mongol shamanists and Christians, one has to take note of the counter-story in the case of Timur the Great (1336–1406). Known also as Tamerlane, the violent warrior overwhelmed Persia in 1379 and killed Christians and Muslims alike in Delhi. So vicious and efficient at opposing dissidents was he that eventually he stamped out the remaining Nestorians and Jacobites, other Christian sprouts, wherever his reach extended. Some Christians who claimed lineage back to the apostle Thomas did survive on the Malabar Coast in India, and a few more hung on in a city on the Upper Tigris River. By this time we are reduced to talking of "hanging on." When the great Christian centers of the East, Jerusalem and Antioch, fell to Muslims and, most significantly, when the capital of the empire in the East, Constantinople, fell to Muslim Turks in 1453, the first millennium-and-a-half Asian episode ended.

## WESTERN ASIA, ASIA MINOR

This Asian story has had to deal with geographical expansion to the east along with accounts of migrations, conversions, and persecutions. These made up some of the externals of Christian existence. It is the internal life of the Christian communities in western Asia that draws more attention for its influence on later global Christians. Having noted one need of Asian churches to invent forms of organizations such as the episcopate, even more important is it for us to account for Christian hungers for definition and conflicts over attempts to address them. Asian Christianity was the fertile ground for producing statements of faith called creeds, which were fashioned by theologians, and which took form in official councils. In part the need arose as Christians and Jews from the first began to part significantly over the question of how faith in the human Jesus as the exalted Lord related to synagogue Judaism. Such Judaism was, of course, also monotheistic, but most Jews could not accept the place or role of Jesus in the godhead.

## CHRISTIANS AND JEWS AGAIN

This part of the story leads us to return to beginnings in the year 70, when the Temple in Jerusalem was destroyed. Decades later, after the Romans crushed a messianic revolt under Simon Bar Kochba in 132–135, they exiled the Jews. The Temple was irreplaceable, but the meeting places for study, the synagogues, were portable, and they became scenes of debate and places for parting between Jews and Christians, both Jewish and Gentile. In them, Christian thinkers opposed Jews for having rejected Jesus as their Messiah. Extravagant and lethal claims followed: that Jews were killers of Christ; that their children must suffer for the belief that their ancestors had killed Jesus; that Jewish law and tradition need no longer be followed. Jewish leadership responded by reaffirming their inherited ways, thus disposing of the Christian challenge. Common reading of the Hebrew Scriptures had kept some of the two together sporadically, as we saw at Edessa, and some Christians did try to follow the Jewish law for a century and more. Still, the breach widened, and Christians, when they came to power later in the empire, persecuted Jews.

Some legacies from Judaism marked efforts by Christians in the east to formulate their own way. With Theophilus of Antioch they drew on figures like Abraham and Moses to show the superiority of biblical witness to Greek philosophy. The opposite kind of challenge to emergent orthodoxy came from Marcion (c. 110–160), a rich shipowner who began adult life as an orthodox Christian but was excommunicated around 144 and declared a heretic, which by any standard of the time but his own, he was. His movement, which took hold in Armenia, Arabia, and villages around Damascus, spread rapidly, lasted two centuries, and ideas from it lived on into modern times. He attached himself to the writings of Paul, and carried his interpretations to the point that anti-Judaism became his main theme. He propounded a radical disjunction between Old and New Testaments, as well as between his Jesus and the Jesus who was revealed as being responsive to the faith of Israel. His Jesus disclosed the true God, who, argued Marcion, was unknown until Jesus came along. The Old Testament God for him was the demiurge, not a devil but not a good god either. Marcion was, paradoxically, a creative force in that perhaps in his time no one more than he forced other Christians to think through the nature of evil and the meaning of Jesus Christ.

In the face of challenges, Christians, accused by Jews of having two gods, had to make clearer their commitment to monotheism. The stage was thus set for the fashioning of creeds, which are condensed statements of faith, to supplement the biblical stories. Theophilus had done much to launch the effort. The invisible God, he argued, was present as Logos, or Word, in the human Jesus. Paul of Samosata (200–275), another bishop of Antioch, added a refinement around 260. His executive style is worth noting, for it demonstrates how the church was growing more complex and its leaders more hungry for power. Paul put to work a set of secretaries, furniture designers who fashioned a high throne for him and a secluded chamber for prayers, and was furnished with a bodyguard. The bishop clung fiercely to the assertion that Jesus was fully human, contending that he did not enter the world as the divine Logos or Spirit, though he came to be anointed as such. Critics heard the bishop say that "Jesus is from below," not born as Logos from the Holy Spirit. He refused to say that Jesus was "descended from above," as the other bishops would. Still, he also raised urgent questions that the other bishops had no choice but to address.

Charges came that he abused his office, that he was immoral, and that he taught a wrong doctrine of Jesus Christ. The critics fired first by condemning and deposing him at a synod in 268. Amazingly, the Christians in contention appealed to the Emperor Aurelian, who evidenced awareness of growing Christian power but knew his own limits, so he turned the trial over to the other bishops. While they again condemned Paul, his stress on the humanity of Jesus and the divine Logos survived to color Antiochian over against Alexandrian (from Egypt) efforts to deal with the issue of Jesus as human and divine. While Paul and another theologian, Sabellius, did not win in the contentions, they had made their point: that Jesus was fully human, and that one dared not deny his human flesh. They helped set the agenda for later councils.

## THE EMPERORS AS DEFINERS

To frame their story, the focus first has to turn to imperial developments, since the power of the emperor played a major role in defining doctrine. The most significant turn in the administration of Christian life for many centuries occurred in the farthest west corners of Asia. It influenced Christian communities everywhere for all the centuries to follow. Its center was Byzantium. All the talk of Christian foci at Edessa and Delhi or Beijing and Persia dwindles in importance when talk begins of the Emperor Constantine (c. 285–337) entering the scene and of his successors dominating. Until now the story has been that of bishops and theologians, worshippers and martyrs, victims of the powerful or those with an eye on the heavenly kingdom. The Christian story, however, is also focused and sometimes dependent upon people of action, wearers of crowns, bearers of swords, sometimes thugs, people with their eye on earthly kingdoms, those who prayed to and claimed the power of the human Jesus and the exalted Lord, whose insignia they placed on their banners, armaments, and thrones.

Constantine is known for having claimed to his favored historian Eusebius (c. 263–339) that he received a vision, if not of the heavenly kingdom, then at least from heaven. Before a major battle in 312 against Maxentius (278–312), a rival for the throne, he looked into the heavens—was it to him still in a way the abode of his other, older god, the sun?—heard a voice, and in a vision saw a symbol, Chi-Rho, the first two Greek letters of the title Christ. The word he heard with it said: "In this sign, conquer." Since the emperor did conquer, he credited it as the sign of God's favor for victory. Whether or not his conversion was complete and genuine is not our question to answer at this point: what he made of and did with the power he gained from his victory and claimed from that sign is of consequence. Until then kings and emperors were persecutors or, at best, tolerators or ignorers of Christians. Now the course changed when the emperor claimed and exerted power *for* and *through* the church, as he saw it and saw fit.

Constantine needed a capital, and in a stroke of genius in 330 C.E. chose the little town on the Bosphorus called Byzantium. Genius it was because this was an easy-to-defend base, located as far east as one could go in the old Roman Empire, and as far west as Asia could take him. He called the soon to be rich city after himself, Constantinople, and gradually replaced the old temples there with Christian churches, the never matched Hagia Sophia crowning them all. As the empire in Asia Minor turned to Christianity from paganism, so, according to records of the time, many Christians in turn adopted pagan customs, purchasing charms and amulets, consulting fortune-tellers, and blending old religious traditions with new ones. Thus the first day of the week became "Sun"day and Christmas was set for December 25, the day honoring the Invincible Sun. Imperial power became involved with naming bishops, and bishops had to advise the emperor. When Constantine died, many of the old beliefs showed their staying power. He was regarded as a latter-day apostle and deified by the Senate. Still no one had done so much as had he to set the course for civil and religious affairs in the Christian world. Fourteen centuries would pass before the Constantinian formula, a kind of unsettled fusion of authorities in church and state, came to be radically questioned and, in some places, slowly displaced.

Many aspects of Christian life eluded the emperor. Force being his game, he soon was directing imperial power to the service of the church, which, in his own way, he would control. His mother, Helena, toured the Holy Land and claimed to have discovered the True Cross on which Jesus had died. Now concern for and visits to the Holy Land became a fashion and a passion. Before long her son was invited to intervene in churchly squabbles and, even where he was not asked, if he chose to, he interposed himself as lay theologian, power-broker, and decision-maker. Soon he was stipulating forms of worship and promoting true doctrine, meaning the teaching of the bishops whom he favored. Just as his pagan predecessors privileged and protected the civil religion, he now would adopt Christianity and work for its success. When there was no one else to whom conflicting parties might turn, he was available, amassing power as he did on each occasion. He took part in inventing a way to address religious agendas and controversies when he called a church council.

Here the story returns to the development of creeds in western Asian Christianity. The place was Nicaea in today's Asia Minor, where in 325, bishops decided on a set of propositions respecting the Divine Trinity in a setting and context we observed when visiting Antioch and points east. It was in this situation that Arius (c. 256–336) stressed the humanity of Jesus in a distinctive way. His key word was "begotten": if Jesus was begotten from the Father, as the creedal formula had it, then he had a beginning and had to be subordinate to God the Father, who had no beginning. Arius lost. The bishops who prevailed, led by the African Athanasius (c. 296–373), made it a policy not to receive back into the church repentant partisans of Arianism, recognized as heretics, so Constantine tried to step in—though also without success. The emperor's great achievement was to help make the empire's eastern sphere become more important than the western, and the site for determining doctrine.

While one imperial descendant, Julian "the Apostate" (331–363), rebelled against the doctrinal and civil settlements, the Christian emphasis prevailed and held for centuries. Successive emperors spoke up for the freedom in theory to believe or not believe in Jesus Christ. In practice they often relied on coercion, and the emperor of the once persecuted sect of Christians now became the persecutor. By 391 under Theodosius I (c. 346–395) they abolished the pagan observances, but paganism lived on away from the official sites. Soon the emperors were busy organizing the councils to decide and then to police their decisions over doctrine. The subject had become urgent because conflict distracted citizens from finding unity and common purpose and because many felt that to teach error would condemn souls under their care to everlasting destruction.

## THE COUNCILS AND CREEDS AS DEFINERS

Now the instrument through which emperors and bishops tried to settle issues of truth with power were councils of the church, called "ecumenical" because they were to deal with the whole church in the whole world. Six more of these followed Nicaea. A historian today may well feel a need to apologize and explain the agendas. Theologians who can think their way into the then current Greek terms which we translate as "substance" and "essence," "nature" and "person," find that mere mention of the controversies is unsatisfying to most modern readers. The vast majority of general citizens are likely to shrug their shoulders, turn the pages rapidly, and long to resume at the point when the story again meets the real world. For better or for worse, however, much of this story did deal with the then real world.

Reports from the time tell of villagers at the barber and butcher shops debating, hours on end, how the man Jesus could be and was "Son of God" or "God." Outcomes led to bitterness and even warfare, while reigns of rulers could depend on how the creedal votes went. Debates that now seem foolish and arcane were the stuff of intellectual and political life. A whole new vocabulary was superimposed almost to the point that it displaced biblical language. The Nicene Creed which resulted from Nicaea drew signatures of all but two bishops. Yet bishops, soon after signing, were scrapping again, until the point that there was almost more dispute over what Nicaea affirmed than over what had occasioned the council. While it was hard to fight the living emperor, Constantine, who was still pleased with his victory, after his death the parties came back with a vengeance—and more councils had to be called.

Other topics than the two natures of Christ were also urgent. Eusebius of Caesarea, the historian who set out to please the emperor with his reports and analyses, helped invent a theology to legitimize power, or, better, a theology for the relation between the two powers. The emperor was the earthly or temporal image of God, while the church represented heaven among people of earth. One attractive and forceful party was still made up of the followers of the Alexandrian Arius, who stressed the humanity of Jesus. Over against him, onto Asian soil and also out of Alexandrian Egypt and thus Africa, came Athanasius. Finally Basil the Great (c. 329–379), Bishop of Caesarea, put energies into defeating heretics and getting the bishops to agree on more elements than they had before. His brother, Gregory of Nyssa (c. 330– c. 395), and a colleague, Gregory of Nazianzus (330–389)—the three were called "the Cappadocian Fathers" after their home base—with him got the churches of the East to agree that Jesus and the father were "of one substance," but they were three distinct "persons," Father, Son, and Spirit. At a follow-up council at Chalcedon in 451, the matters were finally "settled," but by no means to everyone's enduring satisfaction.

## THE TRIUMPH OF CHRISTENDOM

The powerful imperial theology and church life led to the growing independence and authority of the Eastern Church. Constantinople became the main center of Christian influence and organization for a number of centuries: empire and church together ruled the lives of believers. Constantine had learned that to control the empire he had to dominate the church, which meant that he had to work through the bishops, leaders so dispersed that they were at a disadvantage in struggles with him. He and his successors saw to it that little coming from them could counter the imperial, which means his own power. The emperors needed domestic unity because they had to fight off attacks by enemies all around them, such as by Persian Sassanids in the seventh century. Bit by bit the territories of the empire in the East were being whittled away.

At first, one would have expected glory years to follow the triumph of Christendom. To add to the surface luster, early on, Theodosius I outlawed and began to persecute pagans and made

Christianity official. No one outdid Emperor Justinian (527–565) in favoring Christianity. First among the great rulers in this period, this son of peasants but highly gifted and educated ruler set out to abolish vestiges of paganism. He and his churchly leaders became singularly devoted to worship, which climaxes in the formal "Divine Liturgy," a celebration in highly adorned and icon-filled churches. It was opened with processions on great days in the festive calendar. Church buildings were designed to represent the celestial on earth. Great hymnodists contributed to the beauty of worship. Whoever wanted to measure Christianity by its likeness to the simple Galilean ancestry and to Jesus would be disappointed, just as would those who celebrated Christ in glory also feel elated and elevated.

It is easy to see why the imperial agents welcomed the trends, since these represented power. The secular authority of the empire and in the culture were to be displaced by what was intended to be a resolutely Christian state. But "Justinian Riots" and rebellion broke out in the capital city, and great destruction followed. Even the grand Hagia Sophia met the torch, but it was later rebuilt more gloriously than it had been originally. Justinian was ready to turn tail into exile, but his empress, Theodora (500–548), counseled otherwise. Justinian responded to her prodding, organized the army, and sent military leader Belisarius to put down the rebellion, a strategy that led to the death of thirty thousand people. While he could be savage, Justinian is better remembered as the codifier of imperial laws into the Codex of Justinian in 529. His revisers excised everything in the old laws that had represented a hardship for Christians. As Constantine was the wielder of the sword and builder of the cities, Justinian wielded the pen and built the churches. He also preempted many of the duties and attracted many of the honors that would go with churchly office, and considered himself to be the ruler of the church as well as the state.

No one was fooled into thinking Justinian was alone in all this. Theodora also exercised imperial power over the church. Competent and strong-willed, she took a palace in Constantinople and turned it into a large monastery for monks who, as did she, opposed the formula about the two natures of Christ that had been agreed upon at the Council of Chalcedon in 451. She and her followers improvised little insertions into the liturgy, phrases which witnessed to their own theological convictions. The empress commandeered episcopal personnel and authority and sent out defenders called Monophysites, who held that Jesus had not two "natures" but one. It was said that this group ordained 100,000 priests, mainly east of Edessa. Theodora died in 548, but in her succession fights over Monophysitism still raged.

## EURASIA AND THE EASTERN CHURCH

The course of the Eastern Church was led by four patriarchates: Constantinople, Antioch, Jerusalem, and Alexandria in Africa. The territory over which they ruled included Asia Minor, the Near East, Egypt, Russia, Ukraine, and—many called it the "Greek" church—Greece and the Balkans. In the sixth century under Justinian the empire was still intact, but a century later the Muslims had conquered so much that Christian Orthodoxy in the East became a minority faith, and Muslim caliphates governed. The churches, now not only a minority, were themselves divided. The Nestorian Assyrian church of the East opposed and was opposed by five churches that were called Monophysite, those groups which did not accept Chalcedon's terms. Taking them together, one may speak of the Byzantine church as existing from 527 to 1453, when Constantinople fell to the Muslim Turks.

By the ninth century it became hard to contend for a single united empire, as Constantinople went its own way from Rome, or one might say Rome went its own way from Constantinople. One of the strengths in the East was the devotion to icons, representations of Christian saints that in many cases became the subject of what their critics called idolatry. Finally the Emperor Leo III in 726 was moved to attack them, thus becoming known as the "iconoclast," the image-breaker. Naturally, icons had their defenders, none greater than John of Damascus (c. 675–749), whom many regarded as the most profound of the Eastern theologians. He found a way to affirm devotion to icons but to keep that devotion in limits short of idolatry and superstition. In 843 a synod condemned the iconoclasts, but icons continued to draw the support of the faithful in the Eastern churches. At the end of a long process that only looked sudden in its climactic decade leading up to a schism in 1054, the churches of West and East, the latter remaining Asian and Eastern European, split and Christendom has remained divided into our own time.

Reference to the church in Eastern Europe points for a moment to a conceptual dilemma for historians. The continental line dividing the landmass of Eurasia, generally along the Ural Mountains, has been vague and shifting, and what came after the schism to be the Eastern Orthodox Church is also partly in Europe. Since the governance, theology, jurisdictions, liturgy, and "feel" of the Orthodox and Western churches are so different, we shall continue to link the Orthodox with its Asian heritage. While we have paid attention to movements from Istanbul or, earlier, Antioch, all the way to Beijing in China or the Malabar Coast in India, Eastern Orthodoxy also carried on missions to the Slavs and saw to the creation of Slavic churches. Two brothers, Cyril (827–869) and Methodius (825–884), came forward to begin the work, the one a scholar, the other a governor. In 862 Ratislav of Moravia asked the Byzantine emperor for Christian instructors who could speak in and teach Slavic languages, and the brothers were ready to employ the dialect, also in worship. Their main efforts at converting Slavs were thwarted, and neither of the two could have thought of his work as successful at the times of their deaths. Yet they had spread the language, translated Greek texts into Slavic, developed the Cyrillic alphabet, and thus prepared the tools for their successful successors. Some went to Serbia, and found converts after 867. Serbs and Croats, Czechs and Bulgars, and others have revered Cyril and Methodius as saints for centuries.

Finally and most dramatically, these Eastern mission efforts bore fruit when Princess Olga (c. 890–969) and her grandson Vladimir (960–1015) in Kiev were converted, not long before 988. The Kievan church was governed under Constantinople, and its leaders also chose to adopt the liturgies, practices, and theology of Byzantine Orthodoxy. Heirs of these pioneers like to recall that

Vladimir tried to keep the traditions associated with Jesus in mind, and did much to guide work among the diseased and poor. Some speak of these as the most advanced social programs in the Christianity of those centuries and Vladimir was considered "equal to the apostles." For a remarkable sign, scholars notice that after he abolished capital punishment, his sons refused to engage in military action against a relative who had simply seized power—and they suffered death for their refusal.

In subsequent centuries, mystical "fathers" came on the scene, most notably Saint Symeon (949–1022), called "the New Theologian." He founded several monasteries in the Constantinopolitan area, where he was a too rigorous abbot but an effective writer of spiritual tracts. While he did not desert community, he argued that individuals, if guided by a strong spiritual leader, could undertake their own journeys to salvation, if they were disciplined to be ascetic. A devotee of the Divine Light, he wrote in mystical terms that have had wide influence.

Ironies abound in the churches of the East. Subject to the emperor, who always sought unity, and heirs of church councils which formulated patterns of unity, leaders for centuries had to deal with schism and heresy. Orthodox, Nestorian, and Monophysite Christians divided the loyalties of the believers. Yet some themes stressed this unity, for example, of the human with God through mystical experience, as advocated by Symeon and Gregory Palamas (c. 1296–1359). Even more impressive was the widespread acceptance of the Divine Liturgy. Maximos the Confessor (c. 580–662) summed this up well: "God's holy church in itself is a symbol of the sensible world as such, since it possesses the divine sanctuary as heaven and the beauty of the nave as earth. Likewise the world is a church since it possesses heaven corresponding to a sanctuary, and for a nave it has the adornment of the earth." Celebration of that liturgy was often the inspiring and sustaining element as the church of the East faced, among others, pitiless rivals in the centuries ahead.

Balance sheets on Christians in the various parts of the Far East would see the consequences of their inability to find a leader like Constantine to champion them. So Persia and China were rather leaderless, and the believing communities were at the mercy of invaders and a succession of dynasties, not all of them as tolerant as were some of the Mongols. Leaderless, the Nestorians did minister among nomads like the Keraits. Still, farther west in the Eastern Church and empire, martyrs, creed-makers, liturgists, empire builders, artists, and devotees of icons helped develop a form of the church that would survive for centuries, though in different styles, also after the fall of Constantinople in 1453. By then an external challenger, the Muslim, equipped with sword and cause, had conquered and held the churches of Asia and the East in subjection. An episode had ended, though a new one would begin around 1500. That is a very different story which will demand, and later will receive, separate telling.

3.

# THE FIRST
# AFRICAN EPISODE

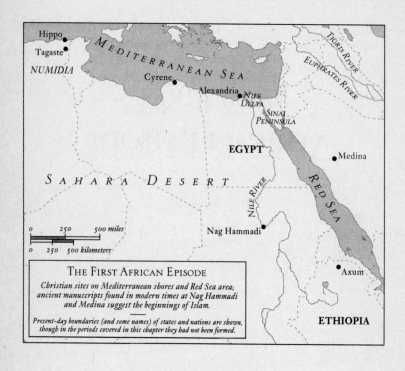

THE FIRST AFRICAN EPISODE

*Christian sites on Mediterranean shores and Red Sea area; ancient manuscripts found in modern times at Nag Hammadi and Medina suggest the beginnings of Islam.*

———

*Present-day boundaries (and some names) of states and nations are shown, though in the periods covered in this chapter they had not been formed.*

While modern concepts of Africa which include sub-Saharan lands differ from the ancient ones, some contemporary African and African-American iconographers understandably like to portray the greatest African theologian, Saint Augustine (354–430), as a black man, though no one knows how he looked. This sort of representation is no more off the point than seeing Mary and Jesus portrayed as an Italian or German Madonna and Child. The African visage in art helps stamp on modern imaginations a sign of the influence of northern Africa in the formation of Christianity. Africa seems remote from Rome and the imperial centers, though we must remember that traversing the Mediterranean to Africa was less arduous and time-consuming than traveling around the eastern end of the ocean by land. Though Augustine was schooled and spent some time across the Mediterranean, once he returned home to Africa and was called to leadership there, he resisted invitations to leave. He suffered seasickness even on the mildest seas, and that fact helped keep him homebound in his Africa, where he traveled much by land.

Reaching into the "uttermost parts of the earth" with the message of Jesus Christ took the Christian movement very early to Africa, the continent which is now becoming one of the two or three centers of Christian energies twenty centuries later. While there may be few continuities between the ancient North African church and modern African and African-American churches, one may stroll into a Catholic campus chapel in modern America and see Augustine pictured in a mosaic as African, a sign of welcome to African-American students. Similarly, seminarians in Kenya, as they trace their spiritual ancestry, make much of the long history of Christianity on the continent.

The ancient moves into Africa were not confined to the creation of mere beachheads or outposts. Witness: six of the most inventive Christian thinkers of all the ages, Augustine, Tertullian, Cyril of Alexandria, Athanasius, Cyprian, and Jerome, flourished there or started from there. From Africa they influenced the other two continents in their time, and continue to color Christian expressions on all continents today. They originated many contributions of style and thought for export and radically tailored imports from elsewhere. Examples of Christian thought were preserved on scrolls and in books, as at the greatest library, in Alexandria, though most evidences of ancient patterns have disappeared. Still one turns to Africa to review and inform some practices, such as early ventures with monasticism. We cannot know whether the pioneers Antony (251–356) or Pachomius (292–348) had an African appearance, however that is defined, but they were or became thoroughly African. We know that despite travel dangers on sea and land routes, African Christians represented the beginnings of what today we would call global awareness.

Three bases with Christian presence were on the northern coast, one in Numidia, another in the Nile Delta around Alexandria, and the third in Cyrene between them. Their records provide historians with data concerning major figures and themes of the faith. The later and larger narrative of Christianity would be greatly impoverished were we not to know of African doings. The New Testament itself already pointed to storied roots of African Christianity. The Nativity account in Matthew described the flight of Joseph, Mary, and the infant Jesus to Egypt. In the gospel story, a man from Cyrene helped Jesus carry his cross on the way to his death. The author of the Book of Acts, eager to show that Jews who spoke diverse languages from "every nation under heaven" were present at the birth of the church on Pentecost, included "Egypt and the parts of Libya belonging to Cyrene" in his narrative. Also according to the Book of Acts, as we read, the apostle Philip encountered and helped convert an Ethiopian eunuch, and the same Acts twice more in passing mentions Cyrene. Nine or ten line-inches of type in a modern New Testament have to take care of the continent.

Africa was not isolated from the rest of the Roman Empire. The seas we call Mediterraneum—Mare Tyrrhenum, Mare Africanum, Mare Phenicium, and Mare Internum—were busy commuting lines, and Roman-style government and military life dominated there while older African cultures lived on. Christian people and events in Africa influenced and were influenced by those on two other continents. Whoever wishes to understand the founding and governance of churches, heresies, monasticism, and a variety of schools of theology anywhere in early Christianity would find well spent the years of studying the traces left by believers in Africa.

## AFRICAN CHRISTIANITY RESISTED

Historians know little about beginnings west of Egypt, but when a synod convened in 220 at the cultural capital of Carthage, seventy bishops were present. Their number would double during the next century. The surrounding Punic culture combined influences of the Phoenician ancestry of some citizens with African elements. Christians had to coexist with worshippers of local deities and gods from Palestine, Egypt, and elsewhere in North Africa. Though the believers knew they had to keep followers of these at bay, they also had no choice but to interact, usually to their disadvantage, with the devotees of the empire's official religion. Imperial resistance to the new faith was spotty at first, but local authorities persecuted and killed some believers. On occasions when the persecutions became empire-wide policies, ready-to-die Christians drew the attention of the public, elicited awe, and, ironically, before the eyes of the authorities, saw their community grow. A faith for which people would give their lives bore looking into.

The Christian communities prospered, which means that most believers survived and set to work to situate the new faith in the old cultures, some of which were highly literate expressions of Greek and Roman ways. Their devotees showed that they were bewildered by the Jewish-based faith in a figure who was somehow both human and divine. How could anyone hold to something so strange? Strict and legal-minded Tertullian at Carthage (c. 160–220), in an often misinterpreted line, said in the face of philosophers that he believed in Christianity because it was absurd. This absurdity proved dangerous among hostile imperial and local forces. Reckoning with the death of Christians he averred that the blood of martyrs is the seed of the church. He knew how risky it was to follow Jesus Christ, who was clearly seen as a rival to Caesar. At the same time, Tertullian advertised the moral potential of Christians, and spelled out to the public that it had need for this influence. Later and further west, Augustine at Hippo decried the "grievous evils of former times," while the "lust of rule" by the "powerful few," he preached, enslaved the "rest, worn and wearied," as the larger population had come to be.

The most effective and generally best emperors, like Marcus Aurelius (232–282) and Diocletian (c. 246–c. 312), turned out to be the worst persecutors, because they could well discern how much of a threat to empire the rule of Jesus Christ could be. Because the emperors were being deified, their domain had no place for Christianity, the rare one among the many sects of the day whose adherents kept their fingers crossed and their mouths shut when it came time to honor the emperor's cult. The persecutions, however few or many lives they took—the figures are always debated—varied in frequency and intensity, depending upon the measure of passions and fears among emperors and their loyal subjects.

Even if there had been accurate counts, to point to statistics might mean slighting the human cost for individuals. A favored story through the ages concerned Felicitas and Perpetua, who were executed in 203 at a time when authorities wanted to stanch the flow of new conversions. Felicitas was the pregnant nursemaid slave of a wealthy young nursing mother, Perpetua, who violated the taboos of her father's society by being drawn to the faith. When tried for her faith and found steadfast despite threats, she was sentenced to be torn apart by animals before crowds in the arena. While waiting in prison Perpetua recorded visions and left accounts, including one on the birth of Felicitas's baby shortly before execution day. To the end she resisted the rituals demanded by the executioners. She refused to wear garb that indicated she was an offering to the gods, and, someone recorded, she approached her death with "an even step as the bride of Christ." When a fired-up heifer which gored and tossed the two mothers did not kill them, a gladiator finished them off with the sword. Again ironically, his instrument turned out to be a virtual recruiting device. Reports say that shouts of praise erupted among the faithful to celebrate "those genuinely invited and chosen to share in the glory of our Lord Jesus Christ!" Many townspeople were drawn to a faith strong enough to produce such responses. Christianity was to become ever more differentiated from other belief systems. By the time of these African martyrdoms it was clear that at this distance from Jerusalem, Jews and Christians, though they were not at war, were growing distant from each other. Gentiles soon made up the Christian majority among believers in Africa.

Some believers lost courage or wandered from what was coming to be thought of as orthodox versions of the faith. Through the African centuries Christians saw their ranks split over policies installed to deal with deviations and what winners in the battle for orthodoxy called heresy. That term comes from *haeresis,* the Greek word for choice. Potential converts certainly had plenty of choices. A chronicler could write a virtual textbook on Christian heresies without taking an eye off Africa. Most of them had to do with the distinctive mark of Christianity as signaled by its very name: the status and role of Christ as the human Jesus, the exalted Lord, but others dealt with moral lapse or wavering in the face of persecution.

## CHALLENGES TO EMERGING ORTHODOXY

For a major example, leaders who defined doctrine and who corraled the votes for an official form of Christianity had to differentiate themselves in the midst of a cluster of adherents to rites and a clutter of philosophies which acquired the name "Gnosticism." Wherever and however these movements began, moderns who have shown curiosity about them have been freshly enabled to study some of their practices in Africa. This is so thanks to a farmer who in 1945 went looking for fertilizer but who unearthed a treasure, the miniature library now known from their site in Upper Egypt as the Nag Hammadi manuscripts. They reveal how Gnostics before the year 400 lived and what they expounded.

Sometimes like the Docetists, who thought Jesus Christ had only seemed to be human, some Gnostics fit their interpretation into an elaborate system of thought as a mirror of the faith in which Jesus often played very different roles than those assigned by these "heresies." Heresies appears this one time in quotes to respect critics of orthodoxy who remind readers that history gets written by winners, and there were plenty of near-winners and bare losers in this time of definition.

One Gnostic leader in the second century, Valentinus (c. 100–c. 153) at Alexandria, propounded the claim that Jesus had not risen from the dead in any bodily way. He and others of his school of thought wrote a variety of short books including two gospels patterned after those that made their way into the biblical canon, plus one "revelation." From such texts one gets glimpses of beguiling alternatives to these biblical writings that the church eventually did adopt as its canon. The biblical Book of Genesis sounded almost matter-of-fact compared to what some of the Gnostic documents described when accounting for origins. While mainstream Christianity had some negative things to say about the surrounding world—witness the monastic pioneers who went to the desert to distance themselves from it—they also saw it in positive terms as the arena where God took on human form and was active.

Most Gnostics described the physical and material world as evil, but did not abandon it completely. Elite insiders, chosen figures known as "spirituals," were seen as God's agents to bring secret knowledge into that world. Gnostic teaching explained what went wrong in the cosmos. In some versions, those who wanted to see how evil got propagated had only to look at women, since women were responsible for evil, and through their children kept enlarging its domain. Gnostics were dualists, for whom the God of Creation and covenant was an evil God or at least a limited one. The good God belonged to the New Testament. While some adherents were ascetic, others offered high times. The father and son team of Carpocrates (c. 145) and Epiphanes, who taught that Jesus was a mere man, pushed behavioral limits into license when they argued that God's law commanded promiscuous behavior.

Another group, the Cainites (c. 175–225), professed that the Creator was so evil that humans should invert and subvert his laws by engaging in licentious and outrageous acts. They praised the serpent in the Genesis story for having stocked Eve's mind with knowledge and insight and chose to follow Judas, the disciple who betrayed Jesus, over Jesus himself.

The impulse to counter the gospel story and biblical explanations with secret knowledge and disciplines survived far beyond Nag Hammadi and Alexandria. This expansive philosophy with a religious hue subtly influenced many Christians, so much so that at Alexandria the majority at one time may have displayed Gnostic leanings. At the same time, the charge of Gnosticism was also often used to accuse anyone who disagreed with orthodox self-definition, just as Gnostic-minded people used broad and fluid definitions to make it attractive. Some Christian leaders saw it as their prime enemy, Tertullian calling it "that bed of poisonous toadstools."

A second major deviating movement was the Asian import called Montanism, a kind of strict obverse to Gnosticism. It was devised around the middle of the second century by new-convert Montanus and two prophetesses, Maximilla and Prisca, who claimed to be vehicles for the voice of the Paraclete, the Holy Spirit. They wanted believers to ready themselves for martyrdom and to provoke persecution, while they waited for the early return of Jesus. Because the time before that return was short, Christians had to be brutally ascetic, as dry as was the bit of food they permitted themselves and as restrained as were their asexual marriage bondings. When an aged Tertullian turned to Montanism, he applied its strictures to other believers. As part of his view of discipline, Tertullian came to oppose the practice of baptizing infants. If he had his way, all Christian women would have been veiled in public and denied a voice in public gatherings, minimal though that voice was allowed to be even away from Montanism. If believers sinned grievously, they were not to be forgiven. If a spouse died, the widowed survivor could not remarry. Tertullian severely judged Christians who, when they shunned Montanism, looked too compromising and relaxed about their faith. The

Montanists, condemned at a synod in 230, went underground and kept exerting influence until they waned in the fifth century.

Another import to Carthage and thus to northern Africa was the more orthodox Novatianism, whose representatives appeared around 250, just in time to complicate the case for those who had taken a soft line to spare being executed during a persecution. Some credit Novatian (d. 258) with being the first formulator of the doctrine of the Trinity, which became a standard measure of the faith. He believed in the deity of Jesus Christ, but stressed, as Paul had in Philippians, that he had "emptied himself" of the reality of his being "equal with God" when he became a human. Novatians called themselves the pure ones; everyone else was polluted. Eventually tolerated by Constantinian decree in 326, they were local embarrassments, also shunned by most African bishops. Their figurative "Faithful Members Only" policy led them to rebaptize converts to their movement.

The presence of these heresies and deviations is in its own curious way evidence of the vitality of northern African believers. It takes energy to question the established forms and to provide alternatives. Thus another separatist group, the Donatists, was made up of self-described "pure" ones, like the Novatians. They surfaced after 312 to attack those they thought had been compromisers in the Great Persecution. While they gathered teachings from African leaders, they also plagued the African church for nearly a century. The Donatists wanted everything in the church to be spiritually lined up, ordered, walled-in, and purified. They made their way in a struggle of wills and became a self-appointed in-group which ruled out everyone else. Sacraments were not valid if the one who administered them was, in their eyes, not in a state of grace. For a time, with their being persecuted as a lure, they probably dominated in the African churches, but at a synod in Arles (314) they were condemned. Still they did not disappear. When Donatists were eventually persecuted they used their banners of suffering to win other converts who were ready for strict discipline, even to the point of death. Some Donatists made foolish and risky choices in civil life, but in the end it was the majesty and zeal of an attacking Augustine, the Bishop of Hippo, which led to their demise.

Still another heresy came later, again by import, into an Africa which by then provided a kind of petri dish for the nurture of exotic growths. As Gnosticism lost some appeal, seekers found an attractive alternative in Manichaeism, whose followers stormed from Persia into North Africa with sufficient notice and caused enough unrest that Emperor Diocletian in 297 acted to extinguish their fires. And fires they were, sufficiently warm that for a time they attracted even the passionate Augustine of Hippo, who later de-converted and put his energies into countering and quelling them. Mani claimed a revelation which posed light against darkness and offered an explanation of good and evil. He kept some room for Jesus in his plot, because Jesus could embody light and minister to the souls of converts, but he was far from giving central place to the human Jesus who was the exalted Lord. Just as the Manichaeans radically divided the worlds of good and evil or light and dark, so they drew a line between two ranks of adherents. The insiders, who saw themselves as the elect, kept the secrets, ate no meat products, and disciplined themselves to shun worldly pleasures. In a larger circle around this tight enclave were all the other believers, regular citizens, growers, and sellers among other ordinary folk.

## AFRICAN CHURCH FORMS FOR EXPORT

Dealing with the aftermath of persecutions was a major issue, in one case led by Cyprian of Carthage (c. 200–258), who had been working his way up in the ranks of civil service in that prominent city. Then his Christian conversion destroyed all his ambitions to gain wealth and power. He was so compelling that, though a raw recruit, he was made a bishop almost instantly, around 250. Carthage, as we saw, did not escape the persecutors' sword, and in the face of it Cyprian wavered, thus for a time gaining the reputation of being a coward or half-betrayer. After things quieted a year later he came out of hiding and, as one might expect, fought for generous treatment of those believers who had lapsed.

On this issue of returnees to the fold, Cyprian had to be generous if only for self-interest for his soul or to put to work what he had learned through his own experience. In his developing viewpoint, the church was necessary for salvation, so it had to be welcoming. He proposed that "no one can have God as Father who does not have the church as mother." He did not want to rule weak people—like himself?—out of the orbit of God's care. As part of his effort to hold together the factions in those stressful days he wrote a work on *The Unity of the Catholic Church*. While predictably lenient with returnees, he was very strict about the boundaries of the church, and did demand rebaptism of those who had wandered from the rule of faith.

By the time of Cyprian some of the Christian communities had developed complex forms. The original disciples or apostles were long gone, their reputed grave sites often having come to be venerated. In the local gatherings there were elders or "presbyters" and "bishops," which meant those who had oversight. To some of their successors theirs were clearly defined and stipulated or regulated roles. In the eyes of others, these were more practical and functional appointments to office of some among the baptized, all of whom were somehow "ministers." In the second century some had claimed that unless a bishop was appointed, blessed, and chartered by someone who had experienced the same authorization in continuity back to the apostles, he could not baptize or administer the Lord's Supper or have oversight. Such arguments over authority and authorization, answered differently in different parts of the church, endure through the centuries.

If the African leaders were fashioning the building stones in the Christian edifice, Cyprian would be remembered as the bishop who put in place the one marked "Governance." He left the more profound theological probing to his colleagues, while he handled the nuts and bolts of church life. On one hand he had to pull in the strict followers of Tertullian and his kind, while on the other he worked to call and lead councils of bishops to work for unity, as leaders of a sort that were hard to find, given all the factions on the scene. While he was a master of the business and administration of the churches around him, he was also a pastor. When the plague came to Carthage, he was on hand with counsel and encouragement. It is hard to picture the development of the church governed by bishops without recognizing his input. His work drew the attention of authorities, and, under the rule and during the persecution of Valerian (c. 200–c. 260), he paid for his convictions first with banishment and then with his death by beheading.

## GIANTS OF AFRICAN CHRISTIANITY

Enough of attention to heresy on one continent, for Africa also spawned and nurtured varieties of orthodoxies that shaped the lives and thought of believers on two other continents. Among the first was Tertullian, by now a familiar figure to us. If he was an irritant, he was also an influence, since his Latin language terms provided much of the technical vocabulary of many believers for almost two millennia. His encounters with heresies sharpened him as a definer, and he exerted an intellectual influence while being in his own way, as we have seen, anti-intellectual. Thinking of geographical symbols for reason and faith, he asked a question that answered itself as a virtual sneer, "What has Athens to do with Jerusalem?" His question came along the way during a century-long dialogue with Greek philosophy. Some opposed such philosophy, others saw in it an anticipation of Jesus Christ among the pagans, and still others used it as a tool to expound Christian faith. In these debates, Tertullian was the anti-philosopher. Other Christians might mix and match elements of faith in Jesus Christ with the thought of the philosophers, but he would have nothing to do with that. Still, he believed that those he called pagans did recognize God's presence. When they responded to it in any way they were proving that they and all people were "naturally Christian."

Of all the Africans, no one did more to address the theme of the human Jesus as the exalted Lord than Cyril of Alexandria, elected in 412 to be one of the four patriarchs of the Eastern Church. His passion was to put down the Nestorians, whom we encountered in Asia. He started a document war with them in the form of anathemas, formal and reasoned curses, twelve of which he lobbed at Nestorius himself, who counter-fired with twelve of his own. When the Council of Ephesus was called to address the matter in

431, it was Cyril who won the most support and who forced the deposition of Nestorius. A man with intellectual street-fighter instincts for whom the adjective "ruthless" might well have been invented, Cyril set out to make the point that Jesus Christ was a single living unity, not divided as the Nestorians professed. In the process he went so far in stressing that unity that critics accused him of leading toward the declared Monophysite unorthodoxy. He is always posed over against Athanasius and the other Constantinopolitan leaders as someone who failed to develop a rich view of Jesus' humanity.

Recognizing, celebrating, or ruing African influences on early Christianity and global faith in our time, it would be hard to find two more influential ancient Christian thinkers than Origen and Augustine. Origen (185–254) was the scholarly giant from Alexandria, the cosmopolitan hub to the east, while Augustine spent decades as a bishop and theologian in Hippo, not quite a backwater but no metropolis, in the west. Origen was a risk-taker and extremist, as evidenced when he once tried to be martyred with his father, Leonides, in 202. His mother thwarted his drive by hiding his clothes so he could not dare authorities in the public square. A rich widow subsidized his education, which led to his becoming head of the Catechetical School at Alexandria. He traveled to Rome and found a home in Jerusalem. Bishop Demetrius (189–232) at Alexandria, who deposed him as a priest and took away the equivalent of academic tenure, thought the scholar to be almost savagely strict, which in some respects he was. To curb his instincts and in line with a word in the Gospel of Matthew 19:12, he castrated himself.

A genius at languages, the pious scholar provided parallel treatments of Scriptures in Hebrew and Greek, and wrote hundreds of sermons and treatises. A champion of orthodoxy, he did not win all his doctrinal battles, chiefly because his devotion to Platonic ideas led him to muse about souls as being preexistent and salvation as a gift to all. The learned scholar even gave evidence that he knew of the Buddha. The orthodox eventually condemned him, but did not and could not purge the scholarly believers of the Greek philosophy he helped infuse into systematic theology, in which he pioneered. Among his legacies were many of the key terms used by bishops when they debated the divine and human natures of Jesus Christ, in arguments at Asian councils. He is the first to have used the term *theanthropos* to signal the divine-human nature of Christ. Origen did less thinking, writing, and acting *as* African than did Augustine. Like so many of his contemporaries, he too was persecuted and in 254 was martyred.

Crowning the African episode is Augustine, usually identified as "Augustine of Hippo," the town name signaling something of the provincial African setting for this titan who was born of Berber lineage in Tagaste. His mother, Monica, entered the gallery of Christian greats thanks to her prayerful influence on her wayward son, who sampled the lures of the world before finally converting to faith, as his *Confessions* classically described it. That he had a superb education is evident from the scope and detail of his writings. In pursuit of wisdom he sampled Manichaeism and stayed with it for almost a decade. Under excellent tutelage, however, he came to distrust radical dualism and Mani's fascination with the power of evil. After tasting the pleasures of classical learning and sampling the philosophies, he was ripe for conversion. The young man had postponed his baptism, as profligate and prudential types then often tended to do, believing that the rite washed away sins committed up to that point, leaving subsequent trespasses to plague the sinner. His conversion, as he tells it, occurred in Milan where he heard a child's voice in a garden urging him to read a challenging passage in Paul's letter to the Romans.

Monica had died before Augustine in 388 returned to Africa, where he stayed until his death in 430. He would have been happy to have remained in semi-seclusion in a monastic cell that he developed in Tagaste. The maturing young man was given no choice, however, since he was all but forced by admiring leaders to become a priest and, a few years later, was appointed a bishop in the coastal city of Hippo. He had to summon all the intellectual and moral power he had accumulated to rouse the apathetic Hippoites and ward off zealous heretics. As a bishop he had to deal with the civil powers, and in his dealings he reflected on the ways of God as tracked in the human city, a reflection that took massive

shape in his classic *The City of God.* In it he addressed the fall of
Rome and the charges against Christians for having brought about
its decline.

In church life, he was busy fighting the array of heresies, including one not mentioned before, and one that did not deal directly with Christology. Followers of the British monk Pelagius
(c. 352–420?) invaded Augustine's diocese to spread the teaching
that humans had an ability to cooperate in achieving right status
with God. In countering Pelagians, Augustine developed drastic
views of human impotence and evil and posed them over against
the grace of a loving God. His own record of success was as mixed
and messy as was his view of human nature. He helped triumph
over opponents on the issue of infant baptism, which he favored
against Pelagians. They believed that humans as free beings had to
make good free choices. Augustine fought them, but then saw his
city invaded by Vandals, and had to console himself, amid destruction, with the witness he had experienced and presented
about how God worked in the mess and mix of history.

Augustine also dealt with faith in Jesus Christ as the mark of
truth. Making much of the fact that believers are saved by grace
through faith in Jesus Christ, he declared that such grace can be
found only within the church. His pupil Fulgentius of Ruspe
(c. 462–c. 533), an Arian who was also active in North Africa, was
most radical: "There is no doubt that not only all heathens, but
also all Jews and all heretics and schismatics, who die outside the
church will go into that everlasting fire prepared for the devil and
his angels." Those who believed in such a mode had two options:
they could hate and kill all such outsiders, or, in love, they must
seek to spread the faith and rescue them. Christian imperial
moves issued from the former; Christian missions more often
from the latter. Augustine supported missions.

## African Co-inventors of Monasticism

One more African invention or at least prime development of an
import was monasticism. A climate in which fasting and self-
punishment of the body, plus promotion of celibacy and anti-

erotic activity, was so extreme that Origen castrated himself, and where purist movements prospered, it was natural for some to take extreme steps to separate themselves from the world and its temptations—and even, at times, from human company. Many new converts did not keep the high standards fostered by leaders like Tertullian. When martyrdoms decreased in numbers and intensity and Christianity came to be favored in the civil order, troubled Christians asked, who would set the standards for a faith that many thought of as world-denying? Of course, monks.

Egypt was the desert home for many of the earliest known Christian monks. In lore and legend no one outranks Antony, a simple man who went to live alone in the desert, where no one should disturb his fasting, prayer, and meditation. He believed he was following Jesus' counsel or command to those who sought perfection: "go, sell..." He "headed for the bush," a translation of his form of monasticism, Anchoritism. Whether or not he was illiterate, his biographer portrayed the unschooled idealist as such. In that account, when people made fun of him because he could not read, he defended himself as being of sound mind and thus not in need of reading. When monks like Antony would overdo their self-punishment, deprived of food and other sustenance, they would dream dreams, see visions, and move into mental worlds of phantasm personalized by the presence of fanciful and always threatening demons. Needless to say, the attempt by male hermits to remove themselves from the lures of women meant that their daydreams and nightmares were peopled by alluring women. If the men were literate, they often recorded their visions, and word of these eccentric but beguiling thrusts attracted the curious. His dedicated way of life must have suited Antony, who lived for more than a century in a time and place where reaching the age of thirty-five was exceptional.

The records of monastic beginnings are sometimes quite specific, especially when hermit met hermit to link in communities of commitment. Best known of these was one founded in the 320s by an ex-soldier, Pachomius, who gathered a community—the "cenobitic" style as opposed to the "anchorite"—and set forth a rule for it along the Nile in Egypt. Communities cannot well or wisely be as fanatic as solitary individuals may be, and what Pachomius prescribed looked moderate compared to what Antony was doing. He mandated common meals, disciplines that were not disruptive of community, and the teaching of literacy. Jerome gave publicity to Pachomius's rule, while the exiled African theologian Athanasius visited and wrote the life of Antony.

Notably, women might choose monasteries rather than be oppressed by husbands, but they came to communal living for a wide range of reasons. Ever the pioneer, Pachomius contributed to the founding of such communities for celibate women, with his sister Mary as one leader. Some women in these communities were of great means, among them Olympias (c. 361–c. 408) of Constantinople, who gave away her wealth. If hermit monasticism was too raw for family people, those in business, or people of moderate temperament, admirers among them were taught to recognize the world-rejecting monks as pathfinders on the way to heaven, people who could petition God for ordinary folk, and thus they came to be well regarded.

Descriptions of Pachomian monastic life are rather rich. All participants ate common meals in silence, prayed several times a day, and celebrated the Eucharist, the sacrament of the Lord's Supper, on weekends. Carefully organized into cells, they pursued study of the Bible and spread literacy to advance this. Thousands of visitors, well known and unknown, made pilgrimages to the monasteries, and many stayed for the rest of their lives. Pachomius did not seek isolation for the thousands who became nuns and monks. They were to serve the larger world around them, and often did.

Behind the monastic moves in Egypt were influences such as that of Athanasius, sometime Bishop of Alexandria before 335 and oft times fighter for orthodoxy. Doctrinal disputes in which he took part led to his being exiled on more than one occasion. After 356, monks in southern Egypt received him back when he needed hiding. He left in 366, a commuter who imprinted his stamp from Alexandria to Ethiopia, and beyond, in famed Christian councils. He had favored Egypt with its famed rich fields of grain and its populace that, growing resentful of outside interference, was turning nationalistic.

Thanks to the monastic communities and the surviving records concerning their activities, it is possible to gain some sense of the makeup of their participants. Palladius's (c. 363–425) history and collection of sayings from Egyptian monastics listed ordinary people such as Paul the Simple, a balsam-growing herdsman, and even an Ethiopian criminal. In the background of this eccentric crew were people with varied careers such as tomb-robbing, piracy, shepherding, barbering, and others whose lives were designed to inspire other simple people to follow them into these patterns of spiritual elitism. The monasteries spread literacy but, where learning was absent, some claimed that miracle-workers were able to read without having been taught. Those who mastered crafts and business brought knowledge from these vocations to the workings and support of monasteries. One Arsenius (c. 350–c. 450), not a native Egyptian, descended from residence in a palace to the point that, impoverished, he was grateful for the gift of even one coin when he faced an emergency—yet, like Antony, he lived for a century.

The women monastics received less attention in the contemporary records. Palladius reported that the women's monastery provided by Pachomius had four hundred members. In early accounts, numbers of these came from well-off family backgrounds. Even women in these communities were perceived as representing the threat of sexual temptation. In one report a monk averted his gaze as nuns approached, in order to prove how holy he was. The abbess took his measure: "If you had been a perfect monk, you would not have looked so closely as to perceive that we are women." Some nuns ministered as nurses to scholars such as Origen, a chaste bet, considering that he had castrated himself.

Eastern Africa matched western North Africa as a shaping place for Christianity, having given birth to those major figures like Athanasius, Clement of Alexandria, Cyril of Alexandria, and Origen. The furthest eastern sweep of Christians occurred in

Ethiopia, where the Book of Acts had located Queen Candace's servant who had visited Jerusalem. The historical traces reach back to around 300 where one learns of the activity of Frumentius (c. 300–c. 380), a shipwrecked slave. His story ranks high in narratives of Christian derring-do, since the drama of a trader taken captive, helpful to leaders in Ethiopia, or Axum, and tutor to the queen's children, was said to have been named a bishop at Axum. People there were believed to have migrated from straight across the Red Sea, and it was thought they brought an Arabian culture and religion with them.

As often was to happen later and elsewhere, when the king, in this case of Axum, became a Christian, most of his people followed, and came to recognize the Bishop of Alexandria as their pope. Attempts to woo Frumentius, who as bishop called himself *abuna,* "our Father," from support of the divinity of Christ in churchly teaching were unavailing. On Ethiopian soil, Jesus was "of the same substance" as God the Father.

Next in the lore came the "Nine Monks" or "Nine Saints," around 480. They were Syrians who arrived to live in monasteries in Egypt but who then started monasteries in Ethiopia. Through the next century these establishments spread and prospered. If one measured vitality by the number and strength of the monasteries, it would be hard to find a better match among Christians anywhere.

Ethiopian Christians meanwhile developed distinctive ways, some of which left them adhering to Jewish customs, including Sabbath observance on Saturday, not Sunday. The biblical monarchs Solomon and the Queen of Sheba were venerated and claimed as Axum's own. One sure sign of such influences was the presence of replicas from the Hebrew Scriptures which described the Ark of the Covenant. No branch of Christianity of any size matched the Ethiopian church as a keeper of ties to the lore and ways of Hebrews, including the practice of universal circumcision of male babies. Famed underground churches came half a millennium later. Never succumbing to outside religious authority, the Ethiopians had their own teachings and jurisdictions, under a pope.

## EXCEPT FOR EGYPT AND ETHIOPIA, THE END

The first Christian episode in Africa, a place where so much pioneering activity occurred, ended abruptly in the seventh century,
long before its conclusion in Asia. This ending does not mean that
there were no holdouts or isolated pockets. One holdout, the
isolated pocket in Africa, was Ethiopia, where a dug-in church—
literally dug-in in some places and respects, in cave churches—
survived.

Across the Red Sea from Egypt and Ethiopia a new faith, Islam,
was rising to complement and compete with Christianity in the
family of Abrahamic or Jerusalemaic faiths. It was soon to rival
and then come into conflict with Christianity. Islamic or Muslim
conquerors isolated Ethiopians from other Christians, and attempts by Ethiopian Christians to be friendly with their conquering neighbors failed. Many Christians went off to hide in rock
churches. From Medina in Arabia, Muslims moved across the
Sinai Peninsula to Egypt and then spread up the Nile to Aswan,
which they conquered in 649. On the coast, Alexandria had fallen
to 'Amr ibn al-'As. Unready northern African Christians, disput-
ing among themselves, were vulnerable, and as they quickly ca-
pitulated, they saw their Christian places soon converted to
Muslim sites. Some Christians were swept into Islam because of
the tolerant face it first presented to fellow "peoples of the Book."
Having to pay extra taxes as non-Muslims, many believers found
no reason or will to remain Christian, and drifted into silence or
converted to Islam. Unpersecuted Christians there did not prosper as the suffering ones did elsewhere.

The Egyptians at first welcomed the Arabs because they could
help free Egypt from Byzantine powers. As time passed, their invaders and now conquerors became oppressive, forcing Christians
to wear heavy crosses around their necks to identify themselves.
They were not free to build new churches or educate the young.
That ruling robbed them of a future in a present that, for the rest
of northern and eastern Africa, by then had meant the decisive,
and from the longer perspective of history, rather sudden and
abrupt end of the first African episode for Christianity.

4.

# THE FIRST
# EUROPEAN EPISODE

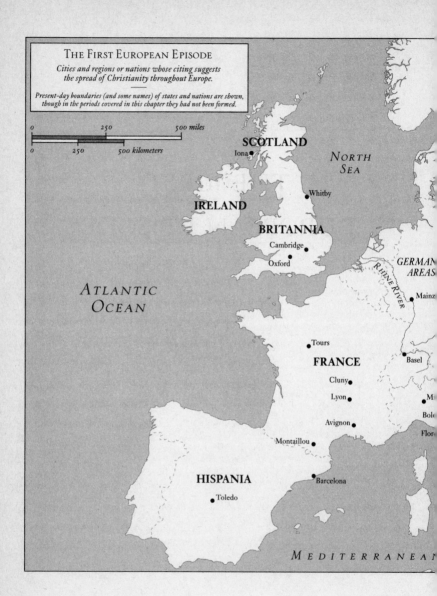

THE FIRST EUROPEAN EPISODE

*Cities and regions or nations whose citing suggests
the spread of Christianity throughout Europe.*

—

*Present-day boundaries (and some names) of states and nations are shown,
though in the periods covered in this chapter they had not been formed.*

0      250      500 miles

0      250      500 kilometers

SCOTLAND

Iona

NORTH
SEA

IRELAND

Whitby

BRITANNIA

Cambridge

Oxford

GERMAN
AREAS

RHINE RIVER

Mainz

ATLANTIC
OCEAN

Tours

FRANCE

Basel

Cluny

Lyon

M

Bol

Avignon

Flor

Montaillou

HISPANIA

Barcelona

Toledo

MEDITERRANEAN

To speak of an episode is to refer to "an event that is distinctive and separate although part of a larger series." To speak of Asian, African, and now European episodes in the twenty-century-long Christian narrative is to refer to distinctive beginnings on three continents and the virtual ending on two of them, Asia and Africa. These are followed in the third, Europe, by changes so drastic that they separate two epochs. It is not likely that anyone living anywhere within the span of seven centuries would consider his or her place in it as being part of an episode. The historian looks back and brings a perspective not recognizable in daily life. Also, no Christian from the first century until well into the fifteenth would have spoken of these episodes as being part of the career of global Christianity simply because the concept of the world as a globe was still lacking. A flat map of "the known world" to whose "uttermost parts" his followers wanted to take the message of Jesus Christ would serve to locate the churches of those times.

By the end of the first century most of the Christian churches had been planted in Syria, Palestine, and Asia Minor, which means in Asia. The map as of that date would quite possibly show only two remembered identifiable churches in Africa. As for Europe, six were in Greece, including in cities to which Paul had written letters—Philippi and Thessalonica. The only two in what would comfortably be called "the West" were in Rome and Puteoli. Even a century later only four communities would be mapped northwest of today's Italy and only four more had been added in Italy itself. A few more by this time appeared in Greece and about ten were added in Africa, but most growth was in Asia Minor and Syria. Europe, which many Western Christians later came to think of as the center of the global Christian community, developed late.

## THE ROMAN ATTRACTION

Reaching Rome, the focus and power center of empire, had been the goal of apostles Paul and Peter, both of whom probably met their death there. It was also the capital of the Caesars, who tried to do away with Christianity. By the time Paul and Peter arrived in the city there was already a large enough Christian community that it drew notice of the classical writer Suetonius. The church there continued to grow under hostile emperors Vespasian (ruled 69–79) and Titus (ruled 79–81), the conqueror of Jerusalem. More than two centuries later, by the time Diocletian the persecutor abdicated in 305, the empire extended west to Hispania, north into Britannia and into much of what became France and Germany. Barbarians in the form of Vandals, Huns, and others threatened the northern borders until one century later, in 410, they brought about the fall of Rome. This imperial expansion did not mean a strong Christian representation by 410. The Germans, by the way, were Arians, and therefore were popular in the eyes of many "unorthodox" Western Christians. Despite Rome's fall and with the conversion of many barbarian tribes and kingdoms, for the next thousand years Christianity expanded through all of Europe.

Rome and the West provided innovations of their own to match those recognized in Asia and Africa. Three essential tasks for the young church preoccupied Europeans, but they had few monopolies on the main development. These began with the task of telling the story of those who witnessed to the human Jesus as the exalted Lord. Second came the inventing of patterns of organization for the churches which gathered believers; and third, formulating creeds which condensed the main themes of the faith, addressed arguments over these, and helped provide ideological boundaries for the community. Most Africans in the Roman Empire and, of course, "Roman" Europeans shared the Latin language. With Rome as the imperial nerve center model, Christians developed an increasingly centralized pattern of church government. The Bishop of Rome, considered an equal or even the first among equals by the other four patriarchates, was busy in the second and third centuries dealing with civil authorities and then with barbarians. As the city of Rome suffered, a church council in 381 at Constantinople stepped up and named that city "the new Rome" or "the second Rome." The bishop of fallen Rome objected, claiming with some warrant that the bishop in Constantinople would be too much under the thumb of the emperor, who at that time ruled not from Rome but from Constantinople.

Claimants for Rome's dominance used history to make their case. While not even everybody in the West went along with the assertion, they heard the pope claim that in the gospel story Jesus turned to Peter and, in their view, showed his intention that that disciple and his successors should be represented as the rock on which Jesus would build his church. In an act that was generous and political at once, the Emperor Constantine paid courtesy to Rome and authorized shrines at the presumed graves of Peter and Paul. For good measure he threw into the bargain the palace of the empress there to serve as his housing and to enhance the status of the Bishop of Rome.

## PAPAL GOVERNMENT IN EUROPE

These concessions did not mean that the conflict was over. Damasus, the Bishop of Rome—the title "pope" became common in the fourth century—from 366 to 384, claiming that his was the "apostolic" bishopric, as he set out to suppress heresies, spoke condescendingly to the East. He called other bishops sons instead of brothers, the latter having been his predecessors' title for them. With such words and acts we can see that the papacy was being developed and consolidated. It took someone greater than Damasus to make good on the claims and names. He was Pope Leo "the Great" (pope from 440 to 461), who, steeped in Roman law and precedent, made the best case yet for a strong Bishop of Rome. Still, he did not persuade everyone. Thus at the council at Chalcedon in Asia Minor in 451 he could not convince the Eastern bishops that he was supreme. His ambassadors felt rebuffed, turned their backs on those sons, not "brothers," and focused on holding sway in the West. Even there it was difficult to assert power because of the exigencies of worldly and churchly misfortunes. Some of these led the papal chair in one case to abandon Rome for Ravenna, in another to see its occupant John I (pope from 523 to 526) thrown into prison, and in both to be frustrated because the emperors in Constantinople downplayed the papacy and sometimes harassed the pope.

Fortunately for Rome, more than a century later came the first great pope after Leo, Gregory the Great (pope from 590 to 604), a needed and revered leader who was not exempt from troubles which abounded when Lombards attacked. Gregory stepped in and, taking over civil affairs, outlasted the Lombards, who were forced to make some concessions. Promoting the domain of Christianity (Christen+dom), Gregory knew that loyalty to this single realm had been strained to the point that the Eastern and Western spheres of the empire were virtually severed. He made an audacious claim against the Patriarch of Constantinople, who had titled himself "Ecumenical Patriarch." Gregory said that *he* was the universal head and ruler. He also knew when to back off in conflict and settle for less than he might have wanted, and on the positive side decided to call himself "servant of the servants of God." The first monk to have become pope, he brought a humble mien to his high office. As the leftover evidences of imperial Rome grew ever more hollow, Gregory's church filled the vacuum. Roman civil law increasingly served as a model for, and in some emphases even became, Roman Catholic law, as the church took over many duties of the state. The pope also demonstrated vision by sending missionaries to extend his papal realm in 597 into England.

Through the early centuries of Christian presence the empire had become increasingly weighted down by decayed patterns of government, was overextended financially, and regularly beset by invasions which the civilized citizens called barbarian. The distracted Roman army and government could not well fight off the Persians in the east and the barbarians from the north while facing challenges to its imperial cult and civil religion. Who was to blame for the troubles? From the time of Nero on, Roman emperors, blaming Christians, sporadically persecuted them, thus creating martyrs in a time-biding strategy that led to widespread citizen reaction which benefited Christians. As in Asia and Africa, when regimes killed believers who remained steadfast, these became alluring objects of curiosity and were attractive to potential converts, who then did convert.

## THE EUROPEAN CASE FOR THE FAITH

The European Christians, late starters in theology, eventually began to assert themselves. Thus Bishop Irenaeus (c. 130–c. 200), born in Asia Minor but a Westerner by choice as he lived among the Celts, took up the intellectual case for the faith when he became bishop of the outpost at Lyons in 177. His work, groundbreaking if not earthshaking, did much to secure the biblical foundations of the Western church. Facing the enduring issue of how to deal with Judaism, he found in the Scriptures a revealed God who dealt with Jews through one covenant and then with Jews and Christians together through another. Arguing against opponents who attacked the faith from two directions, he accented the divinity of the human Jesus and then traced the humanity back to the first human, Adam. Jesus, for Irenaeus, "recapitulated" the human story and incorporated the fate of humanity into his own.

Each of the early thinkers or clusters and schools of theologians in the West developed specialties prompted by particular contemporary challenges and fused these with the philosophies on which the more educated had been brought up. Irenaeus saw Gnosticism sapping Christian energies and threatening Christian defenders. Over against it he envisioned the whole company of Christians, fractured though their communion appeared to be, as a unity modeled after God who was worshipped as a Trinity, but who was in fact a Unity. Irenaeus's classic affirmation began with these words: "The Church, though dispersed throughout the whole world, even to the ends of the earth, has received from the apostles and their disciples this faith," a faith that he said was "ever one and the same." Was it?

The best-remembered advocate of the power of the church against the empire and of the pope against the emperor was Bishop Ambrose (c. 339–397) of Milan, whose family was part of the Roman establishment. Milan itself had become especially significant, because for a century after 305 it and not Rome was the capital and power center. From there Emperor Constantine in 313 issued an edict which gave legitimacy to the long-persecuted Christians. During Milan's century of leadership Ambrose helped the church fill the void left by Roman imperial decline. Educated in the Greek and Roman classics, Ambrose was well along in a civil career when tapped by the church. So gifted was he and so popular had he become that almost by acclamation he was dragooned into becoming a bishop. There was one hitch: he had not yet been baptized or ordained a priest. Other church leaders took care of that problem, and he quickly became bishop in 374.

At Milan he thwarted those citizens who wanted to restore the old gods. Out went the statue of the goddess Victory. When the mother of the emperor set out to promote paganism, Ambrose displayed the nerve, support, and implied power needed to frustrate her. When the Spanish-born emperor Theodosius I, emperor from 379 to 395, had to take up residence in Milan, Ambrose summoned sufficient nerve and voice to get the emperor to repent publicly for having authorized a massacre of citizens in Thessalonica. He also exercised a risky instrument that could force emperors to submit to bishops when he would not grant Theodosius remission of sins. He was in that act forbidding the emperor to receive the sacraments, without which his soul was in jeopardy for all eternity. Theodosius did penance, was then granted access to the sacraments, and because of Ambrose's action, reluctantly participated in a new definition of relations between church and state in the West.

Heresy always threatened a church that also in Europe was defining its teachings about Jesus Christ. Arianism, the theological accent favored by invaders from the north, became attractive and powerful in and around Milan as it already was in Asia and Africa. In the eyes of the orthodox parties, it was seen as downgrading the divinity of Jesus Christ by teaching that he was subordinate to God the Father. Ambrose, putting his learning and rhetoric to work, virtually silenced them. With his good strategic sense he read the minds of the laity. As a way to gather Christians and increase the church's popular hold, he made much of the relics of martyrs, enshrining them in a new basilica. He also composed and encouraged music and song in what today is still called Ambrosian chant. For good measure, we note that this aesthetically inclined and education-minded bishop was also a sort of social activist, forcing emperors to take seriously their responsibility for the poor and the hungry. He established a climate in which Christian charity was attractive because it was capable of facing human need when other agencies did not, while it offered the bonus of the benefits of heaven and perhaps sainthood. Just in case, to back all this and if some of it failed, he was ready to draw on force, as Augustine was to do. In one of the parables Jesus was heard saying "Compel them to come in!" So, compel them Ambrose would, "in," in his mind, representing the church.

## EUROPEAN VERSIONS OF MONASTICISM

If Ambrose stood as a symbol of church power, a soldier named Martin (c. 316–c. 400) can best represent that emphasis on charity. He also played a major role in developing monasticism on models somewhat different from the originals in Africa and Asia. Martin was from Tours in France, at the northwestern reach of Christianity on the continent. His biographer Sulpicius Severus told how Martin had migrated from France to serve in the Roman army, as had his father. The son claimed that the whole army converted with him in 354, but Martin himself subsequently headed for the hills, feeling a call to live alone as a monk. As his popularity ironically led to his growing influence, he was given no choice but to accept a bishopric back at Tours. While some bishops were enjoying finery, prestige, and wealth, he turned his back on all these and dressed as one of the poor, choosing to live at a monastery that he had established. Eager to spread the Christian faith, he took aggressive action against pagan shrines. When he was observed getting away with destruction of some, his audiences determined that had their old deities the power they would have avenged his acts. He could also on occasion make compromises and permitted some favored folk customs to survive even if they were not fully congruent with Christian claims.

Those brought up with modern sensibilities may have difficulty finding and fitting their way back into the worldview in which someone like Bishop Martin drew acclaim. In one word the appeal was miracles. Since his God could outperform the deities and spirits of the competitors, the people were awed by some apparent signs of divine favor. So hungry were both peasants and princes for access to the miraculous that they relished stories of saints like Martin, probably the first Western Christian to have been recognized as a saint without having been martyred. As a matter of fact, monasticism with its rigors and demands for firm witness came to be a kind of surrogate for martyrdom, a status harder to attain when Christian rulers, not Roman emperors, set the terms.

Reference to Martin's monastery is a reminder that during the century in which Latin Christianity began to prosper, Europeans developed monasticism after the initiatives in Asia and Africa. This influence is another illustration of how intercontinental— anticipating "global"—Christianity was almost from the first. Borrowing models for rule from Pachomius in Africa and Basil in Asia, Benedict of Nursia (c. 480–c. 547) led a community that came to be named Benedictine. Reacting against the extreme self-punishment of some other monastic rules, he argued and demonstrated that isolation in the hermitage was not the only way to serve God and pursue sainthood. Monks had been forming communities since early in the fifth century, but he drew notice when he left his hermitages and moved to Monte Cassino, the house where he set forth humane if still strict rules for his Benedictine Order, and where he died.

Some features of Benedictine-style organization did appear to be arbitrary and were still quite severe. All monks swore obedience without question to their elected abbot. As was the case with Benedictine nuns, they were to remain lifelong in the community to which they were first pledged. They were not to become peregrinators, the wanderers that many other kinds of monks were. They were to keep silence, but they could and did sing hymns and psalms and speak prayers in community. The Benedictines were part of an integrated economy, who brought their specialty, concern for spirituality, to the whole community. They were to work to support themselves and thus benefit that economy. Two of their mottos summarize their intentions: to pray and work, *ora et labora*, and to be hospitable so as to "let all guests be received as Christ." Slow at first to attract a following or imitators, Benedictinism eventually came to be the model for most Western monasticism. If among the cultures that were being overwhelmed by barbarians and dulled by slow-thinking Christians, in other words, where cultural and theological shadows and corruptions prevailed, Benedictines often kept the candles and lamps lit in times that later people called the "Dark Ages," and saw to it that the scrolls and books remained open, so learning prospered. They also received some regulations from authorities. Charlemagne helped their cause when he decreed that all monasteries in the empire had to adopt the Benedictine Rule.

The most rigorous Benedictines were the Cistercians, an order founded in 1097 that within a century led to the founding of hundreds of Cistercian houses. They were devoted to silence, hard work, and communal prayer. Many monks paid deference to Bernard of Clairvaux (1090–1153), who was known as a promoter of Christian love but not as well of family life. He was such a charismatic recruiter for the order that parents, it was said, not wanting to lose their sons to monasteries, hid them when Bernard came calling. This promoter of the love of God did not appear to be a lovable figure when he blasted anyone, even a king who might stand in the way of his reform. His softer side was evident in a commentary he wrote on the erotic biblical Song of Songs and when he contributed hymns and devotions that manifested profound piety.

While literacy was rare among most common people, priests and monks were expected to teach the faith and to prepare the children of church members for baptism and a life nurtured by the seven sacraments of the Western Christian church. In whatever mode the baptismal washing or immersion of new believers had occurred in Christian beginnings, baptism of infants along with adults came to be the norm. A second sacrament, Confirmation, which was built on that baptism of infants and newcomers, helped spread education and deepen commitment among people who did not leave all aspects of paganism behind. Since bishops were expected to be in charge of quality control among the faithful, they did the confirming.

The central act of worship in the West as elsewhere was the Eucharist, the Mass, the Lord's Table, or Holy Communion. Since priests feared that they might spill the wine that through their prayers and words and God's action had become the blood of Christ, they offered only the bread of that sacrament—and with it benefits that, they preached, culminated in the attainment of eternal life. Ordinary Christians were expected to give alms, do acts of charity, and lead just lives. It became easy and was common for many to grow spiritually indolent, self-assured because the ministrations of the priests assured heaven as a destiny. At the same time believers had reason to feel insecure, because so many temptations, threats, and pitfalls endangered their path to heaven. Purgatory, defined as an intermediate stage for after-life "purging," took away some of the terrors of hell, but it also easily became a misusable instrument in the hands of the priests who could exact money to shorten the time the deceased would spend there. Corrupt leadership exploited such practices and made it hard for periodic reformers of practice to have much influence.

Accenting the intellectuals and the civil rulers in the early European centuries can be distorting and could lead to overlooking the ordinary people. Yet it was the literate and the powerful who left the records which provide access to the mentality and actions of people of the times, the extraordinary folk called "ordinary" because they did not hold office and may not have been literate. Most of them mingled their practice and belief with inheritances of what people in their time called "barbarian" and, sometimes then and often later, "pagan." Yet the traces they left, their relics, the archaeological remains of churches, and their language as picked up by poets and chroniclers, show that through baptism, the Mass, and the other sacraments, and in the view of stained glass windows in cathedrals, images that drew on Bible stories informed their daily doings and inspired their hope of heaven. They could not keep these stories to themselves, and with sword and spirit or with sword *or* spirit, they set out to turn Europe into a Christian domain.

## IMAGINING A FAN-SHAPED MAP FOR EXPANSION

With theology, the papacy, and monasticism as instruments and agencies, the church in the West prospered. Despite removal of the imperial power to Constantinople, the invasion by barbarians, and the fall of Rome, the time came when with compensatory vigor Western leaders spread their influence north and northwest. After the Edict of Milan and other acts that rendered Christianity official, religion and regime were wed. This meant that when a ruler converted, those he ruled had to be officially converted. If the people had been what the Christians called pagan, they had to be baptized and to abandon the rituals and practices from their past. No matter how radical the administrators and theologians wanted that break to be, all evidence suggests that the people kept many of these relics. Some have suggested that when the official church was too strict an enforcer, the ordinary folk "smuggled in their old gods in plain brown wrappers." And the conversions themselves were not so much one-on-one, face-to-face encounters that led to personal change as they were acts of power advanced by the sword. The development of faith, practice, and argument in support of the faith were expected to follow. The officially favored symbols often depicted Jesus Christ, the exalted Lord, holding the sword.

With such a sword in their own hands, Christians spread their Latin version of faith and observance. An imagined fan-shaped map can serve to show the territories to which conquerors and missionaries spread from bases like Ravenna, Milan, and Rome on the Italian peninsula. To the left on that map was the Iberian Peninsula, especially territories which became Spain. Some of the earliest Christians were believed to have reached there, and

Visigoths, who were Arian, had invaded and conquered some regions, implanting practices which conflicted with orthodox Western Catholicism. In the eighth century Muslims from Africa conquered Spain, and not until the Emperor Charlemagne captured Barcelona in 801 was the strategic Iberian Peninsula brought back partly to the Christian fold. Meanwhile, Christians suffered persecution from the Muslim Moors but, on occasion, they also lived together in relative harmony, as they did with Jews in places like Toledo.

Next, France, peopled most strategically by the Franks, whose King Clovis (466–511) converted. It was told that this change came about because he had married the Christian princess Clotilde under whose influence he bargained: if God would give him a victory in battle against another tribe, Clovis would accept the gift of baptism. After he won, he and three thousand of his soldiers turned the Franks toward a new course. In this pattern other Christian queens and princesses induced or seduced their spouses to be converted, with their troops and subjects expected to follow them.

Clotilde was not the only influential woman among the Franks, though royals and peasants were not as important for this work as were women monastics. Some of them, such as Radegunde (520–587), escaping from imposed and unattractive marriages, found refuge in convents. Radegunde brought her own wealth with her, and was able to establish a convent of her own. She and others like her contributed to the piety of the age by collecting, displaying, and putting to work relics of saints. Recalling that Helena, the mother of Constantine, had claimed to have found the True Cross in Jerusalem, it is interesting to see the premium Radegunde placed on having bits of it made available for devotion—and at a price. Such nuns also advanced profound piety and in some cases had mystical experiences.

When armies of Muslims later threatened to conquer the Frankish lands, Charles "the Hammer" Martel (d. 741) in 732 at Tours beat them back, thus making possible the retention of a line against further Muslim advance in much of Western Europe. His son Pepin came to rule Christianized France after 753, and it was

Pepin's son in turn who came to be called Charles the Great, or Charlemagne. On Christmas Day in 800, Pope Leo III, in an act designed to distance Latin Christendom from the Eastern empire and to enhance the prestige of the papacy, crowned the emperor. At the same time, historians note that Charlemagne, backed by his army and moving forward in ambition, looked for all the sanction he could get, so he had reason to promote this ceremony as well.

Perfecting the pattern that was becoming standard, Charlemagne, against the counsel of his favored scholar Alcuin, kept forcing baptism on conquered peoples, as much out of an interest in unifying his realm as it was out of evident devotion to Christian faith. By 785, before he was crowned, he had completed the domination of the Saxons and then of the Bavarians soon after. Not only a conqueror and also sometimes a tyrant, Charlemagne, though he was barely literate himself, showed his generous side in his encouragement of learning. He developed a royal library and encouraged the arts so much that the word "renaissance" became attached to his achievements. Ironically, the befriended Charlemagne also took steps to subordinate the papacy to his will and whim.

## THE NORTHWESTERLY THREAT

On the continent, Christians were being caught in a Muslim vise between Spain and much of the Middle East. While they fought off the advancing Muslim armies, they put efforts into conquering northern lands. There they were more free to establish a Frankish empire, which meant that they had to win Franks and thus France and then England. The reach of Western rulers against the barbarians is best illustrated by work in the British Isles, where the most remote people were the Celts of Ireland. In the center of all the stories featuring them is the towering Saint Patrick (d. 493), whose story still beguiles. Born Christian, kidnapped by Irish pirates, reduced to being a shepherd in Ireland and then a refugee in Britain, he felt a call to serve the faith. Since his heart belonged to Ireland, he went there to help set up monasteries, thence to spread the faith. Slightly later, a prince named Columba

(521–597) left Ireland and sailed to a little island off Scotland called Iona. According to historian "The Venerable" Bede, in his *Ecclesiastical History of the English Nation,* Columba first converted the king and thus initiated a pattern of endeavor by Ionan emissaries that continued for centuries and did much to shape English Christianity.

As for the "Angles" themselves, Gregory had the vision to convert these barbarians for the sake of heaven and so that they could fall under his Christian rule. Everyone says that a little exchange may only be a legend but then they repeat it: the pope saw attractive children in Rome being sold as slaves. Who were they? "He was told that they were 'Angles,' " it was said, meaning "English," but he turned the word into a partially Latin term: he said they were not Angles but Angels. In 596 the pope sent the prior of a monastery in Rome, who was to be named Augustine of Canterbury (–c. 605), to refound the church in England, where he became the first Archbishop of Canterbury. He too converted a king, this one Ethelbert (c. 552–616), who was married to a Christian princess, Bertha. The palace was turned over to the church and to Augustine of Canterbury. When Ethelbert converted, the people he ruled followed, so missionaries were soon busy baptizing thousands of former pagans. Like other converted rulers, he adapted and made compromises, again applying a Christian overlay on observances such as pagan holidays and festivals. Here the monks were more radical than Ethelbert had been, for they burned the sanctuary of Woden—the name survives in "Wednesday"—and replaced it with their worship.

Getting the Celts to cooperate with the Angles involved a long struggle. The ancestry of these Celts was Eastern, and the earliest missionaries kept some practices from the Eastern Church, for example in their dating of Easter. It was natural that they would clash with the papacy in England. So when Augustine of Canterbury approached them, they snubbed him, also because they thought he had treated them discourteously by remaining seated when first their bishops came to greet him. Celts regarded those of Canterbury as upstarts, since they themselves had been converted long before. The British Isles were, however, finally being Romanized. To help produce some kind of unity between south and north, a synod was held at Whitby in 664. At that contentious synod, Hilda, a converted noblewoman and now an abbess of a monastery that doubled for men and women at Whitby, played her role by working for conciliation and by remaining friendly to both contending parties. The more or less defeated Celts were pushed beyond the empire and grew strong in Ireland, after having agreed to adopt the Roman calendar. Back at Whitby, Hilda's nuns became as well educated as bishops and writers, among whom was Caedmon, one of the earliest known English poets.

Back on the continent, the Irish monk Columbanus (d. 615) sailed for Gaul, where he worked for years in what today is France, and, in advance of Clovis, left a trail of monasteries and churches. Next in the clockwise sweep were the ancestors of modern Germans, tribes such as the Saxons. Here as always there are remembered heroes who became saints, among them Willibrord (658–739), who had served the Friesians on the North Sea coast, and Boniface (680–754), who worked among another pagan tribe, the Hessians. It was said that he confronted the pagan god Thor (as in "Thurs-day"), who was worshipped at a sacred oak. While others bowed or kept their distance from the protected tree, in a display of bravado he simply chopped it down—and no bad fate followed. So the tribe that had worshipped there converted. His fate eventually caught up with him, however, because after years of preaching and confirming, the eighty-year-old was set upon and murdered by pagans. Yet he had become "the apostle to the Germans," as Augustine had been to the Angles and, before those two, Patrick to the Celts.

Slightly further east and far to the north were Vikings and other feared Scandinavian tribes. For two centuries venturesome missionaries, most notably Anskar (d. 865), tried to make gains among them after having been exiled from northern Germany by other pagans. In 1000, after capturing an enemy king, the Christian King Olav gave the defeated tribes the choice of death or baptism, and found them ready to choose the latter as a more judicious option. King Olav and his peers baptized and began the long process of Christianizing them. Among the converts in the north were Olav Tryggvason (d. 999?) and Olav Haraldson (d. 1030), who became fierce spreaders of militant Christianity. In Iceland, Greenland, and other places remote from the continent, expansion was slow, and the stories of the northland usually include chapters in which pagans won back a place from Christians, only to see their heirs re-Christianized.

The Christian spread that resulted from this fanning out was large but in many ways thin. "The Republic of Peter" and the pope as universal ruler turned out to be weaker than the title suggests. Monarchs used the papacy as it used them, and the papal rule was knocked about among the fortunes of petty rulers into the tenth century. Just as the Muslims were attacking in Spain and as Vikings still threatened from the north, Magyars pushed from the east into what became Hungary. The papacy was beleaguered until Emperor Otto I (ruled 936–973) came to its aid and, in the interest of promoting the Germans, helped rescue the papacy from Italian rulers. He did not yield power to the popes, and in 963 Otto even tried Pope John XII and deposed him after calling him guilty of numerous crimes. The fortunes and resources of the papacy seemed all but depleted.

## RETAKING LOST LANDS

If these pages suggest that Christians simply expanded their sphere in the West by sword or witness and that they were free to view the world as their own, they are very misleading. At the very time when across the map they seemed to be outlasting the barbarians, rebuilding empire, erecting monasteries, and developing new forms of piety, they kept running up against an advancing front of those rivals who were neither Christian heretics, Jews, *or* pagans, but Muslims. We recall that these had put a virtual end to Christianity in almost all of North Africa and had beaten back Christian advances in Asia. In Europe they had threatened when they conquered Visigothic Christians in the Iberian Peninsula.

Western Christians did not want to be pinned in between Muslims to the west and to the east. In the twelfth century they gathered forces to take back lost territory in the Eastern Christian world and to recover holy places in the Holy Land. The result was a sequence of conflicts which came to be called Crusades, so named because the *crux* or cross of Jesus Christ was their banner. Appearing on the shields of the Christians, this emblem received constant homage as troops advanced, just as priests and popes also invoked it. The capture of Jerusalem by Muslim forces in 637 meant that their holy city was being desecrated, and they decided that at last it must be retaken. For centuries Christians could make pilgrimages there, but in 1071 some militant Turkish Muslims excluded the pilgrims from as far away as Europe. It was this that turned the Crusades into an intercontinental venture after Pope Urban II (1042–99) in 1095 told European knights that God had willed the recapture. Christians began a series of efforts that led to victories and defeats, corruptions and acts of charity, all in the name of Jesus Christ. The pope set the tone: "I therefore urge and beg you who are the voices of Christ, both rich and poor, to drive the foul vermin from the lands where your Christian brothers live and to bring speedy help to the worshippers of Christ...under the banner of the Lord." Participants who were killed would be granted indulgences, which served as substitutes for doing penance after confession of sins. Forty thousand military men, ten thousand on horseback, left Europe and moved across Turkey, to retake Jerusalem in 1099 and to hold it for almost a century.

All the strongholds that the Europeans had built could not hold off Saladin and other leaders who defeated the crusaders in 1187. The Crusades should have united Christians of East and West against a common foe at a time when the popes and Orthodox leaders were making contradictory claims for their authority. They did not. Plundering Europeans attacked Eastern Christian sites. Under the sign of the cross recruiters for crusaders attracted major figures from Normandy, Flanders, Boulogne, and elsewhere, clad the little men—students of armor average them out at five feet three inches—in leather and light armor, and sent them off. With a new taste for zealotry and blood, Christians from northern Germany attacked Jews as enemies of the cross in German cities such as Mainz. Crusaders went on to trash and loot Byzantine Christian cities and churches as they crossed Turkey.

Moderate successes on military fronts led the pope to encourage a reconquest of Spain, whereupon the inspired Christians recaptured Toledo in 1085, a first stage along the way to future victory. Christians from the pope on down overstepped humane bounds as fanaticism began to mark the whole effort. The question came up: would a crusader who took an oath to support the papal endeavor and then dropped out of the ranks be excommunicated, which in his mind meant, be sent to hell? Still, there were always dropouts and new recruits for future Crusades, and the passion for these ventures spread. Eventually some Slavic non-Christian tribal lands also began to look alluring to conquest-minded crusaders, who simply craved religious legitimation as they lusted to acquire new lands.

More ominous than the Christians' own moral failure was the threat from reawakened Muslims who developed the concept of *jihad*, which simply means "struggle," but in present-day conflicts gets casually translated as holy strife. Such war, often promoted by top church leaders, led to unholy ends, as Christianity and Islam, Eastern and Western Christians, and many factions among each, were driven farther apart, not drawn together. All those promises to crusaders that they could be assured a free pass to heaven and a shorter time of detour in purgatory, according to papal decrees, turned out to include some terms: the crusaders had to renounce serious sin and profess the "right intentions." Popes made much of such intentions, which were basic in the moral theology of their day. For all the heavenly benefits offered, the earthly yields were more elusive. It was the Muslims, eventually united, who by 1187 captured the prize, the city of Jerusalem, which they later lost but then rewon in 1244.

## THE WARLIKE, THE PIOUS, AND THE PEACEFUL

In the frustration born of partial successes and major failures, some Christian minds set out to find new targets for holy war, and leaders in the Western church decided to seek them among heretics in Christian Europe. The Western and Eastern wings of Christianity became ever more hostile to each other and beleaguered and worn down. Constantinople was so weakened that it became vulnerable to Muslim conquest until in 1453 it fell.

Western Christians in many cases had acquired a taste for dramatic action that they used against other believers who displeased them. The crusading impulse found parallels in the other complex sequences of events in the period, also summarized by one word to match "Crusade"; it is "Inquisition." As dissent against imperial and ecclesiastical rule developed, so did repression, as when popes and emperors united in ordering that heretics be burned. Much of the energy of the Inquisition, which started in southern France in 1184, was directed against Jews. When someone was judged guilty, the church did not do the executing, but worked through a special court that itself was named the Inquisition. The inquisitor, completely in charge, was accountable to no one in secret trials where torture was a common instrument of terror. Sometimes torturers went so far that even the pope, upon hearing of the gross excesses, would moderate their punishments. In much of southern Europe the Inquisition operated most efficiently. In such settings accusers exposed witches and dealt with them savagely. The entire two-century episode revealed how little trust the leaders had in the example of the human Jesus or how sure they were when they were acting that they acted in the name of the exalted Lord. Some exceptional documentary records show a slightly more cautious side. In one case at the village of Montaillou in France the inquisitor aimed at educating, not burning, heretics called Albigensian. He interrogated hundreds, but we are told of only six executions. In Spain it was another, almost totally harsh, story. Under monarchs Ferdinand and Isabella the treatment was so savage that the pope tried to restrain them.

Not all records evidence bloodthirstiness in the West. Surprisingly, in the midst of all the imperial and papal traumas, some devotees of Jesus Christ paid attention to the interior life. Mysticism was a sign of creativity in this period. Especially in the monasteries and convents men and women aspired to be lifted above earthly realities to spiritual and transcendent realms, into union with the One, with God. Spain was host to many of the mystics, who carried Christian piety as far as they could, to the point that they created suspicion, since their direct appeal to God minimized the need for clergy and sacraments. In the north, among the greatest was Hildegard of Bingen (1098–1179). Sent by parents to the convent at age eight, she displayed her brilliance when, after learning Latin, she began to write in it, and accompanied her down-to-earth writing with accounts of some heavenly visions. Even the church higher-ups, who had reason to be suspicious of anyone who claimed revelations over which they had no control, could find little fault in her writings. The papacy had to and did regard her as a theologian, the first woman recognized formally by the church. She wrote in defense of the church in a period when it needed defending, yet challenged her readers to let their spiritual imaginations soar above the walls of churches and cities. Remarkably, with the blessing of Bernard of Clairvaux and Pope Eugene, she was sent to preach to clerics, a sign of her talent and achievement and a rare exception to the practice in which only men ordinarily preached. Meister Eckhart (c. 1260–1327) also produced classics of mystical thinking, while saints like the Dominican Catherine of Siena (d. 1380) and Bridget of Sweden (1303–73), who served their orders well, experienced visions of God while they were being energetic in their charities. What was called a "modern devotion" developed, climaxing in a widely circulated classic by Thomas à Kempis (c. 1380–1471), *The Imitation of Christ.*

New spiritually rich orders also were born. Some of them recalled the rigors of the Essenes from the time of Jesus. Two shapers stand out: Francis of Assisi (1181–1226), among the most admired Christians after the apostles, and the Spaniard Dominic de Guzman (1170–1221). Francis turned his back on family wealth and took on oaths of poverty, even as he tried to start peaceful conversations with Muslims. On February 24, 1209, Pope Innocent III gave his approval to Francis and his brothers to organize. Earlier Francis had had an experience that nudged him into what today we would call a vision of mission, as he heard

Jesus say to him personally to "go" and to "preach as you go, saying, 'The kingdom of heaven is at hand. Take no gold, nor silver, nor copper in your belt.' " The words were from Matthew 10:7, 9, but they were rendered immediately relevant now. Not a few Christians would characterize Francis as the one most like the human Jesus among the followers through the centuries. Pope Pius XI officially named him "the second Christ," the other, or *alter Christus.* The Franciscan Order which he founded tried to emulate Francis and thus to embody the life of simplicity. The Franciscans especially carried on ministries among the sick and promoted medical studies. These brothers became agents of mission that led to a second episode of Christian presence in Asia.

Meanwhile Dominic, also a lover of the poor and agent of good works, chose the instrument of proclamation to advance Christianity with his Order of Preachers, which was given papal approval in 1216. Like Francis, he confronted a clergy that often acted as if they were doing magic tricks with the sacraments, ignorant as they were of the niceties of Christian teaching. Dominic's followers were especially interested in learning, while at first those of Francis were not, and out of the Dominican field came the most profound theologian of the millennium, Thomas Aquinas (1225–74), who towered above all others as he developed a *Summa Theologiae* for the scholars and a *Summa contra Gentiles* to inspire missionaries, who also forged ways into new places in the world. His approach would turn out to be helpful more than two centuries later, when Dominicans became advance parties in the spread of Christianity to the Western Hemisphere and elsewhere.

Religious orders like these helped invent universities such as Cambridge, Oxford, and Bologna. Despite what Tertullian had dismissed in Africa, they found ways for learning in the style of Athens to be congruent with faith, symbolized by Jerusalem. As impressive as the newer orders were, traditional Benedictine monasteries also underwent reform and built new centers all over Europe. The monastery founded at Cluny in France was the most important radiating center for renewal, and from it in 1098 a new order, the Cistercians, moved ahead to engage in further reform. Some of the monks were elevated to the papacy, most notably a

Cluniac named Hildebrand, who in 1073 became the great Pope Gregory VII.

## PAPAL STRUGGLES FOR DOMINANCE

Rivalry between the papacy and the crowns, especially in France, led to revolts against papal claims and against the popes. If there was any consistent papal claim, it held that there was and had to be one church with one head, something that had become a kind of fiction to the Eastern half of Christendom. Boniface VIII made the great claim in *Unam Sanctam* in 1302 that "by necessity for salvation [all human beings, including the most powerful] are entirely subject to the Roman pontiff." Matching it was his belief that there were two swords, the spiritual and the temporal, but in Boniface's world the church had the upper hand, because it provided access to the eternal and kings were earthbound. The Eastern Church largely ignored all this.

A high point of the papacy came under Innocent III (pope from 1198 to 1216), an aristocrat and theologian, who often got his way among European rulers. He was Christ's vicar, he claimed, so he could engage in the down-and-dirty practical politics of empire and overrule or undercut civil actions of which he disapproved. He called a council, Lateran IV, which met in 1215. There, tidying up a practical point about the sacraments, the pope declared that "transubstantiation" was the most appropriate way to describe what happened at Mass. The prefix "trans" is a clue to the understanding that the bread and wine were changed into the body and blood of Jesus Christ. Just as what the philosophers called the "accidents" of the bread and wine cease to be the body and blood of Christ, they ceased to be that, for example when they have been swallowed. It can be said that the sacrament was intended for the people, not the stomach. This became a central appeal in the medieval Mass.

Pope Innocent manipulated elections at that Lateran Council, a conclave that joined him in advancing extravagant claims for the papacy while effecting some important reforms. He had nothing to do with the Inquisition and made indirect contributions to the appearance of the Magna Carta, since he helped limit the power of King John of England. From the Lateran Council also came a very rare gesture to Jews, who were to receive papal protection. No one was to attack Jews or their property. True, Jews were to wear an identifying badge, but this was justified as a defense against Christians marrying Jews, just as a badge was to keep Christians from marrying Muslims, the Saracens.

The extravagant papal claims could be backed with power, since Innocent had made some helpful alliances and won some victories, humiliating defeated kings along the way. Such power, however, could not last. The pope, in order to achieve victory at home over his rival, the Holy Roman Emperor, had to form some alliances which strengthened kingly lineages like the one in France and these turned out to be compromising.

While impelling the Crusades and authorizing the Inquisition, popes after Innocent were also often busy with their own territorial and authoritarian interests. Some of these contentions led to papal humiliations, to the point that French-born Clement V in 1308 chose to go into exile to gain security. He thought Avignon could become the papacy's permanent base, but it turned out to represent what came to be called "The Babylonian Captivity" of the papacy for seventy years. France was becoming ever less a friend of the papacy. Clement also saw little hope of restraining power in the mix of Italian city-state politics. While he wanted the power of kings to help him renew Crusades, he and his successors did little belt-tightening and failed to amass resources to advance such causes. They piled up wealth and wanted to display riches that would surpass those of every monarchy.

The popes tried to find new repressive and threatening ways to pay for their luxuries and edifices, efforts that soon became unpopular all over Europe. Through it all the papacy weakened, but after its "captivity" and on its return to Rome in 1377 the popes claimed more power than before among the powers of Europe with which it vied. Some of the rivalries led to schisms, with popes facing counter-popes, each ruling out the other in the process. As councils, attended by bishops, lords, and important laypeople between, acquired new power, they tried to balance and counter that of the papal forces. The regular tugs-of-war between popes and councils indicated how uncertain papal power had become, and the corrupt lives of some of the popes further rendered ever less credible the claims for the Chair of Peter, the papacy itself. At times it looked as if the councils had won in the contests. A council at Basel in 1436, however, caused so much controversy that a later council at Florence-Ferrara (1438–45)—one preoccupied with relations to the Eastern Church—led in 1441 to the bull *Etsi non dubitemus,* which affirmed that the papacy was superior in authority to councils.

Not everything was lost in a time of papal corruption and distraction. On the contrary, much was gained. The arts flourished. Romanesque and Gothic cathedrals became the greatest expressions of devotion and art that Western Christianity had seen. One could deduce the main themes of high theology and ordinary lay life in Europe by studying the stories and memorials in the cathedrals. Their mosaics, tapestries, and most of all windows, illustrating the Creation, the covenant, and the life of Jesus Christ and the Virgin Mary, were the textbooks for the illiterate, the shrines for seekers of beauty, and the focus of devotion. When the cultural Renaissance developed, humanists like Petrarch (1304–74) restored the classics and from them artists drew new inspiration. Now they adorned the church and palace walls of the sanctuary with depictions of both saintly and, curiously, pagan stories. Jesus Christ had to make his way in the company of *Leda and the Swan* or *The Rape of the Sabine Women.* Yet the portrayals of Mary and the infant Jesus or the suffering Jesus himself inspired the response of those who loved art and practiced piety alike.

## ACHIEVEMENTS OF EUROPEAN THEOLOGY

The Western European church was not devoid of theology during the era of the Crusades and intra-European holy wars. Some see the theology of this period as the greatest in Catholic history. Interestingly, while many theologians were concerned with the teaching of original sin or about the sacraments, most important and revealing was the Western church's revisiting of the themes about Jesus Christ that had first been formulated in Asia in the fourth and fifth centuries. Certain leftover issues from the early church had to be dealt with, and were. Typical and most notable was a point not resolved back at Nicaea and Chalcedon in the East. Yes, as these councils insisted, Jesus Christ was both God and man. However, Anselm of Canterbury (1033–1109), the most probing and daring of the new theologians, asked the question that was desperate for so many, *Cur Deus Homo?*, why *did* God become human and why did God *have* to become human? These were questions that monotheistic followers of Allah in Islam or Jews in Christianity's parent covenant could not even dream of asking, but which pointed to the distinguishing mark that gave its name to Christianity.

Anselm acquired credentials to take on the big questions, for example because he provided "proof for the existence of God" in an argument called "ontological." It depended upon some rather tricky logical propositions and dwelt not on physical evidence but reason alone. That approach satisfied many Christians of his period and attracts some even today. Curiously, for many of these arguments, the premium put on reason meant resort to Aristotle, a pagan philosopher whose writings few would have expected to find in sacred Catholic precincts. This was especially so because he had been popular among Muslims and Jews, who had been custodians of his heritage in Spain. Still, Aristotle's arguments appeared to be satisfying and useful, so he was utilized and pronounced satisfying.

Thomas Aquinas, the "Dumb Ox" giant, the greatest and long declared the normative Catholic theologian, made most of Aristotle. Many had tried to deter this Thomas from his vocational path, including his family, who offered a prostitute as a lure who might serve to distract him from his intention, but he remained steadfast and became a sturdy and productive Dominican. Before he made his theological contribution, however, someone had to settle that freshly phrased question as to how the divine and human met in Jesus Christ. Among the "someones" had stood Anselm.

After the Council of Chalcedon in 451 we saw that some Christians of the East claimed that Jesus Christ possessed only one nature, hence we met them as Monophysites. Others, especially the Nestorians, viewed the divine and human natures operating in rather lightly related ways. In Anselm's eyes, however, these approaches kept Jesus Christ from being a perfect mediator, so human salvation was at risk in their hands. To come quickly to the controverted point, as Anselmians saw disorder in God's fallen world, sin in a world that had not been created evil, on biblical grounds they faulted human sinners. Being sinners, people could not get right with a God of justice who somehow had to wreak vengeance on the unjust. From the human side there had to be the sacrifice of a just one, and there were none such. So God entered history in Jesus Christ as God and yet as fully human. When he offered himself up to be killed, he made satisfaction for the human race of which he was a part and which he represented. "Satisfaction" became the key word in describing what Jesus made or gave humans as a human and because of his divine nature. Anselm summarized: "For as there is one nature and several persons in God, and the several persons are one nature, so there is one person and several natures in Christ, and the several natures are one person." This insight or teaching, so arcane and distant from most modern thinking, a mark of the Latin church, was worked into hymns, liturgies, and devotions.

## POPULAR RELIGION AND REFORM

Still another sphere of creativity was popular religion. The laity outnumbered bishops and popes, priests and monks and nuns, and they had lives to live. They partook of the Mass and made pilgrimages, but, according to evidence still being unearthed and explored, they also kept their own counsel and fleshed out their own understandings of the faith, not all of them congruent with official Catholicism. Some historians think that the adoration of relics, the plots of theatrical creations in cathedral squares, the reading of omens and signs, and even the exorcism of devils, all were departures from biblical portrayals. Taking over pagan festivals and rendering them Christian, as was the case with winter and spring seasonal observances of fertility rites that were turned into folk

Christmas and popular Easter, the faithful wanted the best of two worlds. In a cosmos where heavens threatened judgment and where the "Dance of Death" was luridly described in sermons, it was consoling to carry protective physical objects like the rosary or engage in physical gestures like pilgrimages.

The symbols elaborated on doctrines. If the pope was the universal representative of Christ, Mary became the "universal Mother," the inspirer of good works. In a world in which the Black Death wiped out many millions whom wars had spared, it became salvific for those suffering to find the suffering Jesus identifying with them. Doing this identifying was more important than imploring the invisible and often inaccessible divine ruler of the universe. Access to Jesus was often through prayers to saints or appeals on the basis of revering relics, most of which in later centuries would be exposed as phony by Catholics themselves. The inventory of stocks of Christ's blood, Mary's tears, or slivers of wood from the True Cross benefited their owners, sometimes princes and often churchmen. For all the apparent splendor of churches in Rome, cathedrals all over Europe, libraries reborn, monastic orders reformed, the Christianity that prevailed in the middle of the second millennium also displayed signs of weariness.

A new breed of reformers rose: John Wycliffe (c. 1329–84) in England, Jan Hus (1372–1415) in Bohemia, and the Dominican Girolamo Savonarola (1452–98) in Italy attacked corrupt practices of popes and the hierarchy, and tried to stimulate Christian piety in order to realize more of the original gospel story in the life of the church. Clearly, one mode of Christian formation was now virtually compromised and on the verge of being spent. Toward the year 1500, a millennium-and-a-half-year-old structure and synthesis were coming along to the end of what we are calling the First European Episode.

What the Western church could not win at home it sought to gain at a distance, even to the point of attempting to retrieve souls from the Muslims. Some Catholics even looked to Central Asia, where Mongols ruled and where their rulers looked like potential allies against Muslims. Led more than two centuries earlier by heroic Raymond Lull (c. 1233–c. 1315), some representatives of religious orders even dreamed of spiritual reconquest, and succeeded in setting up outposts in northern Africa and in the East. Lull does have to be entered into the record as the most ambitious and capable of the agents who worked to reach Muslims for Christ through the instrument of education. He found much to affirm in Islam, but made few if any converts. He had to return empty-handed, aware after of the futility of their effort to carry out Christ's command to go into all the world. Islam prospered, while Western Christians declined in numbers, power, and will in the face of the Black Death. With stalemates and defeats on other fronts, Portugal and Spain began sending ships to far places, including for the first time across the Atlantic. There they were eventually to find domains on two continents which they called Americas and were to open new episodes of Christian experience and agency.

Meanwhile in once united Western Europe a new episode began, one marked by division, reform, fresh invention, and furtherance of the work theologians like Anselm had charted: to declare the various manners in which the human Jesus as the exalted Lord was to be worshipped, followed, and used to justify actions of princes and hierarchs as well as ordinary people in their various callings and countries.

5.

# THE SECOND
# EUROPEAN EPISODE

THE SECOND EUROPEAN EPISODE

*Locations of major Reformation-era and modern Christian
events in cities, nations, and regions of Western Europe,
as well as Greek and Russian Orthodox sites.*

———

*Present-day boundaries (and some names) of states and nations are shown,
though in the periods covered in this chapter they had not been formed.*

0     250     500 miles

0     250     500 kilometers

SCANDINAV

SCOTLAND

Edinburgh

NORTH
SEA

UNITED
KINGDOM

NETHERLANDS

Amsterdam

Rotterdam

GERMAN

Cambridge

Wittenberg

Oxford

TERRITORIES

BELGIUM

RHINE

Mainz

ATLANTIC
OCEAN

Paris

Worms

Speyer

FRANCE

Zurich

SWITZERLAND

Geneva

Trent

ITAL

R

PORTUGAL

SPAIN

MEDITERRANEAN

While in ancient times (c. 150 B.C.E.) Crates of Mallus, a Greek geographer, had constructed a globe and a few others had described the ways of doing so, in 1492 a Nuremberg adventurer and mapmaker, Martin Behaim, constructed an *Erdapfel*, an "Earth Apple" or globe, which still exists. A curious mix representing mapped reality and fantasy, visited shores and imagined landscapes, it appeared just in time to be of use to the circumnavigators who followed almost immediately in the wake of Christopher Columbus. Also in 1492 that sea captain was busy, more than he knew, helping moderns eventually conceive of the earth as a globe. Alert explorers, traders, colonists, pirates, and missionaries acted on that conception and brought diverse peoples and cultures together as never before. Western Christians, thanks to stories they heard from medieval traders like Marco Polo (1254–1324), already had some dim notions about faraway people, but now they faced the religions of those "others" close at hand. Confronting Africans, Asians, and others who were devoted to their own rituals and gods, came representatives of One God, in contacts that were often deadly but could also be positive.

If belief in One God was the mark defining Christianity over against Buddhism, Hinduism, and many other faiths, belief that the unique mediator between the One God and humans was Jesus Christ marked it off from its monotheistic kin, Judaism and Islam. In the new episode for Western Christianity which began around the turn of the sixteenth century, the religious forces of the continent did remain Christian. Therefore debate over whether the human Jesus was the exalted Lord was less at issue than it had been a thousand years earlier and as it was to become again in later modern times. The confrontations of the sixteenth century were complex, not only because Eastern and Western Christians had split in 1054 but, more important for the extension of Christianity, the West no longer represented some sort of unity whose leaders could engage in missions which would spread the single Catholic faith and its domains.

On their home front, as Western Christendom split—Roman Catholicism under the papacy versus all other Christians as well as those non-Catholic Christians against each other—the issue of Christology shifted to questions about *how* and *by what means* the work of God in Jesus Christ was effected among humans. Later in the modern period, faith in God as Father of Jesus Christ was questioned in ways that forced the churches to respond. The enduring context was with Jews and Judaism.

## THE JEWS AND OTHERS AS "THE OTHERS"

While Islam after 1492 had been pushed back in its western flank from Spain, it still threatened Vienna on the eastern side. Catholic Christendom had few encounters with Muslims over the person and work of Jesus Christ, so Jews remained the "others" for Christians. Suspicion and hatred colored the contacts, thanks to a long history which recalled almost no positive Jewish-Christian relations through the preceding millennium. The Jewish minorities throughout Europe were too small and powerless to count for anything in governmental and military affairs. In the sixteenth century all the old mutual rejections of Judaism by Christianity and of Christianity from within Judaism found new expression. Christians also attacked Jews on cultural and economic grounds. The downgrading of Judaism in that period is still able to be witnessed in the European cathedral art of the centuries. In it *ecclesia* or "The Church" was always favorably portrayed while *synagoga* or "The Synagogue" was depicted as everything from a blinded figure to a sow, the animal most repulsive to Jews.

When the Western church was breaking up in the sixteenth century one might have expected all sides to be distracted from demonstrating hatred of Jews, but that was not the case. The greatest humanist scholar who stayed loyal to Rome in the time of the religious upheavals, Desiderius Erasmus (c. 1456–1536) in the Netherlands, made the typical cultural case: "If to hate Jews is to be a good Christian, we are all abundantly Christian." He envied the French for having gotten rid of Jews by law and banishment after 1348. By the 1540s in the German territories, Martin Luther (1483–1546), a leader of the churches whose ties with Rome were broken, ranted in influential writings which suggest that he was out of control on that subject. He had been a personal friend of Jews in his early years and he still yearned for people of Jewish race and culture to convert to Christianity. He had expected that his translation of their Bible and his preaching which kept the papacy at a distance would be alluring to Jews. When they did not respond and since very few did convert, in frustration and rage he struck out against the synagogue, as did many colleagues and successors.

While historic Jewish-hating Christians had often charged deicide—that is the claim that Jews had been agents or had at least been complicit in killing Jesus-as-God (*deus*)—Luther and most Protestant and Catholic critiques of Judaism centered on the fact that while contemporary Jews might have respected the human Jesus, the rabbi, to accept him as the exalted Lord bred a revulsion among them that can only be called absolutely deep. Their faithfulness to that Christ-less vision of God had to change, thought Protestant and Catholic alike, so they must convert or persecute Jews.

A second challenge to the status and role of Jesus as the church reformation proceeded came from the occasional Anti-Trinitarians who were coming to be called Unitarians. They rejected ancient council teachings that Jesus as one of three persons in the Trinity was "equal with God." Catholics as well as parties which were just acquiring a label or a name and whose presence was soon to be felt, among them Lutherans, Calvinists, Anglicans, and all the rest, united against Unitarians and others they regarded as subversive. Some of the dissenters argued that the Trinity was a post-biblical concoction of church councils. The most notorious instance of persecution occurred when Michael Servetus (1511–53) showed up in the Calvinist stronghold of Geneva, Switzerland. He eventually was put to death for heresy with the approval of the highest authorities. Such Anti-Trinitarianism became a significant movement in Lithuania, Poland, and Transylvania, which even experienced a "golden age" of what later became known as Unitarianism. In all its churches, God, the Bible, and the human Jesus received respect, but Jesus could not be the exalted Lord, the Second Person of the Trinity.

The third rejection of the divine-human status of Jesus came later, in the eighteenth-century Enlightenment, where monotheism on occasion was replaced by Deism. This was a movement whose leaders affirmed the existence of some sort of superhuman power, but not a personal God. Later many of them celebrated human reason as a replacement for divine revelation and hence moved critically into a-theism, which of course had no place for any "exalted" being or person, Jesus-as-God, or God.

## EUROPEAN CHRISTENDOM DIVIDING

To frame the Second European Episode temporarily, one leaps back to the sixteenth century and then ahead to the twenty-first. Back to the sixteenth century: the story of how Christians regarded God's action among them in a new episode begins with the thwarting of Muslim armies and empires between 1492 and 1526 in Spain and near Vienna. Interactions between Muslims and Christians thereafter were rare and remote until the appearance of significant Muslim populations in twenty-first-century Europe helped frame the late years of the second episode of Christianity there. For a variety of reasons defenders of Islam were not able to expand their territories and rule after 1492 as they had during the centuries before. Hence during the period of Western exploration and expansion Christian Europe, having its opportunity to become a presence around the globe, used it well. Now to the twenty-first century: the later arrival of Muslim peoples in the United Kingdom, the Netherlands, France, Germany, Spain, and elsewhere in the third millennium did not overturn the general population balance. Their presence as often thriving worshipping communities, however, served as a contrast to the declining attendances in Christian worship, as cathedrals became museums, churches were nearly empty, and chapels often unused. It is possible to overstate the case for the fact that the Second European

Episode is ending, but the signs are there that the old dominance of Christians is over, loyalties have waned, the cultural influence is smaller, and the faith itself holds less sway than it had for much of the past fifteen hundred years.

If those dates and events are the framing beginnings and endings, there is a picture to be painted between them, a set of complex and exciting scenes so dramatic that the shortsighted and arrogant but talented Catholic apologist Hilaire Belloc (1870–1953) still had good reason to put on the spectacles of a provincial. He asserted in the 1930s that "Europe is the faith" and "the faith is Europe." Europe, of course, was not and is not one thing, and the time about which Belloc spoke did not represent a simple continuity. In the Second European Episode, the peoples of "the papal obedience" had had to yield space to Christians with other loyalties. Between the sixteenth century and the twentieth a new Europe emerged, no longer sheltered under that single old canopy. Such change in Europe had global portent, since its nations and churches were agencies that sent missionaries and exported theologies and liturgies to the other continents and received responses, including new angles of vision and religious languages, from them.

An astute observer could and some observers did see and foresee the coming of drastic changes in Catholicism around 1500. The conflicts between popes and councils that went by the name Conciliarism had been quieted. Before and after that movement occurred it was popes who called councils and who dominated there, often in person and sometimes through legates. Now conflicts between popes and emperors or kings foreshadowed the loss of simple authority in the dominant and, officially, the only church. Stories of corruption high in the church were repulsive to many of the faithful. Theologians began to voice differing opinions on the Eucharist and the authority of the Bible, and doctrines concerning human nature and divine destiny occasioned controversy over divine predestination and human will. Discontent would turn to revolt only when the fight came to be less about morals and more about the teachings of the church, since these ideas had consequences for the fate of immortal souls. Dissenting princes often backed some critical moves toward reform, thus enhancing the power of reformers.

A central idea of Roman Catholic government, which had become vulnerable to attacks, was that God authorized a single earthly authority, the pope as Vicar of Christ, who could counter and punish monarchs. The upper-level hierarchs could bar priests from performing the sacramental acts that were needed for access to heaven while the threat of hell loomed among the fearful. Should such fateful authority, it was asked with ever more frequency, belong to those who lived and taught corruptly?

Questions like that began to find their answers in the fledgling universities where scholars fostered ideas which led to dissent, opposition, and schisms. Students at Oxford and Cambridge, Paris and Rotterdam, and eventually Wittenberg and Geneva, revisited biblical texts in their original languages and became convinced that these were being suppressed or misinterpreted by Rome. They argued that the hungry souls of frightened people would be fed and there would be healing and freedom if pastors and people could read and respond afresh to scriptural words of divine grace assured by Jesus Christ. The printing press, invented by several people at Mainz including Johan Gutenberg in the 1450s, gave access to the larger world so that more and more people could be aware of actions elsewhere. Swift communications offered information that led to provocations against the official church, some of them acted out in the souls of scholars and people of great devotional and mystical passion, but also among the crowds.

While after the fall of Constantinople in 1453 the popes and their armies and agents were fighting off the threat of encroaching Islam, they were also caught between Catholic powers. Notable among these were the Hapsburg and Valois dynasties as they aspired to control much of Europe. They appealed to the spiritual authority of the pope to advance their own purposes against each other, ultimately at expense to his power even as he used or tried to use them and theirs. While popes and princes were busy with such material concerns, a profound spiritual and theological argument was developing. It had to do with how humans, pictured as alienated from God by their sin, were to be made right with God, how they could overcome guilt and face anxiety, and how they would be assured that Jesus Christ was offering grace and thus appeasing a judging God.

The popes found an effective instrument on this front in the preaching of purgatory, which we have seen was a place or situation described as offering a second chance for bliss after death and also after long years of purging before the soul entered heaven. In a sense purgatory reflected a communal notion: if an individual had not fulfilled obligations on his own, those who survived, chiefly family members, could help make up his or her deficiencies in the transaction. The pope claimed to hold the "office of the keys," to use a variation of a biblical phrase that related to the door to heaven or hell. He and his subordinates claimed that they could help shorten time in purgatory or could lengthen it and even aid in condemning sinners to hell. Thus salvation could be managed through forms of politics and economics.

## EUROPEAN CHRISTENDOM PERMANENTLY DIVIDED

Amid all the clashing of swords and armor at the mid-millennium mark came a bookish movement called humanism. Some scholars were putting to use what they had recently learned from "humane literature" that derived from ancient classical literature. They questioned the biblical and theological bases for purgatory. These humanists also unearthed and exposed ancient documents, many of which undercut papal and other official churchly claims for earthly power. They resurrected and translated spiritually rich texts, producing new versions of the basic one, the Bible. Some of the new teachers, like Thomas More (1478–1535) in England and Erasmus in the Netherlands, remained within the Catholic orbit. More used his place there to condemn King Henry VIII for his "divorce." He became a spiritual and humanist ally at a distance of Erasmus of Rotterdam, and was executed in 1535 amid the conflicting-power forces in Henry's time. Before then he and Erasmus fed the reformers spiritual ammunition. Erasmus stayed in his academic fortress which was ineffectively guarded by the Rome that he criticized and satirized most mercilessly.

Best known of the centers of agitation turned out to be in a nondescript Saxon town, Wittenberg, where a cluster of monastics and other scholars gathered under the protection of Elector Frederick the Wise (1463–1525). Highly placed among the German-speaking princes, he tended to local interests, as did many of his counterparts. They came to see how these concerns often ran counter to the preoccupations of the hierarchical church with its Roman focus. As elector, Frederick had a vote in the selection of Holy Roman Emperors, who governed much of Central Europe and Spain. Frederick through the years of his reign had found reason to be wary of an unresponsive papacy. Rivalry between Rome, meaning the pope and his supporters, and the princely forces in the Holy Roman Empire, posed a dilemma for the papacy. The pope could not easily move against princes and kings because he needed at least a fingerhold of their loyalty in order to present a united front against Muslims, "the Turk," just as they, in turn, needed the pope so much that they had to bow to protesters at a diet at Speyer in 1529, whence came their name "Protestant."

The events in that little Wittenbergian corner of Saxony did not appear at once to have potential consequences beyond that realm. The pope dismissed the early signs as squabbles among German monks. Twentieth-century philosopher Alfred North Whitehead called the subsequent upheaval a family quarrel of northwest European peoples. Most partisans in the churchly quarrels were preoccupied with theology and paid little notice to the emerging world of scientists and skeptics around them, to whom much of the future would belong. The Eastern Orthodox churches serenely ignored the stir. Yet world-changing consequences did follow. Still narrowing the focus, some historians have described the action as having begun as a revolt by the junior faculty in that backwater university at Wittenberg. A pioneer among them was the Augustinian Hebrew Scripture scholar, Martin Luther, a young monk who became a virtuoso of self-examination and expert in condemnation of others. This brusque but anguished articulator of what it meant to feel remote from an angry and judging God grew progressively distant from an ineffectual and immoral church leadership. It would never have occurred to him to reject everything in the church. Looking back and around he declared that wherever priests baptized sinners, people could share the Lord's Supper, and clerics would preach the gospel on the basis of the Scriptures, *there* was the church. Along with the rest of the churches of the time, East and West, he and his colleagues cherished the ancient creeds in which the human Jesus the Jew was the exalted Lord and where belief in the Holy Trinity was affirmed.

When Luther added up his problems with the existing church, he found that they all came down for him to the fact that the church had become a barrier against instead of a provider of divine grace in the human community and the individual soul. A genius at translating and projecting his personal agonies, he reached thousands who with him were searching for a gracious God. Their struggles may have seemed more prosaic and modest than his and those of other restless writers and preachers, but congregations could resonate with theirs. In the public side of the church, they found Luther giving voice to their discontent against what was to them a repulsive system in which "indulgences" were being sold. These scraps of purchased paper purportedly effected changes in the transactions which determined the length of time to be spent in purgatory. Where in all this, Luther asked, was the forgiving love of God in Jesus Christ, about which the new translations of Paul, the gospels, and the Hebrew Scriptures had so much to say? The Wittenbergers had to strike out on their own to find out.

Luther experimented with what Rome had to offer, including visits to shrines and relics while on a monastic assignment in Rome. Fatally for his repose within the system, he asked of it all, "Is it true?" "It" meant not the promise of God in the gospel but the whole ordered system of the Western church as dispenser or withholder of grace. By reading the writings of Paul the apostle in the monastery to which he had fled in his search for grace he found his answer in a rather abstract term used by Paul in a letter to the Romans: the believer depended *only* on "justification by grace through faith." In Jesus Christ. Luther interpreted this to mean that nothing he could set out to achieve by good works or spiritual discipline would please a holy and perfect God. Everything instead relied on faith in God's spontaneous and generous grace. Sometimes when explaining this transaction he would speak of a "joyful exchange" in which everything that Jesus Christ is and represents became the repentant baptized sinner's own. The divine-human Jesus left the divine power behind and "exchanged" it for participation in the human condition, even to the point of giving his life for others. He read this in the second chapter of the apostle Paul's letter to the Philippians. In this transaction the human Jesus as the exalted Lord was the only mediator between God and humans, and his gift deprived humans of the need or ability to "work" their way to salvation.

The professor was supported and surrounded by friends but also he and they fought testily with rival reforming powers. In the Wittenberg faculty the learned friend Philip Melanchthon (1497–1560) argued the case more systematically than did Luther, as did the French-Swiss scholar John Calvin (1509–64) in Geneva. Another Swiss leader, Huldreich Zwingli (1484–1531), added some fire. In England and Scotland breaks were to come.

The pope and emperor did not quickly catch on to what was occurring, but before long as they began to understand they at first debated and then tried to put down the revolt by forces of renewal. Significant changes had also been effected in places loyal to the pope, as in the case of pious Queen Isabella (1451–1504), who with her scholars and monks in Spain undertook reforms of their own. Restless peasants and ordinary congregants across Western Europe by the mid-1520s had begun to attach themselves to some of the preachments and practices as these affected them.

In 1521 at a diet in Worms, Luther with a reported "Here I stand!" statement defied the intertwined civil and religious authority by refusing to recant his teachings when pressed to do so. Almost simultaneously others, with different nuances and followings, also began to distance themselves or be distanced from emperor and pope. They were helped by the threat of the ominous

Turk who kept frightening the papal leaders and their allies. Church authorities craved Western Christian unity for defense on the eastern front. More significantly, while the degrees of response varied and should not be romanticized by those in sympathy with them or exaggerated by those who are not, the laypeople in area after area followed the new teachings. Reformers on the continent and in England translated the Bible into various vernacular languages, and the mass-communicators of the day, at that stage being printers and publishers, pirated thousands of their works. They marketed these to people who, often with their princes, walked out of the church of Rome—but, they insisted, not out of the church. While the learned among them replaced papal authority with an appeal to the Bible and shunned some sacraments, almost all retained baptism and the Lord's Supper, though they divided over some interpretations of both.

Understandably none of the rulers among the emerging nations of northern Europe liked to ship money over the Alps to build extravagant St. Peter's church or in other ways to support Rome and bow to its authority. The responses to the agitations in Saxony and other centers of reform were decidedly mixed. Rome, which resisted the calling of a promised church council, was undergoing its own reform of sorts, just as it was in Spain, Portugal, Italy, in parts of France, the Netherlands, and in some German territories. Still, the old Holy Roman Empire had by now been compromised and weakened, while monarchs in the several nations were rising in power. These rulers retained loose ties to Rome when it served their strategic interests.

## NEW SHOP, OLD STYLE

With few exceptions the new church movements set up shop on the old established style. They let the secular rulers determine the religion of their regime—a policy finally made official in 1555—and thus limited the religious freedom that many would have expected from Protestants, who had sought their own liberty. Many joined in persecuting those who complained that most reformers had not gone far enough. They attacked people who came to be called Anabaptist, so named because they rebaptized those adults who converted after having been baptized as a child, or they baptized only adult initiates.

Reform voices were being heard in the Netherlands, Switzerland, Central Europe, the British Isles, and, as noted, even the papal states in Italy. Most of the leaders said they did not intend to rule by the sword but by the pacific call to discipleship and to follow Jesus. There were also stormier, more restless, and by far less pacific sorts among them who did want to advance the kingdom with the sword. Their existence was a threat now to established Protestantism as well as to Catholicism. The established forces did what they could to put down the "heresy," even to the point of burning and drowning nonresistant victims.

The main Protestant-type leaders, often called "evangelicals" because they claimed to follow the evangels, the gospels, looked mainly to their own local interests and went separate ways. An illustrative case is the failure of the party of Luther and that of Zwingli to unite. Most at issue was the understanding of the Lord's Supper. Zwingli and his party said that the bread and wine of the sacrament merely represented the body and blood of Christ in a memorial observance. Zwingli's successor, Heinrich Bullinger (1504–75), moderated that view and rejected the concept of "merely." In Zurich the concept of "remembering" at the Lord's Supper was seen as a powerful act that helped the congregation believe more deeply than when sustained by the word alone. Thus in some senses the congregation became Christ's body themselves.

Luther and the Lutherans persisted in keeping their distance from those among the reformed who argued that "the ascended Lord" could not also be present at the human table. Luther, in a more Catholic style and believing in what his party called "the ubiquity" of Jesus Christ, argued that this Christ could indeed both be, and was, exalted at the right hand of the Father and at the same time also be humbled in the earthly elements of bread and wine. Luther fatefully charged that Zwinglians had a different spirit, and resisted efforts at compromise.

Attempts by the separate parties to be distanced from Rome,

however, spread, as they did most significantly when monarch Henry VIII (1491–1547) in England broke away, after controversies over his marital career and backed by numbers of evangelically minded intellectuals. This king ventured into theology when he struck out in a pamphlet against Luther and was rewarded by the pope with the title "Defender of the Faith." Suddenly the question came: defender of which version of the faith was he to be? Now acting against and in defiance of the pope, he had become head of the Church of England in a movement called, then and now, Anglo-Catholic. This move was of great and lasting significance, given the fact that the Anglican communion was to become the largest Western church sphere except for Roman Catholicism. Since in the centuries ahead England became an imperial force it also was the most prominent agent in spreading non-Catholic influences in nations around the globe.

Meanwhile, back to the cozier space of the British Isles, stern and stormy John Knox (c. 1514–72) led the Scottish churches into Presbyterian government, which meant rule by elders with a focus on the gospel. In the British Isles there was a ready pool of biblical scholars, theologians, and priests who turned Anglican or Presbyterian after the style of their monarchs, whom they in turn educated. Henry VIII, needing revenues, despoiled hundreds of monasteries while his plundering subjects took advantage of the riches in them. Reform tied to monarchy was a chancy affair for Catholics and Protestants alike, since in the succession of monarchs one would be of one communion and the other owed loyalty to the other. Partisans who made the wrong choice at the wrong time suffered silencing, imprisonment, or death.

## CATHOLIC RENEWALS, HOLY WARS

Strong new movements meanwhile emerged within the community loyal to Rome—Luther was put out of it—especially among them one led by Ignatius of Loyola (1491–1556). This young and gifted military man went through a religious experience that led him to become serious about life and by 1534 inspired him to found the Society of Jesus, which was formally approved in 1540.

His was a movement more taut than Luther's, but it was directed toward obedience to the papacy, not against it. One can properly observe that it was his religious order that first took up the challenge of global thinking and acting, since reports had been coming from two decades of explorers who circled the globe and who made room for agents from his Society of Jesus. Ignatius and the order in 1541 sent out Francis Xavier (1506–52), who may have baptized 700,000 people between attacks of seasickness that regularly overtook him as he visited the ports of Asia.

Members of the Society of Jesus, called Jesuits, and some reawakened religious orders, however, could not put Western Europe back together again Catholic-style. While they were trying to do so the Protestants got a major new boost in the leadership of John Calvin in Geneva. The Calvinists provided a systematic theology for Protestantism and enjoyed a more engaged sense of involvements with public affairs than did the Wittenbergers. While influencing Geneva, Calvinist styles eventually shaped the Puritan world in England, then in New England, and eventually around the world.

Mixing political and religious interests, the characters in the main story in Europe, thanks to a political-religious settlement in 1555, for a century had to deal with tumult that goes by the name of the Thirty Years War (1618–48). It was an unholy Christian holy war which sapped the evangelical and Catholic energies of all parties. Mainly Catholic armies opposed mainly Protestant armies for often not very clear purposes. They wrought destruction in Europe unmatched since the Black Plague two and a half centuries before. If the outbreak of Protestantism so divided Europe spiritually that one must treat the time after 1500 as a new founding or a new episode, it was the Thirty Years War that sealed the divisions and led to the drawing of a new map. The Holy Roman Empire, covering France into Poland, could not be held together. Within Catholic Europe, France won out over Spain for prominence. Stories of the war have to focus on Christian fighting Christian, using rape and atrocity as instruments, until more than ten million people had died. Efforts to develop industry and agriculture were aborted. Still, in spite of the conflicts, or because of and in refuge from them, there flourished many pieties, among them serious but reactionary Pietisms and Puritanisms. Just as impressively among Catholics on the continent some of the great devotional and mystical figures of Christian history emerged, among them Teresa of Avila (1515–82) and John of the Cross (1542–91), who remained models for Catholic spirituality into our own time. Alongside these came dedicated and creative religious orders which tended to the sick and dying and advanced the causes of healing and education.

On the military and political fronts, attempts at settlement between warring parties, seldom effective, were especially oppressive to dissenters who suffered from new churchly establishments as they had under Catholics. Meanwhile on the continent and in the British Isles the Protestant nations and parties kept on ignoring the North and South Americas, which Catholics were beginning to reach early in the sixteenth century. Finally in the seventeenth century the Dutch Republic and England entered the global scene.

## INTERCURSUS: THE EASTERN CHURCH AS EURASIAN

If an "excursus" is an appendix, a digression, a "running out" from, what follows could be called an "intercursus," because it "runs between" accounts of Europe and Asia, just as the Eastern Orthodox Church is seen between or across lines of both Europe and Asia. To this point we treated the early Orthodox, Nestorian, and Monophysite churches as largely Asian or at least certainly Eastern, because of their historical bases in Asian cities. Now the story will be more intelligible if, begging the reader's permission, we are allowed for convenience' sake to move Russia west, thinking of Moscow, Kiev, and Saint Petersburg just as we earlier treated Athens, as having location and interests in Europe.

There had been rare and futile efforts to bridge East and West in the centuries after Western European Christendom broke up, but the often snubbed and quite independent Eastern and Asian churches took on a life of their own. Three of the four ancient Orthodox patriarchates were in Asia, and with a more recently designated one in Moscow, represented what the Western Christians call "the East," even as the Orthodox refer to Roman Catholicism and Protestantism as being of "the West."

Just before the Thirty Years War in the West there had been a "Time of Troubles" after the forming of the Moscow patriarchate, but times of trouble remained, as the career of three major rulers reveals. In Moscow and Russia at large, more intimately than in the West, where pope and emperor had long interrelated tensely, the governance and even the spiritual claims of church and state were fused. Occasional attempts to purify the church led to schisms and the rise of sects, but most power remained with the favorites of the tsar. Ivan the Terrible (1530–84), whose appellation accurately describes him, headed a tsarist succession which included Peter the Great (1672–1725), a Westernizer. Most of his subjects were not familiar with Western modes as were the elites that gathered around Peter. He abolished the patriarchate and chose to rule through a Most Holy Synod which he could dominate. The church fit in as a virtual subdivision of the departments of state. Another successor, Catherine the Great (1729–96), preempted church properties and cut churches' income. On the soil thus broken up, any number of sects developed. In the turmoil, Moscow moved some of Orthodoxy's power bases into Siberia, where it also controlled the church. Still, in spite of all the narrowing, there were some revivals of passion for the Bible and developments of piety and theology through the nineteenth century.

Buffeted by Islam for a millennium and more and by Soviet communism in the past century, the Orthodox Church knew more about the suffering church than do most churches in the West. When the Greeks revolted against the Turks in 1821, the Orthodox experienced tensions over governance between Greece and Russia, but in 1852 and after, the Greeks tended to pattern their life partly on the Russian model. Few Christians were left in Constantinople after 1453, but after World War I in now legally secular Turkey the reduced patriarchate there came to be seen as "first among equals" and took major roles in the new ecumenical movement. After 1917 the number of patriarchates in the East grew beyond Russia and came to number one each in Georgia, Serbia, and Bulgaria. Several new patriarchates emerged between the world wars and in Czechoslovakia after World War II.

Theological developments in nineteenth- and early-twentieth-century Russia had an impact felt far beyond that nation. Through the centuries Orthodoxy insisted on and magnified the teaching that Jesus Christ is the Second Person of the Trinity, true and fully God and fully human. Among the great theologians of modern times, Aleksei Khomiakov (1804–60) spoke for both Slavic and universal interests, teaching that the church tradition was "guarded by the totality, by the whole people of the Church, which is the Body of Christ." This was a high-level folk Orthodoxy, which rendered hierarchy, governmental affairs, and formal theology secondary, if they were given a place at all. The new— but really old—concept was called *sobornost*, a communal understanding of the faith and the church. Spiritual and devotional movements also prospered in monasteries, where individual expressions also contributed to devotional recovery. This was typified by those who recited the Jesus Prayer: "Lord Jesus Christ, Son of God, be merciful to me a sinner." Such a prayer and practices associated with it agitated authorities but contributed to church renewal and then to the survival of the faith.

After the Russian Revolution in 1917 and until the tearing of the Iron Curtain in 1989, Orthodoxy experienced drastic legal limits, harassment, persecution, and silencing. Seldom in history had so many Christians suffered for their faith as when the Soviets demolished or closed every one of the thousands of monasteries. Clerics were killed. The Soviet ideology was formally a-theistic, opposed to God-belief and God-language, and it recognized only the human Jesus, while Orthodoxy, through its icons and liturgy, accented the exalted Lord. Other members of the Orthodox family of churches, in Romania, Bulgaria, Serbia, Georgia, and more, were in the Soviet sphere, and also were not free.

Yet the church endured, representing many millions of Christians, in some ecumenical endeavors alongside Roman Catholicism but after 1948 also in the largely Protestant World Council of Churches—in every case under inhibitions. When the Soviet

Union with its atheistic ideology imploded in 1989 and in the former Soviet republics beyond Russia then and thereafter, the Christian churches, which had suffered alongside the Soviet Jews, came out of their inhibited and hidden states, and, though weakened after three generations of discouragement and suppression, resumed their place. They were joined by non-Orthodox survivors—Catholic, Lutheran, Baptist, and the like—and by assertive and rapidly growing evangelical Protestant groups.

## BACK TO THE "CURSUS": INTELLECTUAL CHALLENGES

Following the movements of early modern reform and their aftermath in the vigorous new nationalist forces, a second major cultural and spiritual catalyst altered the mental map of Western Europe. We refer to what came to be called the Enlightenment, along with its precursors and successors. The accent now was on reason, science, and progress in human developments. While the agitation over the gospel and grace stirred the churches of the West, around them a new world of science and discovery had been taking shape, one which presented challenges for which Christian leaders were largely unready. Sometimes they revealed their unreadiness by harassing or condemning scientists like Copernicus (1473–1543) and Galileo (1564–1642). Their new scientific views of the heavens and earth's place in the heavens unsettled those who used biblical geography and geometrical figuring to assess the human's privileged place in the universe. As significant as the resituating in space might have been, the deeper revolution was occurring in the minds of thinkers. If the Renaissance began as a literary revisiting of ancient, classical, Greek and Roman philosophy, history, and other learning, in the eighteenth century what came to be seen as the turning on of the lights of reason, the Enlightenment, was fostered by scientists and then philosophers. They pursued their inquiries unmindful of the biblical worldviews or in direct challenge to them.

Enlightenment figures such as Ephraim Gotthold Lessing (1729–81) also crusaded against crusading and made a holy cause of opposing holy wars. In *Nathan der Weise*, for instance, Lessing dramatically portrayed the idea of the moral and humanitarian equivalence of Judaism, Christianity, and Islam, and suggested how futile conflict among them was. To militant dogmatic Christians this effort threatened to lead to the abandonment of what was valuable in Christianity in order to accommodate and embrace other faiths. Not that the Enlightenment-era rationalists turned out to be all that peaceful. Many of their ideas inspired the French Revolution and contributed to the chaos surrounding it. Still, the ideal of amity among religions lived on, and Christians under their influence evidenced curiosity about Buddhism, Hinduism, and other, to them, exotic religious growths.

In matters cultural, the earlier Renaissance artists and thinkers of the class and talent of Michelangelo served the church but had also chosen themes or lived in styles of life that were frankly worldly. Whoever gazed at the Virgin Mary in Raphael's *Madonna* may have been seeing the face and body of a mistress of the artist. The subsequent Enlightened Europeans were more radical. They often came to question and oppose Christian claims at root. Decisive figures like René Descartes (1596–1650) subjected all inquiry to the employment of skeptical rationality. Though he remained Christian, his approach left problems for thinkers who invoked divine revelation apart from the employment of critical reason. In the Enlightenment-type movements, leaders saw human reason progressively replacing the earlier appeal to the Bible or churchly authority.

## Encountering at Last the Whole World

While aware of the vastness of the globe and increasingly of the diversity of religions on it, one thing most continental evangelicals or Protestants seldom had in mind was the idea of converting the world to Christianity. Some leaders who were aware of the Americas referred to them in their writings, but through various theological twists or because of the wearing of blinders, they undertook little action. Some evangelicals as far back as Luther ducked or reinterpreted the gospels' command by Jesus to make disciples of all nations. They thought that the missionary command had been carried out soon after Jesus uttered it. Now their task was simply to prepare scholarly and consecrated preachers who would beat back the power of the papacy. They were then to go on to support the churches which—they acted as if they assumed—existed everywhere, even if they were not visible anywhere beyond their little European world. In any case, the signs were clear, they preached, that Jesus would come again in judgment and the world they knew would or should keep the believing community pure and ready for his return.

Roman authorities had not sat back in the midst of the ferment, and under figures as far back as Paul III (1468–1549) some worked to set its house in order. In the middle of the sixteenth century he finally called a council, which met at Trent, Italy, from 1545 to 1563. This three-term eighteen-year venture defined Catholicism over against Protestantism and set in hard lines the differences between these branches of Western European Christianity and therefore, later, of the Americas. This council was a long way in time and space from Nicaea, Chalcedon, and the old ecumenical councils. Some historians have seen Trent as having been quite provincial, a "Western Mediterranean" council. Where were the Greeks and the other Orthodox? While a few northern Europeans had influence, Italians and Spaniards dominated and set the terms. The issues that the four patriarchates from the East would have raised were absent. The new tensions did not lead to decline in the West. The Council of Trent, in fact, gave new life to Catholicism, now called "Roman" for the first time. New religious orders addressed the needs of populations under stress, and seminaries manifested new vigor.

Adding to this mix was a set of trends toward the development of modern national states during the later stages of a weakening Holy Roman Empire and wherever else that empire had once dominated. This nationalism was not a mild patriotism but an all-inclusive view of life, with metaphysical sanctions and ceremonies to back it and armies to front for it as a quasi-religious rival to the churches. German territories did not become Germany until 1870, shortly after the time when Italian jurisdictions became modern Italy. England and Scotland, France and the

Netherlands, and most of Scandinavia became assertive, opposing each other as planters of colonies in the Americas, Africa, and Asia and distancing themselves from what was left of the Catholic empire that was making claims in Central and South America and Mexico.

The moves to support nationalism and revitalized territories could not prevail only through the use of reason and in the expanding universities. A new outburst, not of revolt but of revolution, found its key expression in France around 1789 and then in Belgium in 1830, Germany in 1848, and many other places around 1870 down to the Russian Revolution in 1917. Some of the Enlightenment-influenced revolutionaries could echo French skeptic Voltaire (1694–1778), with his shout "Crush the infamy!"— that infamy being the church and its clergy. Restorations after revolutions may have been typed as conservative, and some of the new rulers used the church, but the nation and claims for it challenged and often replaced church authority, and Christian dominance diminished in intellectual specialty after specialty such as medicine, law, and sciences

Roman Catholicism reacted strongly to many of these changes, but it was not alone. While some Protestants in England and on the continent found ways to adapt to evolutionary thought, conceiving development as "God's way of doing things," the more conservative among them opposed Darwinian evolution and many other apparent assaults on their positions. Yet Catholicism was most visibly in reaction against "modernity" and "modernism." This was most manifest in the papacy of Pope Pius IX (1792–1878), who had been moderately open to changes but was then staggered by aggressive acts in the 1848 revolution. During his papacy the Vatican in 1864 issued the *Syllabus of Errors*, a chronicle of what it saw as anti-Christian. Among the movements and themes it denounced were republicanism, democracy, the separation of church and state, and liberalism. Further, in the First Vatican Council in 1870 the pope and assembled bishops went so far as to declare that in matters of faith and morals the pope was "infallible." Infallibility as such was invoked only twice in a century, but it remained a symbol of reaction and a potential weapon against liberals and modernists in the church and many civil issues in the larger publics.

## THE GLOBAL INTENTION

We have spoken of movements that come to us with designations in capital letters; the Reformation and Renaissance, Pietism and Puritanism, the Enlightenment. One force that buffeted the church but provided global opportunities seemed to be only secular in intent, the Industrial Revolution. It was less an ideological than a practical challenge. If revolutions demand the firing of guns, this one meant manufacturing guns, building railroads, and changing the landscape from one that featured the farm to the new silhouette of factories. It relied on the firing of furnaces in factories and boilers in the railroads, which after 1832 made it possible for people to cross great distances quickly and to form new communities wherein machines were used to make machines. Most of these noises disrupted serene country life and drew immigrants from villages to the cities. City life did not always militate against church life, but the settled parishes were not poised to expand and serve the newcomers. Mental energies that once went into metaphysics now were directed to physics, and the industrial age, which saw the upsetting of traditional ways of life, led to the crowding of masses in the city, they being people who were beyond the reach of the parish system when it was strained.

## PROTESTANT RENEWALS

Churches Catholic and Protestant alike did not simply succumb or cling always and only to the old ways. Remarkably, all across Europe there were stirrings called variously revivals, renewals, awakenings, conversions, or in other languages *reveils* or *Glaubenserweckungen*. Some of these inspired new church body names, such as Methodism. It is not a misuse of concepts to speak of the Methodist Revolution within Protestantism. Religious geniuses like John Wesley (1703–91) read well the minds of new generations and their own hearts, proclaiming ways for the soul to be reached and filled with love for Jesus—and then, for the world.

Until then only rare Protestant groups followed Catholic missionaries into Asia and Africa. Most notable among these were the Moravians, a kind of offshoot of Lutheranism, people who conceived of the world as their field. In 1732 they began work in the West Indies and then in Greenland. Discerning leaders among them, clerical and lay alike, sensed a discontent with existing "settled" ministries, the preaching of abstractions, and the routine and remote forms of administering church doings. They now reached for the emotions of individuals and the hungers of masses for faithful company, stirring people to express "heart religion" even to the neglect of "head religion." They also offered more portable means of ministering than those known in the routine parishes and conventional congregations. They made a direct emotional appeal to the minds and hearts of people who were being uprooted amid surroundings that threatened their sense of meaning. Now these publics heard that God cared for each of them as a person, that they were free and were even expected to make a personal decision for Christ to enter their hearts and for their souls to be stirred by the Spirit. Then they could form voluntary communities, not "given" or inherited communities as in Catholic, Orthodox, Anglican, and many European established churches.

These moves demanded a somewhat novel portrayal of God's action. While mystics centuries before and evangelical reformers more recently had long pointed to such a picture, now they boldly showed God seeking a love affair with sinners, who could be purified through faith in Jesus and could form communities under the Holy Spirit. Yes, clergy should still be educated, but their messages were not to be dry academic treatises so much as strong democratic appeals to individuals who had not earlier felt so empowered. Energies that resulted from these awakenings had to spill out, and spill out they did, to be picked up and poured into new containers. Many of them were of a humanitarian bent. The Jesus they preached cared about people who were enslaved and wanted them freed. England's evangelicals pioneered in the abolition of slavery around 1819. Not often directly subversive of authority or revolutionary in ideology, they focused on the vices of individuals who with God's help could change them into virtues, for example by turning from drunkenness to temperance or away from dueling. They led to new patterns of education, fostering Sunday schools for children, who had long been overlooked by educators. Some built hospitals or in other ways performed healing services. They attacked urban ills and tried to face issues of poverty.

All the reports we get from Victorian England or crowding Prussian Germany and much of France or Italy showed theirs to be apparently losing battles. Slums housed the urban poor and poverty became endemic in many places while bourgeois Christians often found solace at a distance from the festering enclaves. They assuaged their consciences or were moved by love and pity—or both—to extend charities and to look for new models of ministry. Among these were some who took account of a Christianity that stood the potential of being seen as global.

The map figuratively took on life among people who were singing hymns about reaching inhabitants near "Greenland's icy mountains" and "India's coral strand." They heard the call to deliver the people from error and paganism and idolatry. It is easy and in place to criticize them and the missions for their blatant claims of racial superiority and imperial outlook, and many of them were used by commercial and capitalist or even military interests. It is impossible to deny, however, that many were inspired by a love for the people they came to convert and serve, and that they were moved to save them from divine condemnation and for living within the realm of Christ. For present purposes it is important to note that most of this tardy endeavor among Protestants began to promote global consciousness among Europeans. Notable were the British, who after the formation of mission societies beginning in 1792 were represented also by laypersons in Indian Christian enterprises. Roman Catholics also adapted to the new times and new settings, producing religious orders which accented the love of God more than divine law. The Sacred Heart of Jesus came to be represented as an icon and to serve as a devotional focus and an inspiration for new missions.

## PITILESS AND PERSISTENT RIVALS TO THE FAITH

If the appeal to the heart meant a neglect of the appeal to constructive reason, as it often did, this suggested that once again the Christian fronts were neglecting the new scientific and philosophical critiques. Assaults came on many fronts. Charles Darwin (1809–82) was voyaging and returning to write *Origin of Species by Means of Natural Selection* in 1859, *Descent of Man* in 1873, along with other scientific works exploring evolution and implicitly, more often explicitly, calling into question biblical accounts of human origins. Many in the churches found ways somehow to welcome this new understanding of evolution as what they thought of as God's way of doing things, though when "natural selection" came to prevail in Darwinism, they found doing this more difficult because its randomness apparently belied the acts of a provident God. They had bought into biblical literalisms of sorts that Augustine had warned against 1,400 years earlier, literalisms that would make dialogue with educated unbelievers unnecessarily difficult.

Another challenge from a pitiless and persistent rival to Christianity came on the social and political front, when figures like Karl Marx (1818–83) issued documents such as *The Communist Manifesto,* which was co-written by Friedrich Engels, and *Das Kapital.* These radical books which grew out of German philosophy were designed to be and were purely materialistic in outlook. Marx and Marxians called religion the opiate of the people, something which numbed their revolutionary impulses and kept them in slavery to capitalist exploiters. Some of his ideas were later transmuted by V. I. Lenin (1870–1924) and others to inspire the Russian Revolution in 1917 and Soviet anti-Christian organization of life until 1989 and, in extensions, elsewhere.

If Copernicus and Galileo resituated the human in the universe and Darwin, Marx, and Lenin in new social understandings, still another typical critic was Sigmund Freud (1856–1939), who late in the nineteenth century in Vienna developed theories, sometimes on the basis of shaky scientific grounds but with almost mythic powers of intuition, to reach for the inner person and develop whole new vocabularies for dealing with the human. No longer to be interpreted in terms even reminiscent of Christian ones, the human was of interest mainly for his psyche, his psychological imprisonment, and Freud's efforts to help him find release that had nothing in common with the divine grace that once colored European personal lives.

Another category of assaults was typified by Friedrich Nietzsche (1844–1900), the most bold, articulate, and in a way poetic of the "God-killers," who attacked Jewish and Christian "slave morality" in the interest of seeing an emergent "Super-Man." Not all followers and epigones precisely aped these five critics and challengers, and some came up with variants that opposed these in brutal ways, but taken together, and often in milder forms, they came to prevail in the universities that shaped so much of the cultural life of Europe when it was coming to be thought of as "post-Christian."

It was clear that while Christianity prospered in many parts of the world, Europe was being challenged by forces usually called secular. This meant that progressively people took note of and explained their world without resorting to supernatural explanations or without a transcendental reach. They may or may not believe in God, but they arranged their lives the same way whether or not God existed and whether or not they owed obedience to God. Thus while the teachings of Karl Marx or Friedrich Nietzsche represented a formal assault against God and the churches, much of the turn to the secular was made without much ideology. People drifted from the churches and cared ever less about the explanations of science and history they had offered. In some eyes, the Victorian era in England was a time of considerable prosperity among the churches, yet those who read the signs of those times with care could foresee decline in church participation and in allegiance to Christian teaching. Agnosticism—a new word coined by a Darwinian social thinker, Thomas Huxley (1825–95)—meant a "not-knowing," not an overt thought-through atheism, but a keeping of the fingers crossed in the face of Christian claims. All the while, within still imperial England, missionaries reported new conquests for Christ in Asia and Africa.

## MODERNITY AND MODERNISMS

Just as with the awakenings and revivals a century earlier, Christians in the nineteenth century were not merely passive, and many put talent and genius to work to address Christian faith and thought in the new contexts. For instance, new schools of theologians, call them romantic or subjective or anything else, addressed the new situation by replacing scholastic formulas and arguments about God. Most notable was Friedrich Schleiermacher (1768–1834), who pioneered by turning theology on its head and by not beginning with reasoning about God so much as by observing the human. Content to be thought of as a philosopher of feeling(s) in the origin of his thought, he ambitiously revisited all the main Christian teachings and came up with fresh interpretations of God's action, Christ's meaning, the life of the Spirit and the church. Roman Catholicism also produced some thinkers in this mode, but as they and Protestants alike began to adapt to modernity and to adopt modernistic approaches, they often appeared in the eyes of authorities, including at the highest levels of Roman Catholicism, to be testing the edges and breaching the walls of faith and becoming heretics. Condemnations of modernism by the papacy in 1907 served to hamper the imaginative work of Catholic theologians, and many of them for a time came to be virtual museum-keepers of the faith, while Protestants were more free to explore, and many did.

Not all the exploration was further into modernism, and some instead even came to be called "neo-orthodox." Thus World War I, a Christian war in that all sides appealed to the Christian God and used their interpretation of Christianity to justify their killing, left millions dead in pointless barbaric activity. It is hard to read accounts of the cruelty, the carnage, and the atrocity of the war in the name of God without seeing it as a contributor to the decline of Christian humanism and Christian expression in much of Europe, a decline from which it never recovered. Yet some pastors and chaplains, leaders like Swiss theologian Karl Barth (1886–1968), did not lapse into cynicism and follow the temptations to despair. Instead, while existentialist and nihilist writers prevailed in the secular culture, Barth and others appealed to the prophets and apostles and to the Protestant theologians in order to witness to the authority of the Word of God and to help give new life to the churches.

One form such witness with global consequences took inspired movements toward common witness, action, and endeavor. The formal name for these, ecumenism, received definition as early as 1910 at a missionary conference in Edinburgh, Scotland. It climaxed first in a Protestant-Orthodox federation called the World Council of Churches, which met in Amsterdam in 1948. One of its agencies, the Faith and Order Commission, offered for its time a formula as old as the early church councils and consistent with what we have been tracing through the centuries: it bid "all in each place who accept Jesus Christ as Lord and Savior" to give expression to it by realizing a fully committed fellowship. Some movements such as Unitarianism, which had difficulty speaking of "Lord and Savior" and was devoted only to Jesus the Jew among other great teachers and examples, opted out or were excluded by definition.

This breakthrough was matched by the hugely significant Second Vatican Council. Called by Pope John XXIII (1881–1963), it met between 1962 and 1965 to set new terms for Roman Catholic life and to encourage better relations with Orthodoxy and Protestantism. Both of these moves had global intentions. The World Council sorts were inspired by needs from the fields where missionaries had been competing, and encouraged church unions as far from Europe as India. The Catholic style alerted visitors at Rome, where the council met, to the fact that very different but still loyal forms of Catholicism were developing, not all of them aping European models. Eclipsing the reality of new relations with non-Catholic Christians were the unprecedented moves to affirm Judaism and build better ties to Jews. The council no doubt did more to effect positive change in four years than Catholicism had initiated for many centuries before.

Between the ecumenical landmark years of 1910 and 1965, however, Europe faced another, this time more vicious, scene than it had during World War I in 1914–18. There was, however, more point to the conflict called World War II in 1939–45, since much of it was inspired by the need to react against totalitarian and, in the end, anti-Christian movements like Fascism and Nazism in Europe. Totalitarian and anti-God communism in its Soviet version during the war was strategically allied with Western Europe and America against Nazism. As for the Nazi influence, much of it supported by the Protestant and Catholic churches, more of it directed against them, and some of it making its way in the face of silent or silenced believers, traded on millennia-old religiously anti-Jewish traditions within Christianity and turned demonic in racially anti-Semitic efforts to purge Europe of Jews.

Significant voices of Christians were raised against the Nazi moves toward genocide and anti-Semitism, especially by those who, like theologian Karl Barth, said that anti-Semitism was an act against Jesus Christ the Jew. A Lutheran pacifist turned activist, Dietrich Bonhoeffer (1906–45), charged that whoever did not speak up for the Jews had no right to sing Gregorian chant— by which he meant to participate in all serious forms of Christian worship. A reflective theologian, he posed a question that reflected twenty centuries of pondering and answers which inspired action: "Who is Jesus Christ for us today?"

Curiously, after Soviet communist empires imploded, Christianity was left without an enemy to galvanize and unite forces for the liberating message of Jesus Christ. In Poland the church prospered longest, but in places like East Germany, where churches had been the centers of silent revolution, when the regime fell, so did church participation. At the turn of the third millennium, Islam in its radical forms began to present a challenge in Western Europe, but it was unclear whether its threat would move Christians to counteract or whether the church was too apathetic or even comatose to resist the signs pointing to the end of this second episode of European Christian life. The monuments remained. It was said of the late Polish-born Pope John Paul II (1920–2005), who acquired celebrity status and drew massive crowds, that he could fill the streets but not the pews. Affluence, prosperity, materialism, consumerism, relativism, the various "isms" on which the pope blamed the distraction and displacement of the church, were proving to be more lethal for Christian life than Nazism and communism had been. The greatest burst of creative theological activity in four centuries, signaled by names of French Catholics and German Protestants, spent itself and left little vitality in its train.

There were some gains, as Christians reached across Protestant-Catholic divides and made moves toward recognizing more fully the role of women. Even though ordination of women was restricted to most Protestant and Anglican bodies, the contributions of women were recognized more than ever before. Among the ruins of a destroyed Europe there were new stirrings of Christian activity, and one would do an injustice to lay movements, theological endeavors, and recoveries of biblical thought and vibrant forms of worship not to notice them. Despite all the valid and creative endeavors, however, after the Cold War and in a time when "guest-workers" and immigrants from northern Africa and elsewhere led to growth in Muslim communities, a complex of forces, often tabbed "secularism" and "militarism" or "consumerism" and "relativism" by Popes John Paul II and Benedict XVI and a host of Protestant counterparts, it was hard for what was left of Christendom to find its old place. It remained true that, counting whole populations as "Christian" because of their heritage and lineage and the almost automatic enrolling of newborns into Christian registers and ranks, Europe had by far the highest number of at least nominal Christians. Europeans who visited the Americas, southern Africa and southern Asia, or the rim of Asia, could not fail to note that Pentecostalism and prophetic movements, among others, were filling churches and having influence in the lives of converts and laypeople in general. These were unimaginably more devoted, active, and, as they would say, "Spirit-filled" than were the vestigial Christian presences in the chapels and cathedrals which number among them still millions who looked for ways to turn Europe around, see it revitalized, and to hope for a replacement after the Second European Episode. Fewer European citizens, in any case, in the third millennium, posed the question or tried to answer it as Bonhoeffer framed it for so many: "Who is Jesus Christ for us today?"

# 6

# THE LATIN AMERICAN EPISODE

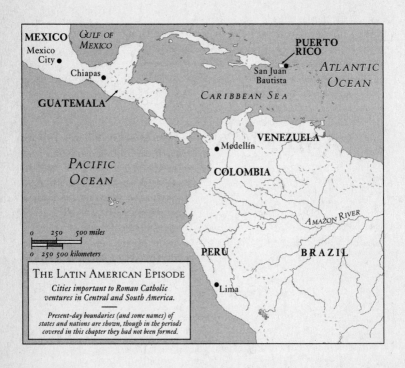

MEXICO GULF OF MEXICO
Mexico City
Chiapas
GUATEMALA

PUERTO RICO
San Juan Bautista
ATLANTIC OCEAN
CARIBBEAN SEA

PACIFIC OCEAN

Medellín
VENEZUELA
COLOMBIA

AMAZON RIVER

0   250   500 miles
0   250  500 kilometers

PERU
BRAZIL
Lima

THE LATIN AMERICAN EPISODE

*Cities important to Roman Catholic
ventures in Central and South America.*

*Present-day boundaries (and some names) of
states and nations are shown, though in the periods
covered in this chapter they had not been formed.*

Forty-five years after Europeans began to become aware of what came to be named "Latin America" in a hemisphere called "Western," Paul III (pope 1534–49) expressed a concern over the fate of the native peoples. In a papal bull dated 1537 he urged that "the Indians, like all other peoples, may not be deprived in any way of their freedom or property (even though they do not belong to the religion of Jesus Christ), and can and must enjoy them in freedom and legitimately." By then millions of them had already been deprived of freedom, property, *and* life, as consequences of the arrival of Spanish and Portuguese conquerors who sailed under flags identified with Catholic Christendom. By 1550, according to most estimates, over ninety percent of the indigenous population had died or been killed.

The papal document was matched by others through the decades in which Catholic leaders charged explorers and exploiters, colonizers and settlers, to help the natives henceforth to "belong to the religion of Jesus Christ." Earlier the pope had reminded the Spanish king that he and his people were to "bring to the Christian faith the peoples who inhabit these islands and the mainland." Queen Isabella, a supreme ruling force in Spain who died a mere twelve years after Columbus brought the existence of the New World into her consciousness, wrote: "Our chief intention was to attract the peoples of these regions and to obtain their conversion to our holy religion." Columbus himself saw the natives as being "very ripe to be converted to our Holy Catholic Faith." This meant, he said as he planted crosses in the harbors to show that they were now Spain's and existed for Catholicism, they were "principally for a token of Jesus Christ Our Lord and the honor of Christianity."

Not all the newcomers shared this sense of mission and some were bold about distancing themselves from it. Francisco Pizarro (c. 1476–1541), a major conquistador, made that clear: "I have not come for any such reason; I have come to take away their gold."

The priests and brothers who arrived often did side with the people they hoped they could help survive. They were supremely confident in their faith and faced no competition among European adventurers. What the Catholics brought was considered a doctrinal finished product and package deal. The Protestantism that was taking shape in Western Europe by 1537 was not yet of significance for the missionary venture. Absent it and Orthodoxy, to speak of exploring, conquering, and converting whole new races of people by Catholic regimes and with Catholic adventurers did not and could not mean engaging in debates over how the human Jesus was the exalted Lord. Doctrines about that were settled. The bewildered "Indians," which is what equally bewildered Europeans at first thought they were, had—and many still have, five centuries later—their own "holy religions," which looked unholy, nonreligious, and wholly barbaric to the Catholics who confronted them on unexplored shores. Of course, that holy religion was "the religion of Jesus Christ," so he figured into all that happened.

## CHRISTIANS AS CONQUERORS

In place of searching for theological debates to see who this Jesus Christ was, an inquirer does better to look at representations of him in the images presented in the quickly erected chapels and the grand cathedrals, on banners and shields, and then in folk art favored by "the peoples of these regions." They characteristically portray an unquestionably human Jesus, usually a gored and gory biblical "man of sorrows," with whom the poorest among them could identify. They portray him being whipped, crowned with thorns, crucified, or held in his lifeless condition by his sorrowing mother, the Virgin Mary. She was also characteristically seen in local and intimate settings, thanks to an apparition, as the Virgin of Guadalupe. She became as much an object of devotion as was Jesus.

The conquerors, cruel and greedy Christians almost to a person, defended their depraved and murderous acts by identifying unthinkingly with the conquering Christ, the exalted Lord of that "holy religion." It did not take much imagination for them to connect their taste for plunder with the power which they assumed came with both the might of Spain and Catholicism backing them. On such grounds the second in command to the first among conquistadors, Bernal Díaz at the side of Hernan Cortés (1485–1547) in Mexico, matched Pizarro's summary with his own: "We came here both to serve God and grow rich!" If the description of these willful bearers of the sword and unwitting bringers of diseases that wiped out whole tribes sounds hyperbolic, let it be said that historians writing as descendants of conquerors or the conquered, Catholic or non-Catholic, seem quite benumbed by what they find in the records. And yet, and yet: out of the sixteenth-century beginnings there have grown cultures and civilizations in which Jesus Christ remains the central figure among the hundreds of millions currently numbered as Christians of many sorts in those Americas.

Native faiths lived on, sometimes fused with Catholicism and often in rivalry or resistance. Classic Protestantism, imported by Lutherans and others from the European continent or North America, has a minority base in several nations, and, as we shall see, evangelicals and Pentecostals in recent times challenge Catholic hegemonies. Catholics often claimed that God had reserved these Americas for Catholicism, and that the fact that Mexico as well as South and Central America became Catholic was a near miracle of timing and military or imperial chance. Now it seems that Catholics must make room for other Christians at their side or in competition with them.

Back to beginnings: had the "discovery" of the Americas occurred a century earlier, Muslims might have been better poised than Christians to exploit the continents. Islam, or as we prefer to call it Islamdom to match the domain called Christendom, had been expanding across northern Africa and into the Iberian Peninsula, chiefly into what became modern Spain, which was the first sending center to the Americas. Iberia was not only Spain and Spanish-speaking. On its Atlantic coast was Portugal, harboring Portuguese-speaking Catholic explorers and conquerors. To minimize rivalry and to help assure that all the resources possible could be committed to the conquest of new lands, Pope Alexander VI, who would enrich himself and his throne with loot from the New World, in 1493 drew a line. East of it was the Portuguese domain and west of it were lands open for Spanish exploitation. The pope did this not in humble service of a simple Jesus but claiming the authority of the exalted Lord, calling himself *Dominus totius orbis,* or *Vicarius Christi,* Lord of the whole world and Vicar of Christ, because he was the "legate of the absolute and universal will of the Son of God." One can imagine the resentment this "gift" to two nations meant to the monarchs and merchants of others.

The papal dividers and mapmakers had no real sense of the geography of the continent, so Portugal came up short, since on this map of the continent it basically had been given only the eastern parts of Brazil to conquer, convert, and "civilize." The Portuguese settled Brazil in 1500, after Pedro Alvarez de Cabral (1467–1520) staked the king's claim for the land, carrying with him the assignment to Christianize the native people. On his ships were a company of religious missionaries. They found work among the Indians to be dangerous, and most contented themselves with ministering to the conquerors and earliest European landowners. Given Brazil's later prominence and influence, this division did not represent a bad bargain. Ships with priests and brothers bearing flags with crosses on them regularly disembarked to establish themselves, fight their battles, displace the populations, and overlay Catholic culture on the survivors of native South American cultures.

In 1492, the year in which Muslims were driven out of Spain, Christopher Columbus inspired the parade of explorations and conquests in the name of Christ and Catholicism. He had the hard-won backing of Queen Isabella, who was taking part in efforts to reach Asia without having to retrek the traces of the old Silk Road from its west to China—or to avoid dangerous passage around the south of Africa. Columbus's Catholic work was not wholly unplanned. He chose the name "Christopher," after a saint who was a "Christ-bearer," and now he would be one. He had read himself and his ventures into the plot and prophecies of the Bible, and considered himself to be an agent of divine revelation and conquest. The promise and then the reward of spices and other lusted-for products were signs that God was blessing and encouraging conquest. Like so many who followed him, Columbus sized up the new potential subjects of Spain and the pope and decided they could be converted.

The idea of separating church and state, religion and regime, not yet heard of in Europe, was simply not entertained in the Western Hemisphere. How to attract, subjugate, control, and make use of the natives that they set out to convert was a physical and spiritual problem alike. Each new intrusion was marked by blatant but not always comprehensible assertions, since they came in languages not understood by the people to whom they were read. The document was called a Requirimiento, a "requirement." From the very beginning there had been native counter-actions, for example at San Juan Bautista in today's Puerto Rico. To put the Indians in their place the Spanish document stated the terms: the conquerors who came in the name of the One God were descendants of the first pair of humans, created by God. Somehow from Adam and Eve the line of transmission went to the pope in Rome, a locale that would have been hard to conceive among the Americans who typically would hear such words in languages they did not know. The pope was "prince, lord, and master of all the peoples of the world." It was God who had deeded the islands and the land of the ocean sea to Spain's monarchs.

The church came out well in this document, for it was to be recognized as "the superior of the universe." The religious brothers in Alvarez de Cabral's company were authorized to preach and to treat with charity those who obeyed. Submit, obey, do not resist, was the word, but the warning came: if you do not accept the Catholic faith and rule you will be victims of war and made subject to the church and the rulers. Part of the revenge against resisters was the threat to make slaves of all, including wives and children. Policies of making raids and forcing victims into slavery then followed.

The story of the conquest itself is familiar: the Catholics discovered rather sophisticated empires, people who made up Inca,

Aztec, and Maya civilizations. With their superior weapons, the conquerors had little difficulty overwhelming the strongholds, killing the chiefs, and engaging in bloodbaths. The cultures they overran were not pastoral and pacific. Some had engaged in human sacrifice on almost unimaginable scales. In one ritual shortly before the Europeans came an estimated eighty thousand victims were killed to appease the Gods or increase fertility. Whatever else the natives were, they were vulnerable and even in the long range defenseless. The Catholics who came had no interest in preserving even the most benign influences in the native heritage.

One covets more word of the response from natives who were often out of earshot, left in ignorance because of the foreign language. Few cared to report their reactions. One reader of the Requirimiento did hear of a response through his interpreters. The native people thought that the idea of one supreme God was fine with them, but that this God deeded their own land to the king of Spain was an idea that had to have been propagated by a drunken author who had no right to give away what was not his. They thought it would make sense for them to counter-raid and bring back the pope's head, to match those of their rulers whose severed heads were posted when they were captured by the Spanish.

## CATHOLIC ROLES IN THE SOUTHERN AMERICAS

In all the transactions, the state kept its stake, because the kings nominated bishops and dominated most of the administrative life of the church, while the church met this new challenge with the invention of the *patronato* system, wherein uprooted peasants were gathered around a mission church and within protective walls, but in the status of indentured servants with little hope of escaping their slavelike circumstance. Here priests of various religious orders undertook the task of baptizing masses. If their activity meant bringing the waters of life, as Catholics saw it, they also carried two angels of death: first, diseases against which Indians were not immune, and the sword, which the conquistadors wielded mercilessly. Disease sounds like a natural enemy, but the spread of smallpox often resulted from deliberate design, as when the conquerors in deceptive acts of apparent generosity handed out smallpox-infected blankets. Unbelievable brutalities were often part of Spaniards' campaigns to get gold. They experimented with finding efficient ways of killing by attacking villages and cutting up people simply to test their blades and demonstrate their overwhelming power. The model for their advances was of a kind that had shaped growth in Europe for centuries: capture, convert, or kill the chief persons, and then demand conversion of the people or subject them to death. The priests baptized tens of thousands who had no idea what was happening to them. The act made the priests feel that they were accomplishing great things for God.

As the popes learned of the means of conquest, to their immense credit and for a variety of reasons, they experimented however tardily with more humane approaches. Finally in 1622, Pope Gregory XV founded the Sacred Congregation for the Propagation of the Faith, an attempt to bring some order to the contests over trade and colonization. The early leadership of the Congregation took note of the cruel policies against natives, the vicious competition among religious orders, and the role of commerce and politics being fostered at expense to religion. Catholic authorities started training better missionaries and providing materials for their use. Their agents, vicars-apostolic, often had to sneak into a territory because many religious orders were suspicious of and resistant to reformers. Some vicars quickly went home in frustration and disgust.

The new policy fostered *reducciones*, "reductions," which were an invention that deprived peoples of their old faiths, rituals, and customs, and then imposed Catholic patterns on them. The biblically informed scholars gave legitimacy to the invasive policies by comparing the venture to the way the children of Israel in the Old Testament migrated into Canaan, Palestine, and with military means conquered and took over from the earlier peoples. If God licensed that aggression in biblical times, the same God authorized superior invaders and migrants to repeat the policies and procedures now.

From the first, Europeans like Pizarro and Cortés were tantalized by stories of El Dorado, a city of gold, and its counterparts all over the map. Their allure grew as the invaders came upon artifacts of gold, jewelry, images of the divine, and even practical objects that were abundant in the treasures of conquered rulers and chiefs. Unfortunately for the first round of conquerors, known gold supplies as early as 1518 began to run low, and silver, still available, was a less rewarding treasure. To diversify the economy beyond mining, the Europeans turned to farming in the rich soils of many areas. They established plantations which yielded sugarcane and other products. Imported and enslaved Africans on these plantations brought with them practices that Spaniards could graft onto the Christian faith as taught by the missionaries. One typical set of rituals they called "voodoo," which provided access to the spirit world. The native peoples were not alone on the scene, and not the only improvisers. Unappreciated in the sixteenth century but surviving into the twenty-first were fusions such as trance-related religion which featured access to the spirit world in what was called "macumba." This was attractive to many African slaves who were brought to the southern Americas in greater numbers than they were later into North America. There were no voices for abolition and few for humanizing the slave system for centuries.

In Mexico, chiefly Aztec territory, the friars and brothers themselves reported the most dire statistics, often to the pope. As an example, Cortés needed only 550 men equipped with the latest weapons technology, instruments unknown by the Aztecs, to defeat their empire—all in the name of Christ, for whom Cortés was a crusader. Some compatriots saw him as a spiritual leader who was rescuing Aztecs from their vice and superstition. As a soldier of Christ, he could see his victories as miracles of divine intervention, so when he confronted the Aztecs he told them that if they would suffer death, it would be their own fault.

So aggressive were his policies that word of them came to Montezuma II (c. 1466–1520), whose capital was where Mexico City now is. It was there that not long before the conquistadors came, the chief sacrificed thousands of people who were designated for sacrifice and victims he had conquered. Before the conquistador attacked, he burned his own ships, so that any mutinous or deserting men would have no chance to commandeer and take them back to Cuba. Making alliances with enemies of Montezuma along the way, Cortés attacked cultures of people who worshipped the sun, built pyramids, and were determined to resist him. His men kept planting crosses and convincing themselves that they were making converts as they engaged in mass baptisms along the way. When the conquerors arrived in Montezuma's capital, they were awed by what they saw and the treatment they received. With the stench of human sacrifice in the air, the Spanish priests said Mass, to impress the Montezuman cortege and court. Dazzled though they were by Aztec civilization, including its architecture, their leader still wanted to destroy it all. His men attacked and demolished the images on display, thereby provoking a suspicion and rage that meant impending conflict and devastation. In response, the Aztec leaders attacked, but in the struggle Cortés captured and bound his attacker. In 1520, with his own people being complicit, Montezuma was killed. When the conquistadors triumphed there in 1521, they destroyed the signs of anything that contradicted Catholic faith. Their complete victory they credited to the cause of Christ.

## THE GENTLER SIDE OF THE CONQUEST

Rare, almost unique among the defenders of the Indians was a priest and bishop who had come to be regarded as almost saintly, Bartolomé de Las Casas (1484–1566). Probably the first person to be ordained as a Catholic priest in the hemisphere, in 1507, Las Casas crossed the Atlantic several times after 1502, at first as a collector of taxes and next as a landowner, but as his faith grew so did his commitment to the victims of conquest. Called to preach one day on a scourging biblical text, he found himself being chastened and then converted by his own sermon. After 1514 he devoted himself to defense of the Indians and a year later was named "Protector of the Indians" by Cardinal Cisneros back in Spain. As protector, he made it a point to identify with the poor, in whom he saw Jesus Christ, while making enemies when he gave publicity in Europe to the atrocities perpetrated by his fellow Spaniards. As Bishop of Chiapas in 1544–47, he opposed Indian slavery so strenuously—even to the point of refusing the Mass, regarded as necessary for access to heaven, to some slaveholders—that he was almost lynched by his own communicants. His main successor as defender was the Jesuit José de Acosta (1540–1600), whose *Taking Care of the Salvation of the Indians* was a forceful document but a patronizing one, since he wanted the Catholics to think of the Indians as children in faith and culture.

Las Casas had the backing of Pope Paul III, who regarded the "savages" as savable souls and who in 1537 came out rather boldly for Indians' rights. The monarch of Spain also came to see the Indians as his subjects and therefore they were people to be protected. Las Casas's defense of the Americans also led him to be attacked back in Spain. Early on in his career while making defenses there, he had come up with a compromising proposition that became the major stain on his reputation. Let the queen's subjects be freed from slavery, he argued, but, since slave labor was needed to keep the economy going, import Moors, black slaves from Africa. Las Casas soon repented for having promoted such a policy, but he had displayed the mind-set of Europeans of the day, people who could not conceive of an economy without slaves and who found no objection in Scripture or in Catholic practice to slavery. His arguments staged against Juan Ginés de Sepúlveda (1484–1573) in 1550 included overstatements, but only mild ones, when he described the agonies of the Indians. His reports became prime documents when Protestants and others later denounced Catholicism and accepted all the criticisms to the point that they created a "Black Legend of Spain." It helped legitimate the ventures of Protestant nations of Europe which did not want Catholics to prevail in the North American lands that developed only decades later.

On the more positive side, unlike most Europeans in North America, many of the early colonists started families, and a resultant mixed race called mestizos became a substantial part of the population. Also, more readily than the Protestants who settled much of North America not much later, Catholics, while opposing native ritual and belief, adopted some cultural features from the natives. The best example of successful fusion occurred after December 12, 1531, when a shepherd named Juan Diego had a vision which he proclaimed as a realistic meeting with the Virgin Mary, the mother of Jesus. In the encounter Mary left an imprint of her visage, an image of an Indian-featured Virgin of Guadalupe on a serape that is still preserved in the enormous Basilica of Our Lady of Guadalupe near Mexico City. Creative missionaries also learned to make use of some visible resources in Catholicism—objects like little crosses to wear—and rituals that absorbed some features of Indian worship. Laborers helped build magnificent churches and cathedrals, landmarks for the centuries to follow. The missions in villages, the countrysides, the large plazas and town squares in the cathedral cities, became visual displacements of native ritual sites.

Dominicans came as early as 1510 and Franciscans followed. Members of the new Society of Jesus, the Jesuits, arrived in 1549. Among them was José de Anchieta (1534–97), who used scholarly energies and showed his interest in mixing cultures by inventing a written language, dictionary, and grammar so that Christian documents could find a readership. Adept at music, he listened to local languages and wrote songs that gave voice to the fused faith, since the melodies and rhythms were local but the stories in the hymns came from Asia and Europe. The bishops criticized such practices in their effort to keep the faith of conquerors pure. The Jesuits went their own way, turning their back on the dioceses and the bishops and taking control of their missions and strategies. Their efforts were certainly expressions of a colonialist mentality, and their vision of native peoples reflects their own sense of superiority, yet there are accounts among them of growing sympathy for the people they served. Being a priest in the dangerous wilds of the Americas was not an attractive option for most young Iberian Catholics, but the religious orders had ways of motivating missionaries to be ready to make sacrifices, even to death.

In the course of time some of the converted native people rose to prominence, including Isabel de Santa María de Flores y de

Oliva, "Rose of Lima" (1586–1617), who before she was twenty became a Dominican. Following a practice that her order lauded, she punished herself as penance, disfiguring herself so no male would find her attractive. She wore the hair shirt and nettle-filled gloves as she walked in the byways of Lima, Peru, welcoming the ridicule of mobs along the way. She was only thirty-one when she died, an exemplar of the suffering-filled life and faith set forth as ideal in Latin American Catholicism. She was named the first saint in the Americas.

## THE CHURCH ESTABLISHED AND THREATENED

Through the sixteenth and seventeenth centuries and longer, the Catholic Church retained its place as the established and official church, where records of baptisms, marriages, and burials were kept after the rituals associated with both had been performed. Still, much of the clerical leadership took its place for granted and made too little effort to put imagination into its ministry. Many of the intellectual currents issuing from Europe to the Western Hemisphere reached South America, including the Enlightenment, Romanticism, nationalism, and other major "isms" that changed the character of populations on the continent. One feature of the more radical Enlightenment thought was anticlericalism and even anti-religiousness. Therefore when revolutions finally occurred, as they did under Simón Bolívar (1783–1830) in South America, disaffection with and distancing from the Catholic Church were manifest. The great Baroque churches of an earlier century often emptied, and seminary enrollments plunged. While the peasants and ordinary folk retained loyalty to the Virgin and Christ, many in the elites turned to secular thinkers for inspiration. In some nations churches were confiscated and public presentations of the faith prohibited.

Events in Europe often impinged on Latin America. Napoleon's armies forced the Brazilian royal family into exile in Brazil, and when it returned, left one of its sons in position as King Pedro I. His rule inspired counter-activities. An independence movement in 1824 revolted against a tired clergy. Secularist philosophies and movements in Europe gained ever more impressive followings in South America, especially in Brazil, and these progressively hemmed in the clergy and deprived many of their rights and privileges. A minority of clergy supported the revolts. Millennialist movements took hold among some clerics, as they envisioned a kind of Christian Utopia once the corrupt leadership was displaced. While the Vatican had gained power over the monarchs of Spain and Portugal who had held much of the domain in the first two centuries after colonization, some foresaw more Roman power in the Latin American churches.

Then came formal clashes between Rome and the new nationalist governments, some of whom claimed authority to appoint clergy. The church was allowed to survive, but it was to be restricted to the realms of private life of prayer and was not to be a public presence or critic of rulers. Governments on occasion suppressed the religious orders which had for so long led the church. No longer would the state perform treasury services for the churches. By the mid-nineteenth century the secular forces had gained so much that many in the church fought back, arguing that only a conservative church, allied with economic elites, could survive. The conservatives returned to a stress on devotion, the supernatural, miracles of the Virgin Mary, and other popular themes that could be revived. Through all these movements, the Virgin of Guadalupe was claimed by forces from the left and the right, and even secularists knew better than to fight against the cults of the Virgin or the images of Jesus, the peasants' friend and brother.

Latin America had always paid special attention to the Virgin. Catholicism, Portuguese- and Spanish-style, transplanted to the New World, had featured dependence upon prayer and intercession by women, mothers and wives. Let the theology and governance be male, the devotion was matriarchal, which meant that it counted on intervention in human affairs by the Virgin and women saints. Thus Rose of Lima had been named a saint, because she worked outside the convent to deal with the needs of the poor. The liturgical and devotional objects from this time and place demonstrate how much the church in the southern Americas was devoted to the Virgin. In a time much later, in the second half of the twentieth century when many Latin Americans were devoted to Liberation Theology, religious sisters, who engaged in works of charity, teaching, and healing, were often on the front lines of the pious activists.

## LATIN AMERICAN REVOLUTIONS AND LIBERATION

After a revolution in 1857, Mexico was declared to be no longer a Catholic nation, and, despite a subsequent Catholic restoration or two, new philosophies and revolutions inhibited the religious expressions. As the Latin American citizenries became more free and some nations more prosperous, the gulf between rich and poor became ever wider, more noticed, more demanding of notice. In the cities new technologies were popular, a fact that favored the already prosperous and equipped. Promises of development often left the poor further behind and the moderately rich scrambling for resources. Some studies found poverty rising among large populations, showing over 180 million poor and almost ninety million more who were extremely poor. Population grew, but distribution of wealth was always very narrow.

In the early twentieth century some Catholics began to adapt the social teachings of Pope Leo XIII and his successors to Latin American situations. In 1894 Leo had issued a papal letter, *Rerum Novarum*, under whose impetus Catholic leaders supported the rights of labor to organize. He was open to involvement of government in issues of justice, though he opposed socialism. Conservatives countered such social teaching by citing his predecessor, Pius IX, whose demand that church leaders stay above politics often meant that they became part of the status quo. As such they were unable to free themselves from identification with economic conservatives and oppressive forces. In 1910 a Mexican revolution, devoted to Marxian visions of the future, attached its themes to ancient Indian symbols. While it did not bring about revolutionary change, it did succeed in suppressing the church in public life. Even priestly garb was forbidden in public.

Some Catholic leaders first took it in hand to try to break up the system. They did anything but turn secular. Instead, they reappropriated some features of the pre-Columbian religions of the continent and fused them with biblical and Catholic motifs and strategies. Announcing that "God has a preferential option for the poor," and having learned from the diagnoses by Karl Marx, they spoke of Liberation Theology with Jesus as human brother and divine connector or mediator. Never encouraged by Catholic leadership in Rome and, in fact, barely tolerated from the first, the liberationists invented new forms, among them "base communities" of face-to-face believers who studied the Bible and church teaching, and then linked up with radical agents of change. Over against intransigent landlords and factory managers, they developed a theology which identified Christianity with the poor at the expense of the ruling classes.

The liberationists were, on one level, very popular for their social policies, but on another, in the pattern of church authority, they could only push so far. Radical clergy were seen as enemies of the upper social classes and as forgiving, benign leaders to the lower, with priests serving as intermediaries and even agents of revolution in the name of Jesus, newly pictured as a spur to radical activity in South America. In the base communities laypeople put to work the teachings which they heard on the radio from leaders like Dom Hélder Câmara (1909–99), an archbishop who chose to live and dress like one of the poor. The faithful also followed seminary priests and sisters who identified with the struggling.

This face of Catholicism was aggravating, even repulsive, to landowners and others who prospered even, or especially, in times of crisis. A conference of bishops at Medellín, Colombia, in 1968 gave encouragement to anti-colonial and anti-imperialist movements. This meant that they tried to distance themselves from those Catholic institutions which they saw as being too bound to political and economic establishments and elites. Gustavo Gutiérrez, a Peruvian priest, in 1971 published the best-known book in the field, *A Theology of Liberation,* which gave intellectual depth to the popular movement. Not all the efforts at economic liberation stood up to attacks by right-wing governments and conservative church members. Many Catholics began to imitate the Protestant evangelicals by stressing the supernatural, contact with God through intimate groups, and local efforts to alleviate poverty. At the time of the Second Vatican Council (1962–65), not only ordinary laypeople but also and even the bishops put some of these teachings to work. They also naturally aroused Catholic opponents, especially among churches dependent on and related to large landholders, who claimed that Liberation Theology was a disguised form of secular philosophy, and must be resisted by the churches. The Vatican may have regarded God's preferential option for the poor a good slogan, but it disdained Marxist philosophy. As theologians were silenced by the Vatican when it discouraged the base communities, laypeople and priests tried to fill the gap with prophetic preaching and action. Still, the church kept losing some members to those Protestant churches which offered hospitality and helped them find a place in emergent economies. In El Salvador, Archbishop Oscar Romero (1917–80) was gunned down, most likely by government death squads. Numbers of priests and men and women in religious orders were also killed.

Some bishops after the Second Vatican Council tried to promote Catholic social teaching which would support moderate reform, but where free enterprise advocates prevailed, many turned to evangelicalisms that favored it. The Catholic public responded through an array of movements, many of them marginally Christian or explicitly seen as survivals or revivals of faiths that antedate Catholicism in the Latin American scheme. Therefore while Catholicism took on the marks of ever wider diversity, the Vatican and bishops appointed by Pope John Paul II late in the century turned more conservative and defined Christianity more self-defensively.

## PROTESTANT AND PENTECOSTAL PRESENCES

Perhaps we have overplayed the picture of South and Central America and Mexico and the Caribbean as Catholic, since Protestants also were present for centuries. For instance, German immigrants to Argentina and Brazil created an enduring Lutheran presence. To understand Latin American Protestantism it is important to differentiate among three terms and three camps. First are the heirs of European and North American missionary work and immigration. They are often called "mainline," and while they hold the loyalty of significant numbers, they yielded their historically prime place to evangelicalism and Pentecostalism, the two other camps.

Some of the liberal political figures, reckoning that they had to pay attention to spiritual needs, favored Protestantism explicitly in Brazil, Venezuela, and Guatemala in the later decades of the nineteenth century. Some of the stresses and opportunities of the time led to the splintering of established Protestantism. It was in this climate that evangelicalism and Pentecostalism began their surge. Well-off conservative Christians in the United States sponsored some of these movements, but their great strength came from their appeal to what someone described as "the upper lower class and the lower middle class." Attachment by many converts to free market ideology and practice further complicated the picture of Protestantism in South America. In any case, the cluster of Protestantisms shattered the image of monolithic Catholicism on the continent and in Central America.

Evangelicalism is a form of conservative Protestantism which in Latin America as elsewhere stresses the inerrancy of the Bible, literal readings of the book, impulses to convert others, and a readiness to testify on one's own to the salvation converts have experienced. Pentecostalism is a movement born early in the twentieth century which seeks and claims to experience the immediate presence of the Holy Spirit, as did followers in the time when the New Testament was written. Pentecostalists cultivate the practice of "speaking in tongues," unintelligible syllabic sequences which they believe are prompted by the Holy Spirit. Most believe in supernatural cures for illness and other miracles. Evangelicalism is somewhat nearer the mainline historic Protestantism, but its adherents also stress personal emotional engagement with God, and are aggressive witnesses seeking to convert others. So successful have these groups been that some progressive Catholic leaders first encouraged cooperation among them and the Catholics, and

Catholics sometimes "took lessons" from the Pentecostals on how to become more engaged and energized. As time passed, the Pentecostal surge became so strong that rivalries developed and some spoke of spiritual civil wars between these two kinds of Christians.

In part, evangelicalism and Pentecostalism prosper because in many places the Catholic churches are passive, understaffed, and not alert to the emotional needs of people. Some estimate that only ten or fifteen percent of Latin American Catholics are regular Mass attendants. Up and down the block from their often nearly empty churches are evangelical storefronts or Pentecostal house churches where the music is pulsing and awareness of God is cultivated. In a continent where access to the "spirits" and spirit world has been sought and claimed, these Protestant movements prosper. While it is likely that predictions about Pentecostal and evangelical takeovers of prime place on the continent are overstated, these Christians continue to meet needs that others do not. Almost obsessive is their stress on the Jesus of the gospel stories as a human among them—and Jesus as the Christ, the exalted Lord among them and within them.

# 7.

# THE NORTH
# AMERICAN EPISODE

Since Christianity around the globe draws its name, its distinctive features, and its central themes from Jesus Christ, its story focuses on what he meant to believers and how they related to others. Such a focus may sound too simple and its choice by a historian obvious and naïve, yet through all the tales of Crusades and Inquisitions, creeds and treaties, explorations and retreats, under all the symbols of aggressive power or winning humility, somehow Jesus Christ was at the root and base of thought and action. That word "somehow" suggests that in different cultures one receives diverse answers to questions about his role. Thus in North America, with its diversity of populations and churches, the questions about him and the new setting have also had to be: *Whose* Jesus Christ? *Which* Jesus Christ? What did the multiple answers to these questions have to do with various Christian and national outcomes in the history of what became the United States and Canada?

In both Eastern and Western Europe for more than a millennium, and in Latin America from Christian beginnings there, the answers to such questions would have been something like "Orthodoxy's Jesus" or "Roman Catholicism's Christ." Other representations than those official ones were in the hands and voices of outsiders, dissenters, and resident aliens in matters of faith. Most of the early settlers in North America from 1607 in Virginia or 1608 in Quebec instinctively and by intention carried over European patterns. This meant that they naturally privileged one religion per one government, fostering one interpretation of the work and meaning of Jesus Christ as chosen by the one prevailing and usually legally established church. Latin America "belonged" to Catholicism, where devotion to Jesus Christ was complemented by adoration of the Virgin of Guadalupe, or of myriad saints. In North America, Quebec aside, the focus in piety, theology, and outreach was on Jesus Christ alone.

Four other continents house more Christians than does North

America, and United States law does not name Christianity as its officially chosen faith. Most citizens and many demographers and political observers around the globe call it a Christian nation. The original colonizers had more in mind and more to do than save the souls of the Native Americans who were there when the Europeans arrived, nor were they there chiefly to bring solace. They busied themselves with the ordering of society. They had to invent forms of government and make judgments within them. Some pioneer leaders liked to claim that they were fulfilling a covenant with God in the name of Jesus Christ. Problems arose from that insistence. In the gospels that they cherished, Jesus was quoted as having said that his kingdom was not of this world. He tended to disdain civil authorities like those who could not comprehend or tolerate him, specifically King Herod, governor Pontius Pilate, or the Roman emperor. He sustained ambiguous relations to producers and owners of wealth. His message in the New Testament was also so radically focused on the immediate end of the world that it offered little guidance or impetus to support public or civil codes of ethics and advice on marketing. Therefore, for their task of ordering society, the colonizers relied more on the Hebrew Scriptures or Old Testament than on the New. The name of Jesus as Lord was mentioned at best perfunctorily or not at all in most official public settings, especially when the time came in which leaders had to recognize spiritual diversity and religious pluralism. The United States coins could not have used the motto "In Jesus Christ We Trust," and the Pledge of Allegiance to the flag, revised in 1954, does not say that the nation is "under Jesus Christ" but "under God." That the name of Jesus could still make many uncomfortable, that it could offend, was apparent whenever school boards or courts in the twenty-first century wrestled with the choice of a divine name or presence to be invoked at public events.

The official case aside, Jesus Christ has been at the front of the mission and the heart of the message for the majority of citizens. When in the nineteenth century a small but very significant Unitarian movement developed, it fostered devotion only to one God, or to God the Father, which in fourth-century language meant the

"First Person of the Holy Trinity." Theologian H. Richard Niebuhr in the twentieth century accused many would-be orthodox evangelicals of being so devoted to Jesus that they were guilty of being "Unitarians of the Second Person of the Trinity." Interestingly, the people whom United States citizens call "founding fathers" were devoted to the human Jesus but rarely spoke of the exalted Lord. George Washington, "the father of his country," was a very religious and moral-minded churchgoer, but in scores of references to "Providence" he avoided biblical terms for God and Jesus received bare mention. Another founder, Benjamin Franklin, averred that some good people believed in the divinity of Jesus and some did not. Some bad people did not believe in the divinity of Jesus, and some did. As an old man, he said, perhaps with a twinkle in his eye, he would soon die and could then find out the truth or falsehood of claims about Jesus' divinity. Thomas Jefferson was so devoted to Jesus the moral teacher that in his White House years he clipped from his New Testament all supernatural references, all miracles, all claims for the divinity of Jesus, and pasted together a scrapbook in four languages of teachings by and stories about the human Jesus. Jesus Christ was a stumbling block, in their minds, if reference to him divided the godly citizenry or alienated those of faiths other than Christian, or of no declared faith at all. Meanwhile, all around them, in private and churchly life, most Americans remained devoted to Jesus Christ.

When Catholic evangelizer Matteo Ricci encountered the Chinese in the sixteenth century, or when Bartolomé de Las Casas did the same with the natives in Latin America, or in the seventeenth century when Robert de' Nobili pioneered with people in India, they made some attempts to understand the rites and beliefs of native peoples even as they repudiated them. Among North American Protestants, the dominant colonists everywhere but in Quebec, or in what became the United States's Southwest, there was virtually no attempt to understand or to do anything but destroy all traces of native religion. While the people of China and India lived on and dominated in Asia, in North America the new settlers brought with them diseases, guns, and policies that led in many places to the virtual extinction of the natives, or the newcomers saw to the natives' removal to remote reservations in others. The treatment of native people by the government and by agents, often supported by the churches, is now universally regarded as disgraceful. The government broke treaty after treaty and inhibited or prohibited Indian sacred rites, while non-Indian American majorities forced the native people onto usually barren reservations, without resources or status.

Between the arrival of the seventeenth-century colonizers and the twenty-first-century pluralists, the North American scene within global Christianity prospered and unfolded in rich detail. Concurrent with the settling of the Atlantic Coast colonies, horror stories were told of troubles such as the Thirty Years War (1618–48) on the European continent and the English Revolution (1642–60) in England, and colonists did not want to replicate them. In most conflicts between whites and Indians the victims were the natives. In the first American century it was the Spanish conquistadors and colonizers who did the killing in the Southwest, and later it was English settlers who killed Indians along the East Coast. Heirs of pioneer whites in New Mexico, California, and Arizona like to remind visitors that the church was planted, built for, and given a chance to thrive in the borderlands. A church in Santa Fe, New Mexico, antedates the Anglican settlement in Virginia, recalling a time when Catholics more than Protestants began establishing missions among the native peoples.

In the Western Hemisphere, Islam, a threat to European Christendom, was hardly a presence at all. Some world historians speculate that the calendar was the Protestant anti-Muslims' best friend. They suggest that had discovery, exploration, and settlement occurred a century or two earlier than it did, there might have been less point in analyzing the fortunes of Protestants and Catholics in North America. Islamic cultures and societies instead had been expanding. No one can know what the Muslim armies could have done, but we do see much that they did set out to achieve against Christendom. Muslims possessed the armies, the ambition to match, the imperial designs, the resources, and the hunger for more, to drive the Indians west. Then, fortuitously or providentially, as the North American Protestants would say,

Islamdom was pushed back from Spain in and before 1492, and it was Christendom that was able to produce the effective military forces. Many of these Protestants also argued that God had hidden their favored "virginal" continent until the Catholic Church had been countered, compromised, and checked in the northern European nations by the Protestant Reformation.

## THE NATIVE AMERICAN ON THE SCENE

The people the newcomers called Indians had peopled the continent for tens of thousands of years. Not one of them was Christian in 1492. They performed rituals, held beliefs, and prescribed practices and ceremonies which most of the newcomers from Europe regarded as savageries, needing to be replaced by the true faith in Jesus Christ. Many of the later comers sincerely did intend to make Christians out of the people already resident there. Explorers and settlers from Spain and France did their converting under Catholic flags, while others, those who populated all the colonies except Maryland, flew Protestant banners. Almost everyone in both agreed that nothing in the native spiritual expressions was valid, and that their own versions of the Christian replacements to them had to prevail, still under European national flags and at the expense of other types of Christians.

For all the talk, some of it sincere, about bringing the savages into membership in the domain of the gospel, the effort was largely a failure. The diseases Europeans brought, smallpox being the best example, wiped out much of the native population, and swords and guns did a good deal of the rest. Even the policy of "reservating" the Native Americans on ever reduced, always monitored, and beleaguered set-aside lands did not bring about healthy relations. In the Southwest that became Arizona, New Mexico, and the California coast, architectural relics of missions survive to enchant fascinated tourists. Catholic priests had performed numberless baptisms and provided new if restricted ways of life for the people they sequestered. On the East Coast and in Canada Catholics had some successes at "civilizing" the natives, but the Protestants among them talked a better game than the one they played. They justified their adventures as efforts to extend Christ's kingdom and bring new peoples into it, but few colonists actively supported such ventures among the people they were displacing. The Massachusetts charter listed among its purposes "to win and invite the natives of that Country to the knowledge of the only true God and Saviour of mankind, and the Christian faith." However, between 1607 in Virginia and 1620 and 1630 in what became New England and the birth of the nation in 1787, only a few outposts of "praying Indians" thrived. It is believed that there were fewer than a dozen Protestant ministers working on the frontier among Indians by the latter date.

Why their drastic failure? First, the newcomers brought higher priorities than spreading the gospel. These included expanding European empires and bringing back riches such as gold or tobacco or other products in demand in Europe. Second, they misunderstood and underestimated the hold of the religious practices of the natives, and found it difficult to attract them to the only ways the Europeans considered valid. Add to this the fact that Indian survivors of conflicts could not consider responding positively to those very Christians they regarded as plunderers and killers. The white person's God was repugnant. Finally, all but a few missionaries failed to understand any part of the worldview, the cultures, and the aspirations of the Native Americans, most of whom resisted Christianity. Some who did convert blended Indian and Christian ways into fusions that the missionaries found repulsive.

When the thirteen colonies that became the United States broke free of England in their revolution after 1776 they had the task of nation-building, an act centered in the acceptance of a constitution between 1787 and 1789. In the conspectus of global Christianity, the most significant feature of this constitution was the fact that for the first time in 1,400 years, ever since the days of Constantine and Theodosius, religion and regime were officially rendered distinct and separated in constituting documents. While religion influenced politics and vice versa, it was not to be legally privileged. Citizens argued over variations of this polity for the next two centuries and more, but meanwhile missionaries or evangelists did not sit on the sidelines. They became free to spread their gospel, to compete with each other, and to invent or develop new forms of voluntary churches called denominations. They could produce a republic in which Christianity prospered as it was seldom to do where the faith remained established by law and the subject of even gentle and often not so gentle coercion.

### AFRICAN-AMERICAN SLAVES AND CHRISTIANITY

Add to the mix of natives and white European settlers another set of peoples who also were present almost from the beginning. In the myth of many Americans the year 1620 and the arrival from England of the *Mayflower* with Puritan ("Pilgrim") dissenters represented the beginnings. However, one year earlier a ship brought a load of Africans to Virginia to start a slave trade that kept most Africans in America in bondage until 1863. These slaves were regarded almost universally as inferior forms of human beings, undeserving of freedom or opportunity, and not always even valid prospects for baptism. One of the near miracles of later life on the continent was the fact that the majority of these blacks, later African-Americans, adopted and then customized the religion of slaveholders, even though the oppressive owners' Bible gave legitimacy to the slaveholding program. What kind of God, it might be and was asked by blacks, would grant privilege to persons with white skin who wielded whips, condemning those from Africa to a world of unending servitude and misery?

Despite the handicap that the slaveholder and a passive larger society brought to the interaction, most Africans became Christian, borrowing practices and themes especially from Baptists and Methodists but also improvising their own rituals and meanings. Some masters taught Christian faith and Christian ways to the slaves on their plantations or in their houses because the Christian story could be an instrument of terror. Who dared violate the will of that Holy One who must have been bigger and more powerful than the slave ship captains and the slaveholders who worshipped that God? Others, of more humane sorts, began to regard slaves as human beings. So they provided opportunities for them to worship, though seldom for gaining literacy. Still, as noted, many slaves adopted and adapted the Christian faith. They often found covert ways to translate the symbols of faith to their culture, to pick and choose the biblical stories that most inspired and ennobled them. Their distinctive songs, called "spirituals," often were full of code language which employed biblical terms that acquired new local and, to establishments, upsetting meanings. Meanwhile, some blacks purchased or won freedom to start churches of their own well before Emancipation in 1863, and many more enjoyed liberties and found possibilities for creative living despite their segregation. They cherished their own versions which later became visible to the larger public as vital and authentic versions of Christianity. Theirs was a Jesus-centered faith, and biblical images of pilgrimage and liberation colored all that they sang about or said.

While slavery existed in North and South alike, by the 1830s it had come to be seen as integral to the national economy, another fact that made the work of Christian emancipators or abolitionists ever more difficult. White preachers, especially in the South, declared that slavery was the will of God. Still, in the face of untold suffering, slaves and those who had bought or won their freedom retold and lived by biblical stories which best addressed their dream of a promised land. They employed as models and inspiration stories of God's ancient people who had become free from Egyptian bondage and who had suffered as they had, but still triumphed in the end, as their hymns and spirituals promised that they would. Some adopted the language of liberation from both the Hebrew Scriptures and the New Testament. Freedmen like Richard Allen (1760–1831) invented and nurtured denominations such as the African Methodist Episcopal Church, Colored Methodist Church, or the National Baptist Convention. Finally after the Second World War (1941–45), in which so many had participated, their churches became prominent and sometimes dominant in northern cities. These had been their creations and had served them faithfully on many plantations, in little shack churches for sharecroppers, or in urban poverty areas. Four centuries after their arrival many shared with Hispanic peoples the crowded circumstances of slum dwelling, their Christian faith often representing both the sign of vitality and the very symbol of the cross that whites had used to enslave them. Now those who had been left out in so much of society embraced something that could serve as backbone and banner for their religious life.

## THE WESTERN EUROPEAN HERITAGE IN NORTH AMERICA

Most of the visible and recorded Christian drama, of course, was in the hands of whites. Beginning in 1608, French Catholics arrived in the heart of eastern Canada, settling what became Quebec. English Protestants occupied the rest of the Canada that was known among Europeans by the time of the colonial or French and Indian War just before the American Revolution. Canada remained a British dominion, a Protestant form of provinces wrapping around French Canada. In the times of the revolution that produced the United States, both Canadas welcomed loyalists who fled there from the warring United States. These refugees were usually Anglican or later Methodist and Baptist, but in the course of time, thanks to Scotch-Irish immigration in the nineteenth century, Presbyterians also found a home there. Though Anglicans were assigned to instruct the children of natives, few of the churches tried to do much work among their Indian parents.

Having experienced no war of revolution to provide myths of national founding, Canadians in their varying degrees of loyalty to French monarchs or the English crown did not develop an elaborate public or civil religion alongside the faith and practices of the churches. The thirteen colonies that became the United States did experience a revolution, developed and responded to a set of myths of origins, and honored a pantheon of their military leaders and other patriots. They also came to regard the United States Constitution in almost religious terms. Before the Revolution and the Constitution, however, much had to happen to ready the people for nationhood and a civil faith of Christian origin.

## Two Styles Begin to Fuse

For centuries, two stories of United States' origins prevailed. The first accounts for the arrival of English colonists to the James River area in Virginia, where in 1607 the first Anglican service was held. The New England story has acquired almost mythic status. The arrival of separatists—radical congregational-minded Puritans on the *Mayflower*—in 1620 and the larger and more influential Massachusetts Bay Colony that settled around Boston in 1630 set the terms for much of American theology and church life for three centuries and more. They may have been dissenters against the Anglican establishment in England, but in New England they became the establishment. As such they thrived on tax support, eroded many lines between religious and civil spheres, and hampered or even excluded and persecuted others who did not share their faith. These included the Anglican minorities who were beleaguered when the colonies after 1775 fought the motherland with its and their own mother church. In some other circumstances they penalized dissenters who split off from congregationalism, some of them forming Baptist churches. On their own, not depending upon clergy and leadership from the British Isles, the Congregationalists and Presbyterians invented colleges like Harvard and Yale. The Baptists did something similar, establishing Brown in Providence, Rhode Island, a Baptist colony that, uniquely in New England, chose not to have an established church. From these centers came native-born elites, clerical and lay alike. They and their contemporaries developed trade colonies whose citizens grew increasingly restive about paying revenues to the crown.

The middle colonies, doing without church establishment, anticipated the eventual national solution to questions of church and state relations. Of particular interest was the case of New Netherlands, later New York. Leaders among its colonists had intended to foster a Dutch Reformed state-supported church that would exclude others. Governor Peter Stuyvesant in 1654 became irritated and felt threatened when a French ship, the *Ste. Catherine,* sailed in from Recife in Brazil. Its "twenty-three souls, big and little," were refuge-seeking descendants of the Jewish community that Spain had forced into exile in 1492. Some had lived in England, the Netherlands, and then in a Dutch colony in Brazil, where they usually had been harassed. The Portuguese had recaptured this colony and expelled the Jews. Would New Amsterdam take them in? They were poor now, but they wanted to settle and to "navigate and trade near and in New Netherland, and to live and reside there." Now, Stuyvesant asked himself and then the Dutch West Indies Company, if these "deceitful" and "very repugnant" Jews, "hateful enemies and blasphemers of the name of Christ," who threatened to "infect and trouble" the colony, were allowed to stay, there would be no way for him to exclude "Lutherans and Papists." The company, which included Jews among its shareholders and whose leaders knew what assets these traveled Jews from Recife would bring, insisted that they be welcomed. They were even permitted to worship in private homes, something Lutherans were not yet permitted to do. Commerce and markets became agencies for religious freedom, without much ideology or doctrine to reinforce it.

Meanwhile, in five southern colonies, notably Virginia and the Carolinas, Anglicanism, often in weakened forms, remained the establishment. Being a cleric on that southern frontier was not attractive to prospective priestly candidates in England, and the quality of southern Anglican church life is usually pictured as less than vital. Still, on its soil there developed a generation of political leaders, many of whom combined Anglicanism or Episcopal faith with Enlightenment ideals, to play a major role in shaping the nation and its constitution. In the four middle colonies that did not have church establishments, non-English-speaking Europeans—Lutherans, Reformed, Anabaptists, and Moravians, among others—found their home and their freedom, as did the English-speaking Quakers who settled in William Penn's colony, Pennsylvania. The one southern exception was the proprietary colony of Maryland, deeded to and further invested in by the Catholic Calvert family, but this Catholic dominance did not last long. By the time of the Revolution it is believed that only about thirty thousand Catholics and three thousand Jews were citizens among the estimated 4.5 million free white colonists. The minorities and dissenters had soon found that the majorities were not flexible. Many in New England spoke nostalgically about piety in the "olden days" of the seventeenth century, and rued the "declension" in the eighteenth.

## THE GREAT AWAKENING AND ITS STYLES

Then beginning across the colonial map there occurred a cluster of happenings that eventually acquired the name "the Great Awakening." One finds beginnings of these stirrings in mid-colonial New Jersey in the 1720s, but more evidence appeared in North and South alike in the 1730s and 1740s. Suddenly, established and settled religion was put on the defensive. Revivalists like Jonathan Edwards (1703–58) in New England, an agent of conversions and the most highly regarded theologian the hemisphere ever saw, and George Whitefield (1714–70), a commuter between England and the colonies, attacked sin, preached the gospel of Jesus Christ, and evoked the Holy Spirit in efforts to produce warm hearts and to build new-style communities of faith in their congregations and among their audiences.

Some of these changes occurred under new forms of Calvinism, the main style of Protestantism in the North, but which was also not without influence in the southern colonies. If Calvinism had seemed to its critics to be a passive and fated faith whose adherents depended only on a predestining God, now it had been renovated and for the Awakening stressed the human will and agency: people were to become active in "accepting" the reach of God, seeing themselves turned and warmed and activated. At the side of Calvinism was also a form of Protestantism often called Arminianism, which did place far more accent on what humans could do to be saved and made holy. Out of it grew Methodism, a renewal movement within Anglicanism in England, which did not surge in the colonies until after the War of Independence because the earliest Methodists had to be true to their oaths of loyalties to the crown and were loyalists who opposed the Revolution.

The Great Awakening is a hard-to-account-for movement, since it spread among local pastors and through the activity of notable traveling evangelists alike. It attracted young people to giant meetings from Boston Common down through Carolina plantations, from Harvard and Yale campuses to the quiet villages, attracting both elites and simple citizens. While the connections are not always easy to trace, its influences were complex, and almost every feature of the Awakening has been debated ever since, there is no question but that the gospel of freedom was preached in churches that were restless with the policies of the church establishment. They became an element in calls for independence. Awakeners, though not essentially politically minded leaders, provided inspiration among conscripts and volunteers who fought the English to a successful conclusion and to win independence after 1776.

Making one nation out of this mix of colonies and versions of the Christian faith was not easy, since not all colonies were ready to give up their religious establishment. On their own, the insistent Christians were not good at inventing a republic, rich as their churchly doctrines of freedom might have promised that they might be. However, their leaders were influenced by ideas associated with the Enlightenment, enough to produce a constitution which did not mention God or Jesus Christ or allow religious tests for office. The founders also saw to the production of the Bill of Rights, which assured religious freedom. Some historians suggest that this creation of what founder James Madison called a line of distinction between religion and the civil authorities was the most dramatic widespread change in governance since the era of Constantine 1,400 years earlier.

## THE SECOND AWAKENING AND THE CHURCHING OF AMERICA

In activities following the initiatives which combined Awakening and Enlightenment as well as post-established and never-established forces, a set of institutions sometimes called "the Voluntary Church" took form. Not all the churches brought theologies which were congenial to this concept, most notably among them being the Catholic Church. Catholics began to arrive in large numbers from Ireland, Germany, and elsewhere in the 1840s, bringing a doctrine which did not include the notion that human response and initiative created the church. In practice, however, as priests and missioners worked among nominally Catholic immigrants, signing them on to parish rosters and getting them to build churches, it is clear that they had to work with what we might call a "doctrine of choice" almost as much as the revivalists on the frontier posed evangelical and Protestant versions of choice. The churches were free to compete for loyalties, and did so, in moves that led the churches in the United States to attract church members in ever-increasing numbers and with developing measures of participation and loyalty.

The voluntary churches, as mentioned, also invented the denominations as their chief instrument for connecting churches and transcending the local scene. One might think of these bodies in three main clusters as they filled up the land west of the Appalachian Mountains all the way to California. First was the colonial "big three" of Congregationalism with its northern Baptist offshoots, Presbyterianism, and Episcopalianism. A second cluster included the revivalist Methodists whose "connectional" polity made it possible for them to start thousands of churches in the West; the southern Baptists, who forgot their New England roots and became a kind of native growth; and the Disciples of Christ, a "primitive" back-to-the-Bible movement also at home on the frontier. Third were the non-English-speaking traditions from the European continent including the Lutherans, the German and Dutch Reformed, the Anabaptists called Mennonites, Moravians, Brethren, and others.

The Enlightenment did not prevail as a spiritual force, though its teachings about freedom and equality infused later national life and played a big role in a Christian-inspired civil religion. Instead, the heirs of the Great Awakening, refreshed after the birth of the nation and during the settling of the West and the South, moved with such a pace and were so attractive that their converts soon outnumbered both the heirs of those colonial-era churches which did not find the revivalist style attractive and heirs of continental faiths that never had been revivalist. This meant that Baptists and Methodists won out among the whites and, curiously, also among the southern blacks, be they slaves or ex-slaves.

Not only did "voluntary churches" develop within Protestantism, but radical innovations occurred alongside more conventional frontier Christianity. With so much wilderness and so many prairies to transform, it is understandable that some spiritually inventive leaders came up with faiths unknown elsewhere in the Christendom of the times. Utopian colonies of non-Christian outlook suggested that humans could start afresh and build colonies exempt from troubles imported from Europe. Most of the colonies quickly failed, victims of extravagant dreams and considerable naïveté. More successful were movements closer to conventional Christianity. They have acquired worldwide significance.

Thus the Church of Jesus Christ of Latter-day Saints, or Mormons, has realized the global challenge better than most, and is planted and prospers in many places where ordinary Christianity languishes. The Seventh-day Adventist movement developed concurrently, with plans to match those of Mormons to spread the gospel globally. Under the leadership of Mary Baker Eddy, the Church of Christ, Scientist drew the hopes of many who were threatened with illness. They also faced the antagonism of challenged church members who saw the Christian Scientists, with their appeal to metaphysical healing, to be attractive to some of their prospects and some of the members of the denominations themselves. In all these cases the now developing ethos of evangelicalism combined apparently contradictory themes. They were to compete in order to grow, but also to cooperate in efforts to form lay groups that help reform the United States and make it attractive.

For all the growth of these upstart and often despised groups, mainstream Protestantism and Catholicism were successful in achieving what some projects and book titles call "the churching of America." The attractions of Enlightenment-style religion were quite confined to eastern colleges and salons, while robust, democratic, and experience-centered "homegrown" devotionalism prospered, especially among Baptists and Methodists, winners of the competitive wars to attract and hold the South for the faith. They developed an informal patent on various new forms of gathering: camp meetings, revival weeks, and youth attractions. They succeeded in doing some "taming" of the frontier even while introducing new conflicts among quieter church members in various bodies.

Sometimes the First and Second Great Awakenings, names given to the stirrings in the middle of the eighteenth century and through the first half of the nineteenth, get written off as nothing but emotional and anti-intellectual. Much in them may have been ecstatic, but more remarkably, the "settled" churches, heirs of the colonial East Coast, also brought learning with them as they went west. They established academies and colleges wherever they moved. If the curricula at such schools sometimes made them look like vocational schools for training missionaries, it must also be said that their schools kept the light of larger learning on in modest ways, just as Benedictine monasteries had done a millennium and more earlier. From the schools issued classes of missionaries and teachers who hurried from colleges like Amherst and Brown to the Sandwich Islands, Palestine, and China alike.

These voluntary churches were not content merely to save souls and package them for heaven. They also took responsibility for activities in society, some of which had been the duty of governments in Europe. Educational impulses inspired some, as in Sunday school and Tract associations. Others were moralistic and reformist in character, as when they promoted temperance in the face of life in what some called an "Alcoholic Republic." Still others focused on charitable work among immigrants and the poor, social service agencies, and, most controversially, addresses to the problems that came with slavery and then with slavery itself. There were slaves also in the North, the heart of the slave trade industry, where some abolitionist movements made their case within economies in which slavery—though not the slave trade!—was not the key to the economy.

In the South, however, slavery on rural plantations and in urban life was so much a part of the economy, the slave so much an element of the population, and the numbers of slaves so large that few southerners could picture what to do should the inconceivable happen—that those in bondage become free. The southern churches found plenty of biblical warrant for supporting slavery or at least opposing anti-slavery moves. The Baptist, Methodist, and Presbyterian churches split on sectional lines in the 1840s. What became the Union in the North and the Confederacy in the South, in turn saw the developments of such competing versions of faith and rationales for ways of life that they represented two worlds and in effect two nations. Clergy and political leaders in the South combined pro-slavery and anti-North sentiments to the point that they argued for the secession of their states from the Union. In the North, while abolition movements were small, they were noisy and visible in the wars over conscience. Anti-southern sentiment developed while the Union itself acquired a kind of mystical status, best expressed in the language of Abraham Lincoln (1809–65).

Guns went off in 1861, initiating among Americans the bloodiest conflict and the costliest in terms of lost lives, properties, affections, and futures. In the middle years of that war President Lincoln issued the Emancipation Proclamation, which began to assure freedom for blacks. The war ended in 1865, with both sides exhausted, impoverished, and sure that they had been right in serving God-given causes. For a twelve-year period, postwar efforts in the South called Reconstruction offered churches the opportunity to interpret their defeat and to counter its effects. The churches themselves, meanwhile, were defined on racial lines. Emancipation and northern victory did not by any means produce the end of segregation, a policy that continued to call for theological defenses, always southern and sometimes northern in representation.

During the remaining third of the nineteenth century, the West opened, as pioneers and missionaries pursued new destinies on the Oregon and other trails, across plains and prairies and over mountains, leaving a landscape marked by steeples all the way to the West Coast. After the Civil War, President Ulysses S. Grant (1822–85) authorized a policy in which various churches were assigned responsibilities or given privileges to "work" the various

Indian reservations. New arrivals from Ireland or the European continent crowded eastern cities and western plains, creating social problems by the sheer weight of their numbers, the competition for land and jobs, the disparity of customs among them, and theological disputes as to how each of them was the one true religion.

## NEW TIMES, NEW DIVISIONS

A new divide, no longer between North and South but between rich and poor, also now became ever more visible. Industrialization occurred, as large manufacturing companies and complex corporations took the place of small farms and village enterprises. Among the leaders were enterprisers whom critics called "robber barons," most of them church members who used their interpretation of the gospels to justify their ways. Names like Rockefeller, Pullman, Vanderbilt, McCormick, and many more symbolized the policies which made workers dependent while they hampered the development of labor unions. They also represented philanthropy and the building of higher educational institutions. Andrew Carnegie helped build libraries in many communities. John D. Rockefeller devised a "Gospel of Wealth" to justify his approach to the market. What came to be called "Social Darwinism" prospered among the magnates as a representation of the economic survival of the fittest.

So sudden was the rise of this economy that it took some decades before other voices and forces were heard and organized. When James Cardinal Gibbons, the most notable Catholic leader of the time, dragged his feet when pressed to suppress the unions as secret societies and refused to condemn the Knights of Labor, a fraternal proto-union, he made it possible for laborers, most of them of Catholic stock, to remain loyal and not to have to fight the church as many had back in Europe. To justify and support their actions, Gibbons and his heirs cited social teachings from the Vatican, where popes were trying to come to terms with industrialization and the need for labor to organize. Meanwhile Protestant leaders, often in seminaries and away from the front lines of middle-class churchgoers who thought organizing labor meant violating natural law, began to formulate what came to be called the Social Gospel.

This Social Gospel, as formulated by the Baptist professor Walter Rauschenbusch (1861–1918), the Congregationalist minister Horace Bushnell (1802–76), Episcopal advocates of "Christian socialism," and other leaders, sided with workers and advocated labor unions to give poorer workers a voice. As did Rauschenbusch, they combined piety and prayer with liberal and modernist theologies in support of social justice. Their favorite symbol was the Kingdom of God, with Jesus as the exemplar of justice within it. Their critics called them all socialist and tried to stigmatize theirs as radical Marxist-type movements. Others noted that "they did not get their hands dirty," as so many of those called evangelicals did. For instance, evangelicals promoted the Salvation Army, a church-based but streetwise reform and charities movement.

Mention of tensions or splits between North and South, Social Gospel and salvationist movements, liberals and evangelicals, or between Catholics and Protestants, "Know-Nothing" anti-Catholics, and creators of anti-immigration sentiment and action points to the fact that the Christianity that prevailed in the United States and Canada a century after American independence and a half-century after Canadian confederation (1867) was anything but united. Its elements were estranged from each other and rivals of all others. The cause of the disunity was often celebrated, for it represented religious freedom and the numerical results of competitive Christianity, especially among Protestants. The result of all this striving and bragging, however, was dismaying to many. The advocates of policies designed to do something about it; agents of church unity in a movement later called ecumenism argued that the disunity violated the New Testament pictures of the one church as "the body of Christ." It thus represented sin that had to be repented and practices which had to be changed. For others, the disunity was both a spiritual and a practical issue. By this time many American Christians were sending missionaries to Asia and other continents, and some of these came back with reports of what competition on the mission field did to the credibility of Christianity and how duplication of efforts among rivals was inefficient. Coupled with this was also an imperial impulse among many of those who were out to enlarge the domain of Christians, civilize humans, see the triumph of white people in a nonwhite world, and demonstrate Christian superiority.

The ecumenical movement, born in this era, ushered in a century of invention of bureaus, agencies, and international connections: a Faith and Order movement linked with a Life and Work movement combined to help form the World Council of Churches in 1948. All along in a number of nations there were mergers, such as the one that led to the Church of South India or the United Church of Canada, as well as federations and councils, which predominated in the United States. Advocates of these movements were consistent: unity should advance missions. Ironically, it was often the competitive and anti-ecumenical missionary forces that attracted more converts through the twentieth century.

## MISSIONS ABROAD, MISSIONS AT HOME

Mention of the missions calls to mind the rise early in the nineteenth century of a missionary movement in which American Christianity, originally dependent upon Europe for its own Christian impulses, was beginning to "go global." Inspired by millennial visions which urged them to convert others and bring education and healing to the non-Christian world, through the whole nineteenth century they envisioned and supported agencies to take the gospel of Jesus Christ to India, China, and Africa. Bright and dedicated college graduates, often with their wives, headed for tropical posts or situations of danger anywhere. Their abundant gravestones on several continents, testimonies to the effects of disease, suggest something of their dedication. It can be and has been argued by critics that their missionary endeavors were part of an imperial scheme. No one can deny that their efforts were combined with those of commercial and sometimes national interest, but archives full of letters, writings, and sermons suggest that for most of the missionaries, regard for the souls of the unconverted was the moving force. That their attitudes were often condescending if not racist goes almost without saying, but it is not the only thing to be said about them.

Back on American shores, in 1908, the Federal Council of Churches, made up of bodies that were heirs of eighteenth- and nineteenth-century movements but not including the more conservative groups, was organized as one instrument of church unity on practical levels. Some leaders worked to form actual mergers among competitive groups, especially within the denominational houses. Earlier in the twentieth century the Lutheran version of the gospel, for example, was being preached in almost two dozen languages, and in pulpits that represented denominations which had been formed on Swedish, Slovak, or other ethnic lines. They began to try to consolidate the churches of those whose parents had arrived on different boats from different shores. The main council-style movements tended to neglect evangelism and to stress good works plus social, educational, and charitable activities. The leaders of these remained in their denominations, but in their liberal theologies they were more interested in stressing what they had in common than in what separated them.

Evangelism, therefore, became largely the activity of more conservative church bodies, for whom the belief that the world would end soon, and that they must save people in a hurry before Jesus returned to judge the world, crowded out witness to the essential unity of Christianity. These drew on eighteenth- and nineteenth-century revivalist traditions, now deftly moved from village to city environments. Dwight L. Moody (1837–99) at the end of the century and Billy Sunday (1862–1935) in the 1920s were geniuses at attracting and holding large crowds and getting thousands to repent and commit themselves to Jesus Christ. In their neglect of Social Gospel ministries, they were not necessarily inhumane, but they argued that saved individuals who would choose to be generous and moral were the instruments for meeting the needs of a changed world. The more doctrinally stringent among them also did battle with ideas and practices that came along with modernity.

Charles Darwin and the Darwinists called into question bibli-cal accounts of the world's creation and the special creation of hu-mans. The progressive Protestants criticized literal interpreters of the biblical visions of the end of the world and the second coming of Christ. Many thought that critics of the Bible, who treated the Scriptures the way they would any other ancient document when they went about probing how its books got written and who called attention to its contradictions, threatened the truth of its witness. To counter them, early in the new century some wealthy lay oil-men subsidized a set of pamphlets which were mailed to every Protestant cleric they could track down. Called *The Fundamentals*, these gave the name to a new movement formed around 1920 and coming to public awareness in 1925 as some denominations split over "fundamentalist" versus "modernist" issues. The highly pub-licized Scopes Trial, which dealt with the teaching of evolution in a Tennessee high school, engrossed citizens. The schism within Protestantism was now obvious, and there was little communica-tion across the chasm separating the two styles.

## POST-PROTESTANT STYLES

If evangelism, new-style, and fundamentalism were challenges to the once established denominations, these saw other movements chipping away at their monuments. For one thing, Roman Catholi-cism in the twentieth century, portrayed as a domain which aspired to rule America, was a galvanizing force that kept the mainstream Protestants mobilized and focused. Add to this Pentecostalism, a movement that drew attention during a revival on Azusa Street in Los Angeles after 1906. Its advocates believed that evidences of the acts of the Holy Spirit in biblical times could reappear now. God had never announced the withdrawal of the Spirit. So the Pente-costals, on their way to becoming the fastest-growing movement within global Christianity, "spoke in tongues." Many experienced and claimed miraculous healing. While Pentecostalism was at first a largely southern phenomenon, its effects trickled north where it had particular success among African-Americans, as in the bur-geoning Church of God in Christ late in the century.

Two distractions of two world wars and the hardships of the Great Depression in the twentieth century made it more difficult than before to promote liberal and progressive causes, and the revivalist evangelicals with their message to convert people out of the world prospered at the expense of liberals after mid-century. Most of the council-type churches bore the genes of church establishment in their systems and they did not organize to convert people the way the mass evangelists did. So they lost their primacy on the American scene. Better phrased: they had to share power with all the others inside the rich mix of American pluralism. In the Social Gospel era they had been most interested in effecting change within the political, social, and cultural worlds. A century later it was a coalition of evangelicals, Pentecostals, Baptists, and conservative Protestant denominations in linkage with certain kinds of Catholics on certain kinds of issues that was most ambitious at trying to "run the country," especially in causes such as opposition to abortion or homosexual rights.

One great issue in which the place of Jesus and the prophets figured in an immense way was the civil rights revolution. A United States Supreme Court decision in 1954, insisting that "separate but equal" facilities for African-Americans were insufficient, helped trigger a complex of responses which by 1965 led to major legal changes. Black clergy were leaders, long prepared to work for change but not given an opportunity until the late 1950s. Demonstrations by supporters, black and white, Christian and Jewish and everyone else, helped bring about change, but not until after violence by opponents of the movement had taken its toll. Leaders like Martin Luther King, Jr. (1929–68), rather deftly combined two motivating themes. On the one hand, the preacher treated the Declaration of Independence and the United States Constitution with almost religious fervor, arguing the case for realizing human rights on their basis. On the other hand, the Baptist pastor opened the gospels and was devoted to Jesus Christ not as a mere teacher or example but as the divine agent into the world that needed radical change. The African-American churches came to be more vivid than they had been in the general public's consciousness. Public performances that were rooted in black churches now were celebrated in the public square, where songs about Jesus Christ as liberator were part of festivals marked "Soul," "Gospel," "Spirituals," and the like.

The missionary and ecumenical movements had done well to give American Christians awareness of global Christianity, motivation to deal with it, and impulse to seek justice everywhere. Christianity, Catholic and Protestant alike, by the third millennium had become a local-based phenomenon in the era when the globe, thanks to commerce, enterprise, media, and rapid travel, had figuratively shrunk. As Christians in many places faced the challenge of radical Islam or, in some cases, as in India, radical Hinduism, they had to think through their policies in respect to missions, their decisions about whether to carry on dialogue with other faiths—including those represented in ever greater numbers in Canada and the United States themselves—and their approach to extremist and terrorist life. They found that they had to draw on resources of the Christian church elsewhere to understand the times and plan strategies at home.

Change is a constant in North American churches, and some changes had been almost impossible to envision decades earlier. Who could have conceived that after the Second Vatican Council, Catholic-Protestant dialogue would become urgent and strongly encouraged? Who foresaw the ordination of women in most churches beyond Catholicism and the large Southern Baptist Convention, and the expansion of the roles of women in changing the agenda or offering fresh voices, that appeared late in the twentieth century? What will one make of an episode in which Christians are coming to know each other across denominational lines and religious boundaries, yet many are turning more withdrawn and hostile to others?

## INDETERMINATE CHRISTIANITY WITH GLOBAL CONNECTIONS

One hesitates before blithely leaving a scene and an episode with a set of such questions. Yet the record of surprises in a nation of Great Awakenings readies one to see indeterminacy in much of the North American future. Advocates of this position or that in theology or political life often sound sure about where history is going and what their part in it is. The complexity of witnesses and actions by American Christians inspires caution about prediction. Movements have their day. Catholics have been repositioned since the Second Vatican Council. In their officially approved epochal document *Nostra Aetate,* the Roman Catholic Church speaks well of elements of non-Christian religions and looks for a new dialogue with them. Evangelicals and Pentecostals are also having their inning, African-American churches are strong in their independence but weak because they often lack resources to help subsidize movements advocating social and racial issues. The large number of Mexicans and other Latin peoples are suddenly turning America into a bilingual nation, with millions of new Catholics, evangelicals, and Pentecostals among them.

"Christian America" is strategic in global issues when it comes to relations to two religions or peoples in particular. From 1654 to the present a small but influential Jewish community has thrived alongside the Christian majority. While evidences of anti-Semitism, whether based in Christian theology or in the general culture, were present, it was never a governmentally sponsored program and Jews won ever greater measures of freedom. Many Jewish leaders said that they were hard pressed to think of a nation in which Jews were better regarded or more free. After the birth of Israel in 1948 and increasingly as the twentieth century wore on, fissures developed in the Christian communities vis-à-vis that nation. Most curiously in the eyes of those who recalled theological anti-Semitism in conservative Protestantism, some forms of fundamentalism, evangelicalism, and Pentecostalism became most friendly to Israel. One can call this curious because the friendliness of "Zionist" Christians is based in a theology and a hope that Jews do not welcome. In their version of biblical literalism a state of Israel must thrive as a precondition of the return of Jesus Christ to earth, to complete a plot in which Jews as Jews will have a negative role if they have one at all.

Meanwhile, Christian relations to Muslims were minimal until almost the turn to the third millennium. Muslims in America were few, and they had not been expressive or visible in popular arts or the world of celebrities and headlines. Their presence grew, alongside larger Arab Christian communities, especially after immigration laws changed in 1965. When radical Muslim movements, most of them described as fundamentalist, created problems for the United States, more Americans became alert. Embarrassed by a hostage-taking in Iran in 1979 and threatened to the core by jihadists, extremists inspired by selective Qur'anic depictions, who attacked American sites on September 11, 2001, Americans at large and Christians among them reacted. Some, like William Franklin Graham III, son of the century's most notable evangelist, Billy Graham (b. 1918), less tolerant than his father, dismissed Islam wholesale as a "wicked and evil religion." At the same time thousands of Americans, evangelicals among them, worked to establish better relations with local Muslims and new interpretations of international Islam.

In both cases the place of Jesus Christ was prominent. Christian anti-Semites based their theological rejection on readings of the New Testament which they interpreted as including self-condemnations by Jews. Twenty centuries of negative and even murderous treatment of Jews in the name of Jesus Christ made it hard to promote theological, personal, and communal relations, but many Jews and Christians worked arduously to bring about a new relation. The Qur'an, the Muslim holy book, respects Jesus, but regards him as a prophet among the prophets. Christian-Muslim dialogue almost paradoxically finds that it best advances when the role of Jesus in both faiths is openly confronted and presented.

For the larger scene, including the arrival of more Asians and people from Africa—very many of them intense Christians—one looks back to the change in American immigration laws in 1965. Immediately immigrants by the millions arrived from the non-Western world where the Christian population is small. Their presence forced rethinking by Christians, who had taken Jesus Christ for granted in public affairs, since few were around to protest a monopoly by believers. Now in Catholicism and Protestantism alike, in their encounters with neighbors of non-Christian faiths, leaders and laypeople had to rethink what their commitment to Jesus Christ as divine mediator meant to neighbors. Recalling early Christian language, Jesus Christ became an offensive reference to minorities in public schools, civic ceremonies, and on the calendar. "Who is Jesus Christ for us today?" became a newly urgent question. Advocates of a new spirituality admired Jesus the teacher and exemplar, but resisted any claims by Christians that he is the exalted Lord of all. Thus ensued a series of adjustments to a new era with devotees of Christ in the midst of pluralist affirmations contending with those who wanted public life to be officially devoted to Jesus Christ. The arguments became court cases, in a pattern not likely soon to be left behind.

The concern with new spiritualities is strong in much of North America, but the obverse side of their coin is the new secularities, the fresh ways in which the North American nations relate to modernity. In the United States prosperity and consumerism have not replaced Christian and other religious voices. Somehow its citizens mingle frankly sacred and manifestly secular faces. In recent years, a "prosperity gospel," fostered over television, attracts many who see no contradiction between it and the gospel calls to discipleship. If the United States sees a pattern of monitored or controlled secularity, one might call it, as I have, "religiosecularity." Canada has followed more closely the career of churches in the British Isles, which means "down": down in membership, participation, and national influence. Its United Church of Canada, while dwindling in size, still commands much of the mainstream. Sudden drops in participation in Quebec and the Maritime Provinces indicate that a secular culture pushes religion and church further afield. Many Canadians, especially in Quebec, follow the trajectory of their counterparts in the rest of Canada.

Many Americans, including American Christians, had long conceived of the United States as being exempt from many problems and issues that affected the rest of the globe. If its first colonies were like a "city set upon a hill," as John Winthrop conceived Massachusetts Bay Colony to have been in 1630, it became popular to apply such language and such a concept to the nation as a whole. The Monroe Doctrine was to keep it from foreign entanglements, while American "exceptionalism" and "isolationism" were invoked by Christians along with so many others who assigned special virtues to this self-conceived newly chosen nation. The rest of the world did not see the United States that way, but pointed to exceptions to exceptionalism and intervention instead of isolation. Involvement in two world wars and placement as a main agent in a global economy compromised the mythic pictures.

While the story is complex and the record mixed, it must be said that thanks to the constant inflow of immigrants—with a kind of suspension between 1924 and 1965 during legislated limitations—and the missionary movements that began in the early nineteenth century, Christians who were alert to the actions of their churches and voluntary associations were better informed and had more connections than most other citizens when economic globalization came to prominence late in the twentieth century. This involvement did not make them more sophisticated in matters of foreign policy, but many of them had established ties of empathy and sympathy, examples of teaching and learning, and personalization of efforts and agencies in faraway lands.

In the 1950s, Reinhold Niebuhr had said that America was a paradise suspended in a hell of international security. The terrorist attack of 9/11 in New York and Washington in 2001 meant a cutting of that cord. Americans were dropped into the world of insecurity that had always been known by most people in most places at most times. How the Christians among them would deal with the new environment is fateful for American and global Christianity alike. In any case, American Christians were better poised than ever before to be partners in a global Christian movement at a time when the most explosive growth and change among Christians was not in Europe or North America but in poorer worlds, mainly to the south.

8.

# THE SECOND
# AFRICAN EPISODE

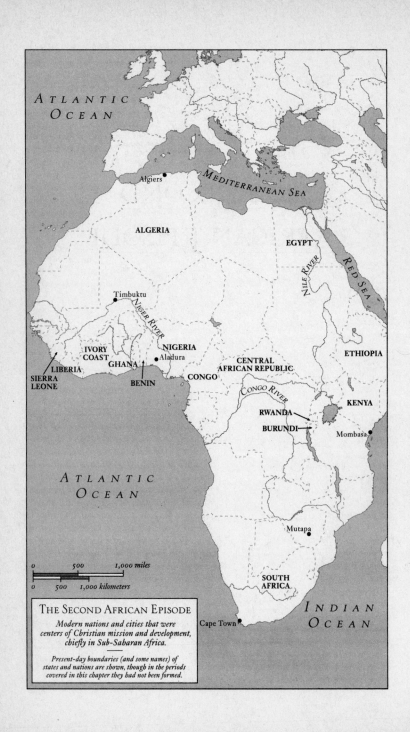

ATLANTIC
OCEAN

Algiers •

MEDITERRANEAN SEA

ALGERIA

EGYPT

NILE RIVER

RED SEA

Timbuktu •

NIGER RIVER

IVORY
COAST

NIGERIA

CENTRAL
AFRICAN REPUBLIC

ETHIOPIA

LIBERIA

GHANA

• Aladura

SIERRA
LEONE

BENIN

CONGO

CONGO RIVER

KENYA

RWANDA

BURUNDI

Mombasa •

ATLANTIC
OCEAN

Mutapa •

0        500      1,000 miles

0      500    1,000 kilometers

SOUTH
AFRICA

INDIAN
OCEAN

Cape Town •

THE SECOND AFRICAN EPISODE

*Modern nations and cities that were
centers of Christian mission and development,
chiefly in Sub-Saharan Africa.*

*Present-day boundaries (and some names) of
states and nations are shown, though in the periods
covered in this chapter they had not been formed.*

The episodic character of Christian presences on various continents was never more apparent than in Africa and Asia. Northern Africa, whose story was integral to early Christian accounts, saw a beginning and an end by the eighth century to Christian churches and cultures everywhere but in Ethiopia and Egypt. Centuries later came change of a most radical character as a new episode began in what was at last truly global Christianity. To many ears in the northern worlds it sounds disorienting when someone points to Africa and calls it the new center of Christian growth and source of innovations. Here African Pentecostalisms and other emergences are magnets for scholars and worshippers who visit from elsewhere. Africa is the best place to go for anyone who wants to observe how Christians live in the face of poverty, disease, and almost constant warfare. All signs indicate that, in the decades ahead, more and more Christians on other continents will be studying, supporting, and learning from Africa.

So dumbfounding is this concept to those who have been spiritually and intellectually remote from Africa that we pose the issue again in question form: how can Africa, especially sub-Saharan Africa, be a new center of the Christian world? Not by drastic growth in the northeastern corners of the continent. The Ethiopian Orthodox Church, a legacy of Frumentius and his cohorts in the fourth century, does number almost twenty million members, despite inhibitions and restrictions created after a military action in 1974. Typical of these harassments was the deposition of the church's leader in 1975 by a Marxist-style government. In Egypt the Coptic Orthodox Church remains independent enough to go its own way, never having accepted the ancient Council of Chalcedon's definition about Jesus Christ's nature. While this church is besieged and suffering, it is also vital. The enmity and prohibitions of some Muslim governments after the year 642 have always limited Christians, but today there is a precarious version of religious freedom.

## ENTRY INTO SUB-SAHARAN AFRICA

Christians, having long lost their bases in northern Africa, entered sub-Saharan Africa in two waves. First, late in the fifteenth century, Portugal, newly a sea and market power which needed resources, found them in Africa. Some of the Portuguese Christian efforts were frankly designed as a counter-Crusade to block the still fanning out efforts of Muslims and to gain territory for the Catholic domain. For a time Portugal, with papal backing, was given a monopoly on those African coasts. For two centuries, papal licensing of its missionaries was a boon to Portuguese rulers and traders. Spiritually the Portuguese were naturals for doing religious work in such settings. As Catholics they called upon unseen saints for health and protection, in invocations which evoked or matched Ghanaian practices and rites. Such Christians, intending to destroy traditional religions, did some adapting to them and won some converts. The effort was, however, largely a top-down mission which stayed largely at the top, meaning that it was not a successful reach to the hearts of ordinary people so much as a mutually beneficial exchange among priests and kings. Similar transactions were also visible in Kongo, where in the late fifteenth century the newly Christianized king, upon receiving favors from Portugal, kept his part of the bargain by trading away his best crop, namely human candidates for enslavement. The Portuguese needed slaves to work their expanding territories, and Kongo chiefs and others were only too happy to produce them.

The story in Benin was somewhat happier. The king, by refusing to deliver people into slavery, for a time thwarted Catholic expansion efforts. A very small and later almost forgotten kingdom, Warri, also produced conversions but saw its chief turn humans over to the slave market, about the only product he could use for trade. In places like Mutapa, the royal family converted, but there was no popular turn to Christianity with them. Those who cheer Christian expansion would find little to encourage them among the ordinary populations. Portugal could not sustain its own empire beyond two centuries and with its decline came the virtual end of the slave trade. Only a small number of Catholics stayed on in ports there, and efforts at converting Africans of any status ended. The two-century effort had to be counted as a failure blighted by the slave trade.

When well into the eighteenth century Europeans made sporadic new attempts to control and convert Africans, they demonstrated that they had learned little about the heart but remembered much about power. They once again aimed directly at royal courts, justifying their practice and strategy on the grounds that masses might follow converted rulers to the faith. This was what their own ancestors had done in Europe a thousand years earlier. Yet the royal new Catholics usually turned out to be only partial and sometimes conniving converts who had much to gain by adopting and merging their own and old rituals with Christian expressions. Before long most of the leaders became barriers to, not agents for, Christian growth.

Among both royals and the rest of the populations, some cultural customs abhorred by European Christians were so taken for granted and supported by native Africans that churchly efforts to abolish them were futile. Polygamy was the most visible and, to European Christians, most notorious among these, favored because kings had long used the practice of taking numerous wives as a way of building alliances. On another track of conflict, when Africans called on ancestral spirits, European Catholics, not noting how much such invocations resembled the Catholic practice of calling on saints, shunned the ritual and again failed to connect.

## THE SECOND ENGAGEMENTS: THE NINETEENTH CENTURY

The most competitive stage for Christian missions in Africa was finally set when in the nineteenth century Europeans came to regard Africa as a continent ripe for spoils because it was rich with resources—how rich, few yet knew at the beginning of this colonial period. When slaves were in demand in the Americas, African kings, as we saw, would trade off their own young. They could justify this using rationales associated with the market, arguments which were not utterly beside the point. They claimed that their economy and the ability to provide food for people depended upon their having something to trade. Needless to say, this African leadership was inhumane, its ways of life matching those of European slave traders in their readiness to exploit and dehumanize those they traded. Later discovery of other resources such as diamonds and gold attracted more colonialists, who competed to boost their own and their nations' fortunes. Native peoples, aware of what was going on, found good reason not to convert to the God of the exploiters and bringers of terror.

In the most notorious case, King Leopold II (1835–1909) of Belgium after 1876 personally came to own the Congo and to determine its policies to his own taste and interests. The king's agents forced Congolese men to work the rubber tree plantations to meet European demands for their products. Those thousands who did not reap enough of the raw material fast enough had their right hand and forearm cut off. Some people of conscience in Europe and the Americas eventually became aware of this and denounced the barbarism, the slave trade, commercial exploitation, and the flag-waving of imperialism, but they were long ineffectual in their critiques and responses. Estimates of those killed in Leopold's ventures range from two or three to fifteen million.

Evangelizers there and elsewhere in southern Africa characteristically arrived on the ships of colonialists and merchants. Some were in effect chaplains to the imperialists who justified the brutal policies, provided Christian services, and assured good consciences for the exploiters. The story of their cruelty and hypocrisy should be familiar, having been told by Africans who have spent centuries freeing themselves from the devastating effects of such practices. Now let it also be said with emphasis also underscored by many Africans: more of these agents of Christianity, while taking advantage of the transportation, protection, and sometimes the subsidies of government and commercial interests, and instinctively bringing with them racially inspired attitudes of superiority, were generally moved by their own vision of faith in the redeeming work of Jesus Christ. Their sincerely held motivating vision told them that unless African "heathen" were reached, converted, and baptized, these benighted souls would go to hell.

Reached, converted, and baptized, on the other hand, they would be headed for heaven, meanwhile being motivated to effect good works on earth.

Such missions produced trauma in the form of psychological damage occasioned when, in cultures which revered ancestors as sacred presences, missioners heartlessly preached that the unbaptized ancestors of their hearers, not knowing the grace of Jesus Christ, were suffering eternally in fiery hell. Another downside to their work in many places resulted from the fact that, just like newly developing industries, churches were in competition with each other, whether as Catholic versus Protestant, Protestant sect versus Protestant sect, or even as squabbling theological disputants within the various churches. When some people of conscience among them reflected on their part in what was going on, they began to question their national policies and the way the sending agencies of their churches conceived of what they were doing.

For all their evident faults, the impulse of missionaries to show mercy and serve the Africans to whom they showed condescension produced some positive effects. Archived letters home from the African front, missives by preachers, teachers, nurses, aid workers, and doctors or their spouses are full of comment on the schools, hospitals, agencies, and water systems they developed. The agents of Christianity had arrived with the burden of vast ignorance about their new settings and had to learn with what means they might have to attract people who already had their own stock of traditions, rituals, and behavior patterns.

The records of missionaries balance words of generosity with expressions of prejudice. All this fit the pattern of their attempts to "civilize" Africa through those policies rooted in their sense of superiority and paternalism. Such attitudes were born of a dilemma posed for even the most humble and cooperative missionaries. A natural question was, why bother to convert anyone unless you believe that what you convert people to is better than what they have? Yet your "better" could also rob the potential converts of dignity, uproot them from environments that were valuable to them, and leave them in confusion.

## AFRICAN CHRISTIAN DISTINCTIVES

We are tracing through twenty centuries on all continents a story about a basic issue: what differentiated Christians spiritually from all other peoples among whom they lived, with whom they fought, and whom they converted or tried to convert? From New Testament times on they witnessed in countless ways to the Jesus Christ whose name they took as their mark. They and those who made up their movement and the people who were affected by them found that somehow they were devoted to the human Jesus as the exalted Lord. Addressing that complex concept in the world of Greek culture, as they did at Nicaea and Chalcedon in 325 and 451, was one thing. Now the act of facing African cultures was another. Of course, to speak of "African cultures," not African culture, is to open the door to new complexity, for demographers count over three thousand ethnic groups and thousands of cultures which are at least as diverse as were cultures in the West.

Debates over how to observe, define, explain, and treat the options in Africa or anywhere else in the Christian world are intense and will never be satisfactorily settled. The missionaries for centuries did not know what to make of the gods and practices of people they thought were as simple as children, as untutored as infants, as limited as the disabled of all sorts. The Christians came with dogma and doctrine, catechisms and confessions, boundaries and definitions. They landed among African cultures whose people knew none of these and often wanted little to do with them when they found out what they were. Yet there were not total disconnects, and those forms of African Christianity now called indigenous drew on both. Thus both the newcomers and the Africans made much of the divine act of Creation, but Africans were more likely to see the natural world invested by spirits with whom one must deal. Both dealt with authority, though Catholics and Protestants could produce charts of hierarchies and chains of command, while most Africans reckoned with local chiefs just as they also dealt with local deities. Both had a strong sense of community, but many Africans tended to see the Western version compromised by the accent on individualities.

Then came the issue of Jesus Christ. Many African peoples found ways to translate the concept of the exalted Lord to the tribal chief's High God. Naming and the power of names are concerns among those Africans. Their Jesus could be named not only Chief but also Healer, Ancestor, or Brother, but they accepted what was special about Jesus Christ so emphatically that his divinity often received more stress than his humanity. Many scholars see that without any knowledge of formulas as old as those of Nicaea and Chalcedon, many Africans expressed interests which roughly matched the dogmas. Converted African Christians very much needed and felt the presence of the human Chief Jesus. While Europeans and Americans, using biblical terms, talked about salvation, many in more modern Africa have translated this to "liberation," including liberation from oppressors, who were so vivid in their experience. These new Christians by the millions found the stories in the gospels translatable to the contexts of their own stories, myths, and legends. At the same time they found it necessary to trim many uses of the story which Westerners brought, since it was so tied to strategies for depriving them of dignity, power, and community.

## CONVENTIONALITY AND EXPERIMENT

Two sets of missionaries began to divide up the huge territory of southern Africa, with Protestants clearly dominant in South Africa and along the coast of western Africa, in what became Liberia and its neighbors, and Catholics having more strength in Timbuktu and elsewhere in what became Niger as well as in much of the Congo region, though they also were effective in much of southern Africa.

As we shall see, in the twentieth century new indigenous churches, prophetic and often Pentecostal, erupted so suddenly and with such force that non-Africans who had interests in Christianity had to begin to account for them. As elsewhere, divisions among Christians caused perplexity and rivalry. Incoming Christians made their way among cultures marked broadly as we have described them, chiefly through efforts not only to tell the gospel stories but to produce some of the positive effects they intended. Especially attractive were the medicines and medical practices which manifestly healed many. In the eyes of many Africans here was something like magic. During this phase in Christian competition the newly arriving Protestants were often favored because they used and taught efficient agricultural techniques and put new medicines to work. Those about to be converted might think that these were the work of spirits, while to devout medics from Europe and North America these were the workings of God through science and medicine. Many of the medical advances were in the hands of Europeans who made no religious claims for them, but they were accepted as the accomplishments of the Christian God and God's agents.

During these centuries the Europeans did help reshape cultures, for example through their hygienic and agricultural efforts as well as their spread of literacy and technology. Many accompanied their efforts by preaching and teaching themes that were new and often confusing in sub-Saharan Africa. These included the concept of sin, the call to repent and change ways, and to prepare for means to avoid hell and win heaven in a life to come. Fear and belief in the love of a healing and rescuing God did help produce converts who began to understand the faith apart from those who used it as instruments of power.

Some Christians eventually advanced liberation by working for abolition of slavery in Europe and the United States. Notable were British crusaders like William Wilberforce (1759–1833) and an African, born in today's Nigeria, who claimed to have survived slave ship transit, Olaudah Equiano (c. 1745–97). Known as a merchant and abolitionist in both hemispheres, Equiano was much acclaimed and influential among white abolitionists. Among the white writers, Scottish Zachary Macaulay (1768–1838), like Wilberforce an evangelical, who had become governor in Sierra Leone in 1799, was among those reporters who effectively spelled out the evils of the trade. Some former slaves from the British Isles and the United States who settled back in Africa in the course of the nineteenth century developed some effective town structures. Among them were slaves who had broken into freedom and had lived in Halifax, Nova Scotia. In Africa they sang hymns that were often familiar to converts influenced by Baptist and Methodist missions in Africa and won the confidence of native peoples, as many other returnees from the United States did not. Many of these black evangelists enjoyed some advantages over white missionaries, and in some instances they proved to be less vulnerable to disease and other climate-related problems than were white evangelizers.

## INDIGENOUS AFRICAN CHRISTIANITY

Indigenous Christianity eventually emerged, largely in the hands of newly assertive Africans who were weary of colonial impositions and forms of Christianity whose agents were insensitive to the rights and dignity or the imagination and skill of Africans. If they were Catholic, potential leaders had long had to settle for being ground-level servants or catechists, knowing they could never become priests or bishops. Some of these liked to be called "Ethiopian," because they celebrated the memory and presence of Christians who had been in Africa as long as other believers had been in Europe.

Late in the nineteenth century there emerged a new model sometimes called Zionist, since it drew its name from the claim that Africa was the Zion of Africans. Zionists imaginatively appropriated all that they could from native practices. Most important of these was Pentecostalism, which involved speaking in tongues and claiming that the Holy Spirit, who was speaking directly to believers, healed the sick and cast out evil spirits. Some of these groups borrowed from European and American-based Pentecostal practices. Others expressed what they called "Africanity," prospering behind the backs and away from the altars of Europeans and North Americans.

The Zionist Christian Church spread in the Northern Transvaal, the Church of Nazareth along the Natal Coast of southeast Africa, and Aladura in the land of the Yoruba in western Africa. Some progressive whites working among the Yoruba advanced a spirit-filled convert named Samuel Adjai Crowther (c. 1809–91), thinking that their backing a black man would lead to conversions among his fellow blacks. However, Crowther was so at home with the English customs which he had picked up in his student years that he could not well identify with his people. His story was dramatic. He had been sold into slavery after he had been extricated from a Portuguese slave ship in 1821, but in freedom eventually became a noted educator at the University of Durham. Translating Scriptures and holy books for the Yoruba, he worked with missionaries from the United States and England, places where observers became aware of the creativity and intelligence available among Africans.

An associated effort by a white missionary also led to change. Missionary Henry Venn (1796–1873) invented a "three-self movement," in which the African churches were supposed to be "self-supporting, self-governing, and self-extending." The climax of their teamwork came when Crowther let himself be named Bishop on the Niger, in an event celebrated among those who supported and worked for a more formal native church. Sadly, Crowther, too European in style to gain credibility among most Africans, also failed his backers when his church in Niger disintegrated in the face of charges that focused on his mismanagement.

Meanwhile, native-born leaders, especially in the sprouting Pentecostal churches, prospered in part because they did not have to be college-bred. Some were not even literate. When epidemics like an influenza plague early in the twentieth century spread, Western medical doctors could not make the rounds fast enough or serve effectively, so prophetic movements supplied spiritual healers. A generation of charismatic leaders emerged, some of whom became internationally known. Among the Pentecostal leaders was "Prophet" William Wade Harris (c. 1865–1929), an Episcopalian in Liberia, who emerged as an early leader. The angel Gabriel, he claimed, had visited him in a vision while he was in prison for having taken part in a failed coup in Liberia. Freed in 1913, he went on an evangelizing mission unmatched in African history, converting tens of thousands by 1915. He provided simple Christian answers to their questions. Upon his conversion he disposed of the Western clothes he had adopted and in team with his two wives wore simple white linen while they spread the gospel. Following biblical example, he chose exactly twelve apostles to advance the work. In the 1940s one of his followers, a priest named Bague Honoyo, gained a half-million converts on the Ivory Coast.

In 1921 Simon Kimbangu (1889–1951) developed and gave his name to the Church of Jesus Christ on the Earth by the Prophet Simon Kimbangu, a movement which would eventually attract millions. Like Boniface in Europe, who had startled the local people when he chopped down the sacred oak and did not suffer, Kimbangu challenged converts to destroy their old icons and idols. This they did, always with impunity, so many thought that he was demonstrating God's partnership and availability for them while their wonder-workers and witches were in retreat. Kimbangu made no pretense that his churches derived from the heritage of Europe. They were on their own, and needed no prophets but their own. Belgian authorities jailed Kimbangu soon after his first miracle, a decision that worked against Christianity, especially in the forms he favored. However, he was freed and the movement prospered, though he would be sent to prison again and spent much of his adult life there. Both political and Christian missionary authorities worked to block the fast-growing movement, to little effect. His church was received into the World Council of Churches in 1969. As similar movements to those begun by Harris and Kimbangu prospered in Africa, it became clear that, for all the support it might get from elsewhere, the major initiative for Christianity from then on would be African.

## WESTERN RECESSION, AFRICAN ADVANCE

Such activities and movements served notice on the Western agents that they were losing control. Followers of their prophets rallied and formed movements, informal church bodies on the way toward becoming high-powered organizations, which quickly did outgrow the colonial churches with which they were in competition. Well over two thousand of such movements thrive in South Africa alone. In due course some of them chose to be looked over by Christians from elsewhere, were approved, processed, and became members of ecumenical organizations that challenged the old European bases for mission and church unity. They were in all cases recognizably Christian in historic senses and manifestly African in the eyes of any who knew the background of African rites.

It would give a false impression were we to suggest that all African indigenous Christianity replaced the historic churches. Millions of Catholics, Lutherans, Anglicans, evangelicals, and fundamentalists, upholding a long tradition, attract and hold dynamic followings. First, in South Africa the Christian story went back to the work initiated after 1799 by a Netherlands missionary society agent, Johannes van der Kemp (1747–1811), who traded on his military and medical experience in Cape Town. He offended many by marrying a Malagasy slave girl, but won many others by his effective work against slavery. The London Missionary Society sponsored some of the best-known European missionaries, men such as the tireless Robert Moffatt (1795–1883) and the legendary explorer David Livingstone (1813–73). Such agents irked the Boers, immigrants of Dutch heritage, and those British who did not favor freedom, rights, or a reasonably independent life for Africans.

For another example, in central Africa after 1844, where the Portuguese Catholics had worked long before, Protestants dominated the story. A German agent of the Church Missionary Society, John Ludwig Krapf (1810–81), at great expense to his family—his wife and daughter died in Mombasa—teamed with other missionaries to evangelize in Kenya and Buganda, part of today's Uganda. Like most other Protestants, they patronized Bible societies, and worked as Bible translators and people who could convert others.

In eastern Africa among the pioneers was the controversial Anglican bishop John Colenso (1814–83), who imported and was affected by controversies in England. He was perceived as a radical because of his support for the teaching of Darwinian evolution and what was called the "higher criticism" of the Bible. He used his version of Darwin to oppose another version, one which had legitimated colonization because, it was argued, the Europeans, being fittest, would survive, while less developed Africans could not. Though Colenso stirred controversy over his unorthodoxy back home in England, he won the hearts of many Africans, displaying the difficulty of doing justice to the rights of Africans—in his case the Zulu—while trying to please the sending agencies in England. Needless to say, debates over Darwin were not at issue in eastern Africa at the time, but when a missionary there became controversial "back home," this was distracting in what "home" called "the field."

All this time Catholics were active, in a small way in northern Africa, having been moved to reenter Africa, led by their pioneer, Charles Lavigerie (1825–92). He was archbishop in the tiny surviving Catholic colony in Algiers and thus a very lonely leader in a remote outpost. He organized an impressive group usually called, because of their garb, "White Fathers," but officially the Missionaries of Our Lady of Africa. They did not take a vow to be celibate, but they did vow to be faithful to Africa, which they swore they would not abandon all their lives. The White Fathers, unsuccessful in Algeria, worked in both eastern and southern Africa. After 1879 they had some success among the Buganda, after they converted the kabaka, or king, Mutesa I. A sad and surprising new kind of conflict emerged there when his heir, Mwanga, grew furious because some young Christian men resisted his homosexual advances. In 1885 and 1886 he had twenty-two of them executed. They were later canonized. The story of these "boy martyrs" at the same time inspired more work in Africa just as it terrified many who might have intended to be missionaries in that dangerous territory and then chose not to.

Polygamy was prominent in conflicts among the many cultural clashes, often over sexual matters. Colenso was in the center of some of these too. He argued, against all the impulses of the British churches, that it may be all right to permit polygamy to continue. This would be the case because ending the practice suddenly could lead to suffering among women who would subsequently be turned out of their homes with no chance to marry and thus would face bleak futures. He also bought trouble by making selections among biblical stories, scorning those in Genesis that he thought could not have been true or dismissing some from the Hebrew Scriptures that could be used to legitimate conquest.

The cause of Zulu rights found advocates after Colenso's death when his daughters joined others in starting schools of the sort where notable African leaders were converted, educated, and became prominent in the African church. Many later African liberationist leaders got their ideas from their churches and from the Bible, especially from the impulse and example plus the calls and promises of Jesus. The vehemence with which this generation reacted against the colonialists surprised many in the northern world. Some of them backed off from the support they had provided when the missions still allowed for white supremacy and determination.

## MODERN SOUTHERN AFRICA

After World War II all situations changed during anti-colonialist times, as European nations progressively withdrew from Africa in the face of African nationalist movements. Their departure and absence often revealed the negative effects of their century or two of governing and exploiting tribes and nations. Many in the first generation of African leaders, though trained by missionaries, failed their own people and governed in corrupt and exploitive ways themselves.

The twentieth-century story of Christian success can focus almost anywhere in sub-Saharan Africa, because growth there is so widespread. A backward glance at the prospering but not explosive traditional denominations illustrates how much Christianity's center of gravity was moving south. Mainline Protestants and Catholics remain among the leaders in Uganda, where at the beginning of the century chief Yohana Kitagana jettisoned his honors and donated his property, henceforth to serve Catholicism and to help reform the nation which had produced the "boy martyrs." Anglicans there point fondly to Apolo Kivebulaya, who was ordained a priest in 1903 and served Congolese Pygmies for thirty years. Uganda regularly experienced revivals of Christianity, often thanks to efforts of medical personnel who spread healing and faith. These churches suffered terribly when Uganda came to be governed, or misgoverned, by General Idi Amin, a murderous tyrant, between 1971 and 1979 as, once again, the Ugandan church produced martyrs.

Kenya has also seen mainline Protestant and Catholic growth. Once again, during revivals, the Mau Mau revolution occurred as the Kikuyu people after 1952 became notorious for their violence, also against Christians. Knowing that the Mau Mau oath called for the drinking of blood, one Christian is reported to have shouted that he had drunk the blood of Christ and could drink no other. He was felled on the spot.

The anti-colonial movements began at mid-century, for instance when under Kwame Nkrumah (1909–72) in 1952 Ghana won independence. Nkrumah's pattern was matched in the 1960s in the Belgian colonies of Congo, Rwanda, and Burundi, while colonial dominoes also fell in Tanzania, Kenya, Malawi, and Zambia in the first four years of the 1960s. In the next decade leftovers of the Portuguese presence, Mozambique and Angola, went on their own. While revolutionaries elsewhere in Africa were often secular or Marxist in outlook, leaders here were often products of Christian schools. Some of them, including Zambia's Kenneth Kaunda (b. 1924), were sons of pastors. Their presence and role as Christians did not assure safe passage to the post-colonial world. For instance, Zambia was traumatized by the effects of Alice Lenshina (1920–78), who formed the "Lumpa" movement, a stormy cause that used Christian motifs against traditional religion. It sadly degenerated and produced its own violent scenes in 1964, when the prophetess herself was imprisoned.

The drama in African Christianity that most caught the notice of fellow believers elsewhere was in South Africa in the late years of apartheid and during the transition to some measure of freedom for all races. The policy developed during the twentieth century where white South Africa, dominated by the Dutch Reformed Church and supported by Anglicans, legislated policies that segregated and deprived black Africans, "colored" mixes of races, and others of civil liberties. The Dutch Reformed Church had long justified this policy on the basis of its interpretation of the biblical story of the Tower of Babel, wherein God dispersed the nations and tongues. This interpretation led after 1948 to legitimation by the regime and the white citizenry of a policy of "separate development," one that turned out to produce unimaginable suffering and countless deaths. Interest in this conflict shown by Christians on all continents was an example of the growing global consciousness.

Perhaps because South Africans had more ties than others to white Christians elsewhere—originally the Netherlands and England—and because voices from there came to call the policy into question, some white leaders could emerge. Among these were the novelist Alan Paton, the Anglican cleric Trevor Huddleston, and Pastor Beyers Naudé, an heir of privilege in the white churches who turned against them and formed a group that worked closely with black leadership to bring down the apartheid regime in the early 1990s. The more important and prominent African leadership included Nelson Mandela, whose religious commitments were not always explicit, and Anglican archbishop Desmond Tutu of Cape Town, whose were. While serving his own communicants he was able to gain support on other continents. After the Dutch Reformed synod publicly acknowledged that both its biblical interpretation and the policies based on it were wrong, it was only a matter of time before the white separatist government would fall, as it did between 1990 and 1994. After such a long period of repressive rule by whites, no one expected the transition to freedom to be easy, but in the midst of the turmoil, the prophetic voice of the black, white, and colored churches was heard internationally. The Truth and Reconciliation program headed by archbishop Tutu did much to bring the races into dialogue and help the nation heal.

Among the travails in Africa are those occasioned by wars. Post-colonial realities breed chaos, as long-suppressed people acquire armament and often form militias or insurrectionary groups. In cases like the ethnic genocide in 1994 in Rwanda and Burundi, people brought up in Christianity were on both sides of the outbreaks of violence. Further, many millions have died as a result of an HIV/AIDS epidemic. Such misery deprives the church of much talent and leadership, and creates drastic social problems in the form of poverty and the loss of parents in countless families. Endemic hunger and poor delivery of health care mean that the African church in most places is a suffering church. Numbers-conscious Christians cheer the growth of the church, but many on the scene urge that new converts must become well grounded so that they can face the moral, political, and social problems with their faith as resource.

## WHAT IS AT STAKE?

Global Christianity has much at stake in the destiny and choices of Africans. Thus when the Episcopal Church in the United States late in the twentieth century began to be torn over the issue of ordaining homosexuals, it met rejection by many of its kin African Anglicans, especially in Nigeria. While the churches in America muted their criticism of Anglican adaptation to African ways—polygamy remained a widely accepted practice—African Anglicans were vocal in their criticisms and interventions in American church life. Knowing the background of custom and culture helps one interpret the conflict: wherever African Christians are up against strong Muslim presences, as in Nigeria, where the two faiths fight for dominance, it is easy for the vehemently anti-homosexual Muslims to advance themselves and win among potential converts. All they have to do is to say that the Anglicans have ties to a church that elsewhere on the globe recognizes homosexuals—and troubles result.

From another angle, evangelicals in America, some of the most aggressive supporters of missions, became known for their humanitarian and educational work. Some of the self-styled members of the religious and political right in the United States export American social problems, refashioning them as imports in African Christianity. While African Pentecostalism, including within Anglicanism, appears to have a free-form character, in what are often called "moral issues" it is deeply conservative.

The theology of African churches varies widely from place to place and from tradition to tradition. Ties to the sending nations often remain strong. Thus African Catholic bishops were often highlighted at the Second Vatican Council and in other meetings of bishops. Some foresee the naming of an African pope early in the new century, since this would be a beneficial strategy and a sign of Catholic maturity there.

Through it all, Christianity remained an extension of the story of Jesus Christ, but the story was now radically transformed in cultural imagery. Wars and famines and disease may come and go, as did colonial powers, but visitors report that the stories of Jesus Christ are what bind the otherwise lightly connected and often contentious African churches. Historian David Edwards has conveniently catalogued and commented on some of the vivid images employed. The black Jesus leads off, since, though Jesus as a Jew would not have been white like Europeans, European illustrations in the books of missionaries had generally "whitened" Jesus. Recalling the devotion to ancestors, the Milingo movement evokes Jesus the Great Ancestor who represents "all that our ancestors have and more, as one who is close to the Creator and who keeps his covenant and prays on earth."

Africans who have lost parents to AIDS, famine, or warfare can refer to Jesus the Elder Brother, who draws the young to him, protecting and tutoring them. Edwards moves on also to Jesus the Healer, one of the main images in Pentecostalism and elsewhere. In lands where medical care is primitive, rare, expensive, and often even unavailable, human agents who accompany the ill through suffering and then address the needs of the dying welcome the message of healing. Sick of chiefs who have armies and who kill, they nominate Jesus as Chief, and as their own families are threatened and confined, some speak of Jesus the Head of the Great Family. While women for the most part still live in limited or even lethal circumstances, they can invoke Jesus the Liberator of Women, about whom they have heard in the gospel stories. And while they have their own prophets Harris and Kimbangu and know of Elijah and Moses, Jesus is their main prophet. Some other ancient titles still are invoked. Jesus is the Priest, who sacrifices himself, or the Suffering Servant, who is humble. Some are time-worn images, but appear fresh in new settings. Others are vivid corollaries to or replacements for the titles argued about centuries before at the Councils of Nicaea or Chalcedon, in very different cultures but among humans who share the basic needs and hopes of Christians elsewhere.

Two key words in contemporary African theology are "identity" and "context." John Parratt, an interpreter of Third World theologies, points to "the dynamic search for self-identity, an identity which takes seriously the tradition and cultures in which it is located," and adds that "the agenda must come from the social world in which Christians now live." As for context, Virginia Fabella, an encyclopedist of Third World theologies, emphasizes that today the "African focus [is] on the Africanization of Christianity rather than on the christianization of Africa." In 1977 the "Final Communiqué" from the Pan-African Conference of Third World Theologians urged: "Our task as theologians is to create a theology that arises from and is accountable to African people." This task is well under way. Theologians there speak of seeing Christ in places, thoughts, relations, and worldviews in which he has not been recognized before. Observers of intercontinental actions point out that "missions" is a two-way track, and that some of the biggest congregations in Europe were started by Africans and ministered to by them.

In the bewilderingly varied cultures in Africa, and with myriad variations and interpretations, and in indigenous terms, he remains for them the human Jesus and the exalted Lord. Some surges of converts, especially to Pentecostalism, are believed to be the most sudden and fast-moving ever known among Christians. Let European Christianity languish and North American faiths hold their own, the African versions more than compensate. In the longer perspective of the churches in the northern world, the Second African Episode seems to be still at its beginning.

# 9.

# THE SECOND
# ASIAN EPISODE

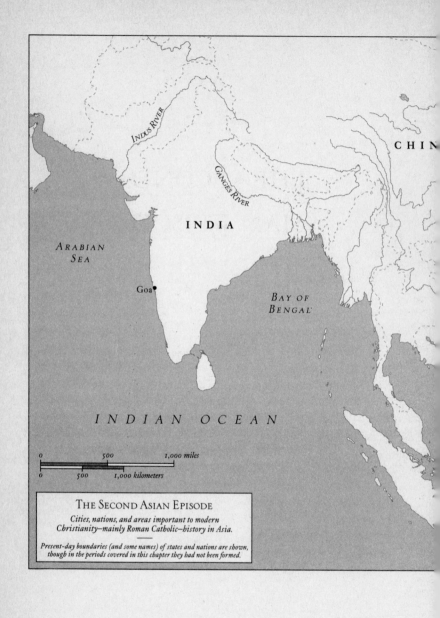

INDUS RIVER

GANGES RIVER

INDIA

CHINA

ARABIAN
SEA

Goa●

BAY OF
BENGAL

INDIAN OCEAN

0    500    1,000 miles

0    500    1,000 kilometers

## THE SECOND ASIAN EPISODE

*Cities, nations, and areas important to modern
Christianity—mainly Roman Catholic—history in Asia.*

*Present-day boundaries (and some names) of states and nations are shown,
though in the periods covered in this chapter they had not been formed.*

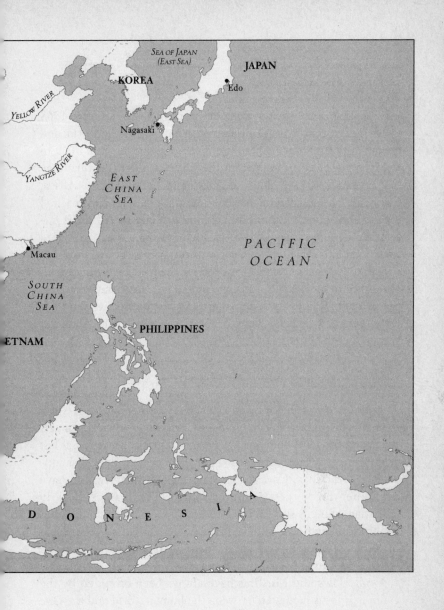

European explorers, colonizers, and missionaries after 1568 could use Mercator's Projection, a flat map of the world, and even before that they had at their disposal globes to help them in their voyages and treks. Within the space of a half-century they had reached the two American continents, sailed around Africa, been able to conceive of that continent as a whole, and reached Asia on both its eastern end and southern coasts. All these encounters brought them face-to-face with peoples who had shared no part of Christian witness or controversy over their central figure, Jesus Christ. Christians for centuries had had experience with two other monotheisms, Judaism and Islam. Now they met people, many of whom were non-theists or polytheists, who did not focus on a god, or who were, in Christian eyes, overabundantly supplied with deities.

## WHEN TWO WORLDS MET

Among uncomprehending missionaries, East Asians were dismissed as heathen, pagan, or godless. Christians wanted to convert them, and began to do so as they became a global presence, at last represented on five continents. The language and ideas that supported Orthodoxy, Catholicism, and Protestantism would have been alien to the newly approached people. Names of early Christian councils such as the Nicaean or Chalcedonian might as well have come from a different planet. Yet Christians kept trying to connect with people alien to them, making their case on the basis of Scriptures, markets, and the sword.

Godly Jews and Muslims have always been offended by the claim that Jesus mediated between the human world and the One God. Missionaries in this new Asian encounter had reason to ask what sense it made to speak of a human as God. Now Christians confronted people who revered many gods or no gods. In addition, where other religions were vital, the question became: how could Christians spread their faith among Hindus in India or Buddhists in China? When confrontations of East and West occurred, both sides had reason to be befuddled or scornful. So the Catholic and Protestant missionaries to Asia who arrived centuries after most earlier Christianity had been forgotten there faced unanticipated and enigmatic cultures, utterly foreign to their experience.

By 1500, Christianity, born in Asia, had all but died in Asia. The first episode in which they gained a strong presence there had long concluded. Admittedly, words like "died" and "concluded" may seem too emphatic, since some pulses of Christianity could be noticed among believers within beleaguered enclaves and in a couple of areas of strength. Also true, three of the four ancient Eastern Christian patriarchates still had their marked places on the maps of what people in the West today call Asia Minor, or in some cases, the Middle East. The Christian minority was powerless in Palestine. The crusaders three centuries earlier had failed to conquer territories that Christians once called theirs. They did not permanently win back sites that, evoking the ancient stories of Jesus, through a millennium prompted pilgrimages by those seeking salvation. The believers were now strangers in Jerusalem. A continuous Maronite Christian community did survive in Lebanon, where faithful communities persisted against all odds.

In what is now called the Far East, Mongols and other attacking groups had brought the Christian presence to an end. One would need a microscope and a strong imagination to find significant enduring traces across Asia along the way of the old Silk Road. As for the regions now called the Asian Subcontinent, where Christians of India claimed origins dating back to Jesus' disciple Thomas, the spiritual domain was largely in the hands of traditional Hindus, Buddhists, and aggressive Muslims.

## A New Christian Episode

While that First Asian Episode had ended centuries before, a surprising new one was ready to begin as Christians returned to create enduring minority presences in Asia. They produced often startling results. Five centuries after the new contacts there remain twenty-one million Christians who make up two percent of the Indian population. They worship in the neighborhoods of Hindus, Buddhists, and Muslims. Many critics dismiss them simply as leftovers from the days of the Raj ("Reign"), the now departed British colonialist empire.

The second relative stronghold remains Southeast Asia, including Vietnam and the Pacific islands, in which the French and the Dutch had a hand. New Guinea and some of the Indonesian islands are home to substantial Christian populations. North of there are the Philippines, Muslim in the south and predominantly Christian in the north, the latter being communities living in the heritage of a Catholic mission that began early in the sixteenth century. Still further north is the only relative Christian success story in Asia, Korea, once formidably closed off from Christian influence, but decades later, with twelve million members, the strongest Christian presence in Asia and now second only to the United States among sponsors of missionaries.

Japan, China, and India, the most populous Asian nations, proved massively resistant to the faith. Today only one or two percent of the Japanese are Christian. The faith prospers in the Chinese underground and in an official Catholic governmentally approved and monitored church. Estimates of the number of church members in this constituency vary from a few million to over fifty million, among them many secret Christians. Today, therefore, even if the percentage of the population that is Christian is small, the huge size of populations across Asia assures that Christianity attracts perhaps 350 million adherents, leaving Asia the continent with the third largest number of Christians.

The natural question is: how did they get to be in Asia a second time? Around 1500 there had not been enough warm embers to be blown back by spiritual bellows into fiery life. Strangers and outsiders had to intrude, and this they were eager to do. Most stories of Christianity in Asia have been tied to commerce and colonialism. Asia possessed products that the rest of the world could use, and the rest of the world provided markets for Asian goods. Second, powers of the West, whether Catholic or Protestant in ethos, were exploring and conquering Asia, vying with each other to be dominant in territory after territory. For the not often attractive enlargement of their mission, they found it profitable to send agents of Christian missions abroad, and missionaries were eager to help secure their own salvation through Jesus Christ by offering salvation to others. It is possible to tell the story of Asian Christianity as an example of the spiritual exploitation of native peoples, as the critics of missionaries have done. Or one can tell it from the angle of vision of the agents of Christianity, who thought they were simply spreading stories of the Jew and winning converts to the faith that he is the exalted Lord, meanwhile not always venturing to assuage the consciences of exploiters and plunderers who were acting for Western crowns and principalities.

## Catholic Renewals Inspire the Efforts

The Catholic renewals of the early sixteenth century in Europe led there to the forming of new religious orders and agencies to team with older ones. While many of their devotees remained in isolation in their convents and monasteries, a large cohort itched to be of service to the cause of Christ in the world. We have accounts of these agents, often training in Italian or Spanish seminaries, studying the unfamiliar names of places on their globes. When new information about those places arrived, or whenever a military or commercial fleet returned from a foray to "the Indies," as Asia was often called, preachers and brothers would go into action. They were spurred by stories of how the pagan peoples there who did not know the stories of Jesus and did not have faith in Christ would, after death, be sent to suffer in purgatory or hell. The heathen and the pagans were to be spared only if they formed ties to Jesus Christ and the Catholic Church. Daring missionaries possessed of conscience or will and an uncommon zest for adventure thereupon found ways to represent the official church, along with the interests of their rulers and merchants. They accepted passage on the boats, and often ventured farther into Asian interiors in the mission of finding people to baptize than did the traders and investors who went to find markets and who, relatively speaking, played it safe.

Christianity had always been bonded with its cultural environments, so now again it took strenuous efforts on the part of young brothers or priests to be pried from their familiar milieus and freed to adapt to new settings. They did this often in the face of criticism by church leadership "back home," as in Rome. There, suspicious monitoring authorities saw no need for Catholic representatives to adapt and accommodate themselves, as the missionaries knew they had to do to survive and be successful. Certain names of pioneers among them stood out because they left a legacy of institutions. One of the Catholic reformers, Ignatius of Loyola, led his followers in the Society of Jesus, the Jesuits. They were to give unquestioned loyalty to the pope when he gave directions for them to undertake missions. Lacking families of their own, such celibate men, often of noble families, sailed away, never very sure whether they might return. Storms took some and illness carried others to death. Those who survived and wanted to be at home in the new cultures could be apprehended by native people for transgressing lines of custom, whipped, jailed, and even martyred, as numbers of them were.

While Ignatius stayed in Europe, he was able to send out courageous or, to their critics, foolhardy souls like Francis Xavier. He sailed along the coasts of southern and eastern Asia, stopping to plant trading posts that really were centers for literacy, education, and training of new "brothers" and "fathers" to carry on the work. Believing, as he and the church did, that unbaptized children would not go to hell or to heaven but to limbo, a place between heaven and hell, a doctrine now repudiated, he went wherever he could to pour water on natives and bless them as baptized children of God, now purged of original sin. Converts were no longer to be threatened by the terrors of hell and their children were not to be consigned to the bleakness of limbo, but were now moved by the promise of heaven.

After 1542 Xavier, beginning at Goa, mass-produced baptisms among people who found him exotic, the promises of baptism rich, and the teachings incomprehensible. The Jesuit coura-geously attacked exploitive Portuguese traders as he set out to ap-proach the ordinary people. While he claimed to have baptized eighty thousand people, only one was a high-caste Brahman con-vert. When later another pioneer missionary, Robert de' Nobili, arrived, he encountered Hindus and confronted a caste system which inhibited his access to many formal classes of people. This limiting liberated him to attract converts from the lower classes and untouchable castes. Still, he persisted in efforts among elites, educated people who found the Europeans curious and alluring. De' Nobili and his successors had to deal with alien customs among Hindu religionists, but they persisted. He eventually broke barriers and in four years claimed to have converted over one hundred high-caste Hindus. Catholic critics charged that de' No-bili had actually become Hindu, but examination of his writings shows that he was a rather rigidly orthodox Catholic under it all, and in the end he was not very positive about the religious dimen-sions of the Hindu culture whose externals he embraced.

Sprinkling water and saying a blessing may be simple acts rich in theological meanings, but culturally the Jesuits and their con-verts faced many complex decisions. The most dramatic example of these forced them to consider how much cultural trapping they brought along from the Europe whence they had sailed, and what to do about it in India, China, or on the islands. Whether the peo-ple they faced were animists, ancestor-worshippers, or devotees of Confucius the philosopher, they had never heard of Jesus and the apostles. They certainly would not have known what to do with the philosophy of giants like Plato and Aristotle. Such thinkers had influenced education and religion among most Eu-ropeans, even those who never heard of those ancient Greeks. The counsel that Christian risk-takers in Asia gave and took was to distance themselves from Western ways and to frame thoughts less colored by Western philosophy.

Some of their experiments were simple enough. One Protes-tant missionary wore his hair in a queue to identify with the Chi-nese. He thus demonstrated his eagerness to belong even as he roused the suspicion of many potential converts in China or India.

He antagonized the monitors of Christian teaching in Europe. If Xavier found Indian cultures problematic, the China that was next in his compass sights was even more sealed and forbidding. Reaching into their cultural baggage, he and other Jesuits came up with revised rules and regulations and offered tangible trinkets and rosaries, which were appealing to natives who had little idea of what these represented. Every Jesuit or Franciscan knew that Christianity was not a religion of trinket-worshippers but, even in these extremities, they helped move people to take the messages and rites seriously.

## PROBLEMS OF EMPATHY IN ASIA

Empathic as they were about many Asian cultural artifacts, none of the Christians saw much to affirm in Asian religions. However engaging their primary appeals for faith might be, they sooner or later had to state the claim on which virtually all of them agreed, basing it on the Bible: that salvation occurred only in the name of Jesus Christ. Whenever they discerned among prospective converts any sense of response to the sacred as they experienced it, they traded on this. At some point in an encounter they characteristically would pray for the people, for the Jesuits and all the other Christians, addressing the One God through Jesus Christ. Usually in the initiating rites of water baptism connected with primal catechism teaching, converts had to slam the door on the spiritual sanctuaries that had previously been theirs.

At the point of prayer, teaching, and preaching, all the agents of the faith who came to Asia faced a dilemma. If they simply mouthed the name of their God in an alien context, people of Asia would scowl and shrug and depart the scene. If they went too far in naming and identifying God in terms that various Asian cultures used, there was danger that Christianity would simply be absorbed or shelved. Some missioners like Xavier tried to explore halfway measures, seeking to adapt where possible, but insisting on the uniqueness of Jesus Christ.

When missionaries didn't denigrate the images of the Buddha or denounce the Hindu names for God, their critics and their spiritual authorities back home attacked them. Communications were slow, so debate was tedious and prolonged. It took some seasons for over-and-back messages to make their way. Tattlers who were critical of those who adapted to the many Asian customs and thought patterns somehow seemed more efficient and speedy than were the admirers and supporters. They saw to it that accommodators were condemned, often called home to Europe, or asked to cease and desist from calling God by names like those the natives used. These wars over rites slowed down the efforts to convert others, but Xavier and his kind sailed on, baptizing and preaching.

## THE CATHOLIC ADVANCES

Catholics who had reached India as far back as 1519 saw their world expanding afterward. In that year Ferdinand Magellan left Spain in an effort to circle the globe—his men completed the effort. He reached the Philippines in 1521, the end of the road for him—he was killed in tribal warfare and, we are told, chopped to pieces—but his endeavor represented the beginning of a Catholic presence there. The missionaries that followed him were among the more successful, as evidenced by an outcome: no Asian nation became or has remained as Catholic as the Philippines. Five centuries after the first mission encounters, the number of all the Catholics annually baptized in Poland, Italy, France, and Spain does not match those christened in the Philippines.

The missionary orders almost from the beginning competed with each other, so to make peace among them the Spanish monarchs assigned various territories to each. Some produced heroes such as Esteban Marin, "the apostle to the Ingorot people." He was an Augustinian who boldly went into the mountains and for seventeen years served among gold-prospecting headhunters. Despite all his positive efforts, in 1601 he was roped to a tree, beheaded, and burned to ashes by resistant natives. Such stories, far from deterring his colleagues, inspired them. By 1600 it is estimated that half of the dwellers in Spanish territories in the Philippine Islands had been exposed to the message of Jesus Christ and a third of the population had been baptized in his name. Catholic efforts to instruct may have been superficial, but the sheer weight of numbers gave the church a base for the centuries of trials ahead.

By 1549 the Jesuits under Xavier had reached Japan, which was to become the scene of highest drama and eventual greatest disaster. Courageous priests and brothers gained footholds in southern Japan where, despite discouragement, opposition, and eventual persecution by people who were at first uncomprehending, they told the stories of Jesus and administered sacred rites. Resistant Japanese leaders knew that commitments made to the claims of these stories would undercut existing religions—in this case Buddhist or Shinto—and, with that, would become a challenge to the emperor, who was considered divine. For all that, the Christian presence grew, until it numbered perhaps 300,000 in areas around Nagasaki. Alluring Jesuit and Franciscan teachers were in the main friendly to the scientific and cultural achievements in Japan as they were in China, and many became popular and felt at home.

Such prosperity could not last, and as Japanese rulers sensed the cultural confusion and perceived religious aggression by the Europeans, they countered their efforts. Many of the priests and brothers were forced by the authorities to return to Europe, leaving behind devout and zealous converts. Persecution became intense after 1612. In 1622 their assailants struck the Franciscan church in Edo, which was to become Tokyo, and there killed fifty-one Christians. Christian apostates fingered believers, and eventually many thousands of believers were killed. As the Japanese grew ever more nationalistic, they viewed Jesus Christ as a competitor to those authorities who were stressing the divinity of the emperor. An edict accused Christians of overturning right doctrine. The claim was that "Japan is the country of gods and Buddha." Devastating to Catholics was the defection of Fabian Fukan (Fukansai Habian, 1585–1621), a Jesuit on whom they had banked because he could defeat any Buddhist in argument. Around 1608 he disappeared, some said to live with a woman. In 1620 he returned as an apostate to write "the first anti-Christian book in Japan."

About the time that church membership reached 300,000 converts, authorities began to expel some believers as Europeans and to persecute Christians of any origin. Within thirty years most identified Christians had been tortured and burned to death. Given the hideousness of the treatment, it is no wonder that many turned from their faith. Relics stowed from that era bear out their testimony. The Catholics had distributed metal images for converts to revere. Some of these bore pictures of Mary or Jesus. The reacting and furious Japanese forced the converts to renounce the new faith. To prove that their renunciations were authentic they were forced to tramp on these metal images to profane them. Surviving objects among these give evidence that many thousands of Christian shoe-scrapings left abrasions that obscured the images. Those who did not trample often were condemned to death. Catholic priests had to leave when Japan closed its doors. Still, a lay-led underground church survived in forms recognizable as Christian more than two centuries later, when Japan opened its doors a bit.

China was another kind of stumper, a cultural scene that demanded accommodation by Catholics. The greatest among the pioneering adapters was Matteo Ricci, who came to Macau in 1582. He dressed like a Buddhist monk and spent twenty years becoming a Mandarin scholar—before he even mentioned Jesus. By the time he did he had gained so much respect that other Mandarins listened. He looked like a scholar, learned the main languages and dialects, taught science across the boundaries of East and West, and contended that the Chinese would easily become Christian because their teachings were compatible with Christian themes. They would find in Christianity elements that would help them fulfill their dreams of a Chinese republic of peace. He was a puzzle to many of the Chinese, most of whose leaders evidently had thought all Westerners were barbarian—but he was learned, scientific, and curious. Chinese leaders had not been very hospitable, but occasionally adaptive Catholics like Ricci won their way in part by expressing genuine respect for the science, mathematics, astronomy, and military craft of the Chinese.

Ricci won attention by giving a Chinese ruler something he

had not seen before: clocks. He spoke of the Lord of Heaven rather than of God. Some of his successors went further than Ricci, choosing to turn Jesus into a kind of Confucian wise man in order to make him acceptable. To the resistant Chinese he would have been the human Jesus but never the exalted Lord. Some critics considered Ricci to be playacting and charged that his approach was a hoax. Others complained that he did not truly learn from Chinese rites and respect them, but was friendly only for strategic reasons. Across all the distances, some authorities in Rome who tracked Ricci were determined to discipline over-adaptive priests and to forbid certain practices. These authorities were also divided. Some Jesuits won favor by permitting converts to venerate ancestors, while Dominicans took such a hard line on such issues that they could accomplish little. While Ricci died in 1610, his approach led to some acceptance of Christianity until finally in 1692 it became a tolerated faith.

## TARDY PROTESTANTS ADDRESS THE GLOBE

All this occurred while Europe was breaking apart as a result of conflicts among Catholics and Protestants. In the earliest decades of Protestant movements from the 1520s on, almost nothing was said or done among them to promote the idea of extending Christian influence into all parts of the world. Often the Protestant clerics possessed or generated no theology to justify an approach to Asians. Thus Martin Luther believed that the apostles had reached all of the world. Christians, he and his colleagues argued, could help supply new pastors and teachers in these places and for such presences, but they were not to make new inroads where Christianity had never been active. In this argument, clergy had to be "called," and it was not likely that Catholics would call Protestants to carry on their competitive work. For that reason and others among other evangelicals, almost two centuries went by before these Protestants were stirred to go to Asia to make converts.

When they finally sailed, they entered with the force of some numbers. Like the Catholics, they were often able to advance best when they were linked to explorers and commercial interests. These they sometimes represented, at cost to specifically Christian efforts, because they were beholden to and thus inhibited by the colonial powers with whom they were thus identified. When on occasion in conscience they broke with these, they did so at the expense of their enterprises. The approach of these Protestants was also different from the strategies of Catholics. They could not hand out images, objects, and trinkets like those the priests used to render vivid the Christian story and scheme. They also could not come teaching reverence for the hundreds of saints to whom Catholics appealed. Saints were figures who often formed a kind of spiritual company for those converts who were leaving their old worlds and families behind. Indigenous peoples found the sacraments credible and attractive, since these often tied in with habits of a devotion to ritual within their cultures. Protestantism in that stage, and for that matter ever after, could not rely on a visible earthly leader, namely the pope, to represent divine authority and provide credentials. Its agents had to stress and impart the biblical story in print. They had to devise dictionaries, produce Bible translations, and help many natives become literate before they could bring them to Jesus. Still, they made their moves.

The question comes, as it has been voiced before and elsewhere: why did they do all this? The motives of the missionaries colored the Protestantism of Asia, and gave shape to theologies, institutions, and the ethos of converts. So, the questions come again: why? Were they mere chaplains to commercial interests and providers of soothed consciences for conscience-stricken colonial powers? That they often appeared to be such and that they sometimes took on such roles had to be obvious in the Raj in India and elsewhere. The many stories of chafing, uneasiness, and independence on the part of so many missionaries showed that they had other missions in mind than the commercial or military sort. They will never be understood until those who study them become aware of how vivid was their faith or their conclusion that the people they would not reach with baptism, conversion, and

Christian rites would be severed from God and punished forever. It was a heady notion for a young priestly or ministerial student looking for life work to realize that he might rescue lost souls.

Add to that motivation numbers of others, many of them born out of genuine interest in Chinese, Japanese, Koreans, and other Asians. While the agents of Christianity discerned high culture among many of the Asians, admiring their languages and the literature, which some of the missionaries set out to translate, they remained convinced of their own cultural superiority and worked to spread enlightenment and learning on that basis. Such activities irritated some commercial interests, since ignorant and virtually enslaved people were not as free to be independent and rebellious as were those who felt they had taken destiny into their own hands by converting religiously.

The register of Protestant preachers of the gospel includes their heroes just as those of Catholics did. In fact, these missionary ventures matched another new interest of many Protestant pioneers. In the eighteenth century a rather novel doctrine about the end of the world was developing. Christians had always had to account for an end to the Creation that had a beginning, and they employed various biblical scenarios to picture these alternatives. One of them came to be called "post-millennial." It held that Jesus would return to rule for a thousand years *after* Christians had achieved much good, converted many souls, and made the human scene attractive to this Savior who would gather his own for the future of blessing during a thousand-year rule.

Interestingly, in the middle of the nineteenth century, another novel version of the end-of-the-world story, called "pre-millennial," inspired another set of evangelizers. Drawing on a few usually overlooked prophecies in Ezekiel and Daniel and dream-passages in the Apocalypse or Revelation, the last book in the New Testament, the Bible readers foresaw a world getting not better and more attractive but instead more wicked, to the point that it merited divine destruction. The exalted Lord would revisit the human world in this chaos, snatch his saints away, and then return with them to establish a thousand years of utopian life. Such teaching inspired missionaries to try to rescue as many lost souls as possible in Asia before Christ returned. These two accents were embodied among two sets of Asian converts. One worked on "this-worldly" projects of education, sanitation, health care, and issues of justice. The other urgently set out to convert others, since the end of the world was near.

## PROTESTANT PIONEERS AND NEW OPENINGS IN CHINA

The Protestant pioneers, moved by millennial and humanitarian visions, arrived with the naval powers, which at first meant the Dutch from the Netherlands, who were developing colonies and encouraging trade. They came on five ships in 1601, agents of capitalism and almost unwitting initiators of a new phase of Christian life in Asia. They drove Portuguese Catholic merchants and priests out of many Indonesian islands. In 1599 they began to realize the need and opportunity to add Christian missions to their doings, issuing a decree that traders from Holland were "to teach the people living there in darkness the true Christian religion." In their eyes, Catholic predecessors had obviously been false. Some of the Dutch, like the Lutherans among them, excused themselves from undertaking mission under the influence of those biblical scholars who said that the apostles had already carried out Jesus' command to "teach all nations." Mission work among them was usually grudging and underreported in the Netherlands. Most scholars judge that the Dutch efforts to engage in mission and conversion was rather perfunctory, yet heirs of the seventeenth century remain as a particular Christian presence in Indonesia.

The English, meanwhile, were developing their global empire. While English chaplains had mingled for decades with non-English Europeans, Moravians and Danes among them, it was 1792 before the English work became serious. The pathfinder in India was a shoemaker, teacher, and Baptist preacher named William Carey (1761–1834), who is still celebrated by Protestants who support the global endeavor of Christianity. He wrote a book challenging Christians to break out of the boundaries of Western Christendom. Amazingly accurate in his statistical estimates, he showed how provincially European the Christian world had become, and proposed ways to get out of the box it had chosen. Urged by extreme Calvinists to leave conversion to God, not crediting human effort, he defied them and preached that they should "expect great things from God," and therefore should "attempt great things for God." Despite opposition on many fronts, he and a small party sailed in 1793. He got no cooperation from English authorities, and can hardly be considered a colonialist. His course of life bordered on the tragic. He spirited away with him a wife who was unprepared for a lonely and dangerous mission, suffered from mental illness, and has to be described as quite mad. A glimpse of Carey's outlook appears in the words of a hymn by Isaac Watts that he chose for his tombstone: "A wretched, poor, and helpless worm, On Thy kind arms I fall." It is not possible here to follow the trail of Carey or others who followed his example, but he had established a basic and simple pattern which the English followed and which was carried over into Baptist-type churches in India and beyond.

The English took over in India, ruling in the Raj from 1847 to 1947, when India became independent. The agents of the British gospel were not nobodies; many were memorable personalities who inspired biographies that in turn inspired new young men and, interestingly, women to join the missionary groups. Unlike the priests, most of the men were married, and, like Carey, they often took spouses and children into unhealthy climates and environments that were threatening to them. Surprisingly, many of the women became leaders, in the face of authorities in Europe or the United States who often tried to follow rule books that restricted and disciplined them, hence limiting their ministries there.

Chief among those who "opened" China was Robert Morrison (1782–1834), a Scottish Presbyterian who arrived under the auspices of the London Missionary Society in 1807. For thirty years he struggled against the British East India Company and imperial China, where trade and missionaries were alike unwelcome. He decided to translate the Bible, an act that benefited all subsequent agents of the gospel there. Not for seven years was he able to report a baptism. Some of the early converts were allowed to go where Morrison and his kind could not. Yet missionary and mercantile and imperial interests often collided in a time of great turmoil and wars, some of them evidence of resistance.

## ENDING AN EPISODE, TURNING A PAGE

Across Asia, then, in spite of tumult, Catholics and Protestants alike were coming to be at home. Though theirs were not indigenous religions, they won at least toeholds and beachheads for their work of conversion. Many of their outposts reflected their European countries and churches of origin. They did erect cathedrals, seminaries, schools, and hospitals, not for purposes of legacy but as entrees to new cultures. In the twentieth century the West kept sending missionaries, but by then the churches were growing independent and becoming indigenous. When China, Japan, and Korea engaged in armed conflict with each other, missionaries often suffered in their spiritual crossfire. When Mao Zedong won control of China in 1949, he set up repressive regimes which strenuously worked to end Christian influence. The "Cultural Revolution" for which he later called did undertake some needed civil reform, but it also produced innumerable martyrs and it inhibited religious expression. After World War II, in which Japan was a major member of the Axis which opposed Allies, including the United States, missions were jeopardized and the churches had to go on their own. After the war, churches became free to rebuild in Japan more than in most places in Asia, but they remain a small minority. Early in the new millennium it was estimated that fifty million Christians worshipped in China and millions more in Korea, which had been a resistant kingdom but one which, when it took to Christianity, followed its ways zealously.

It is not possible to make stops at every place along the way in Asia, Oceania, and the Pacific island world, but some indication of the Christian reach is obvious to observers of Australia and New Zealand. The former was stocked with English prisoners in the nineteenth century who were sent there as a penal colony. They transformed their situation and became a significant member of the British Empire, with churches favored by the British, though Australia later was one of the less "churched" among the Christian reaches. The churches there have been rather open in acknowledging not only the evil ways with which their ancestors kept the native populations out of the way, but also that they still fail to do them justice. The aboriginal people include many Christians, but most of them are aggrieved because of the treatment by the colonials. Surveyors of the scene in the South Pacific locate Christian presences in the colonial and post-colonial worlds in New Zealand, New Guinea, Indonesia, and Malaysia. Significant Christian presences, established by Dutch or English colonial powers, live rather anxiously in increasingly Muslim nations like Indonesia and Malaysia, but they have endured and taken part in the Christian ecumenical ventures, just as they became host to evangelical movements in the course of the twentieth century.

Christians in the Asian nations have generated theologies appropriate to the scene. After the Second Vatican Council in Rome, venturesome Catholics initiated dialogues with Hindus and Buddhists so openly that the Vatican disciplined some for "syncretism" or "universalism," code words for the mingling of faiths at the expense of Christian particularity, leaving behind Christian exclusivism, a move which exclusivists felt would mean the loss of Christian faith. Representative of indigenous social Christianity were figures like Toyohiko Kagawa (1888–1960), who became known for his activism, efforts to promote justice, and pacifism. After conversion he studied theology in Japan and the United States, and became critical of dogmatic and severe forms of Christianity. Arrested in 1940 for having been too conciliatory to China, he was freed in time to go to the United States and try to advance efforts to prevent World War II. He survived the war and became an exemplar of Christian activism on at least two continents.

If the first Christian episode in Asia ended around 1500, the second one shows little sign of ending. Any tour of global Christianity has to include Asia as a major stop, its many varieties allowing for identifications with many kinds of Christians elsewhere. Anyone haunted by the puzzling question which one of the gospels frames, "When the Son of Man comes, will he find faith on the earth?", could find evidence from millions of Africans and Asians that the answer would be "yes."

10.

# UNFINISHED
# EPISODES

*So what?"* is an abrupt colloquial question that can well serve to encounter those who wrestle with the concept and reality of global Christianity. *So,* it is said, the ambition and hope of early Christians to see their faith gain a worldwide reach is realized today. *So,* as everyone can observe, modern communication, travel, and economic forces make it possible for Christians almost anywhere to be in contact with Christians almost everywhere. *So,* further, the political and military situations expose Christians to common challenges, for example those posed by militant Islam, robbing them of security and giving them no place to hide. *So,* the ecumenical movement and the contemporary interfaith endeavors are now available to help lessen tensions based in religious rivalries. *So,* Christians on the various continents can learn from each other and trade hymns, prayers, and gifts. *So,* awareness of human devastation caused by natural disasters or human-made conflict may inspire Christians who have means to share with those who do not. *So,* the styles of Christian worship and witness in one part of the world, say Asia, can inform and color those of Christians in other parts. *So,* continuing our register: all these and many more evidences that Christianity is truly global demand interpretation by people who have acquired a global perspective: *then what?*

Tracing the story through twenty centuries and on six continents is an act that produces enthralling stories, but, one asks, what understandings and actions among Christians and non-Christians alike might follow these? The historians' tasks are complete when they have told the story. The history of Christianity in its second episodes in Africa or Asia has intrinsic value. Inevitably, however, historians and their readers will move beyond the interests of narrative, of telling and hearing tales, to ask some questions of meaning and, incidentally, of strategies. Here the richness of the promise deserves to be mined and appraised. Having done some probing and analyzing of the story, we shall now point in the

African and Asian directions, to what many call the southern world or the poor world, new horizons and renewed homes for Christians.

A word that comes to mind to describe the global venture of Christians is "irrepressible." When ancient persecutors set out to oppress them, the Christian survivors, inspired by the example of martyrs, engendered larger Christian communities. When the first Asian and African episodes ended, the irrepressible Christians became dominant in Europe. When Europeans warred among themselves over faith, some idealists among them helped spread the faith and saw it take root in South and North America. When northern Christianity or Christianity in the rich world began to decline, Africa and Asia became renewed sites for vigorous Christian expression. When modern totalitarianisms attempted to demolish all Christian sites and devastate all Christian presences, the faith survived. Thus in Germany, the Soviet Union, and China, to name only the giant totalitarianisms, rivers of ink were used and oceans of blood were shed. Yet, at the end of the time of suppression, Christianity had survived, often taking on new forms. Many of those who endured persecution and setback showed eagerness to participate in global Christian endeavors.

All speaking of rich promise has to be qualified at once by an assessment of some of the problems facing Christian presences in Africa and Asia. As for the latter of these, which I will now turn into a sort of case study, three continents today number more Christians than does Asia, with its approximately 350 million believers. In a couple of decades that number will likely have shrunk to only two: Africa and South America. The European presence wanes and the promise of Christianity elsewhere rises. The promise of further growth is obvious, but counter-forces are also strong. Much of Asia, beginning with the heartland of early Christianity, is Muslim and shows few signs of opening to Christianity. While there may be fifty million Christians in China, most of them hidden and unrepresented in the state-licensed church, the repressive agencies of the state remain strong and efficient. What some scholars call neo-Hinduism, neo-Buddhism, or neo-Confucianism represent a renewed vigor and often aggressiveness among Asian religions which sometimes had been quiescent and passive during the early modern centuries of Christian growth. To these "isms" must be added the rival ideologies and practices which compromise Christian expressions elsewhere: nationalism, materialism, political ideologies, secularism, and adoption of ways of life inimical or at least indifferent to Christianity.

Despite these forces and trends, the promise for Christians remains. One-fourth of the South Korean population is Christian. There a mixture of Pentecostals, mainline Protestants, Korean native religionists, and Catholics are productive and in some cases able and inspired to send missionaries to other continents. Three-fourths of the Philippine Islands population is Catholic, prospering but, as mentioned, also beleaguered where Muslim populations threaten. Philippine Catholicism is also transportable, its leaders even being able to export some clerics and members of religious orders to other continents. Christians elsewhere take lessons from the way these make gains.

Similarly, Christians who are equipped and motivated to engage other of the world religions find Asia more promising than Africa. This engagement must be differentiated from efforts to proselytize and convert people from other religions to Christianity. Instead, Roman Catholics in particular seek some kinds of common ground with Buddhists in Japan or Hindus in India, never expecting that the two partners in dialogue might someday in some way merge. Instead, they wish to draw upon resources of the other, as when Christians learn techniques of meditation from Buddhists or Hindus. Similarly, these experimenters seek to minimize the potential for conflict among faiths. The dialogue they favor is much more difficult to pursue in the Islamic world, so non-Muslim Asia will likely remain the best laboratory for interfaith inquiries.

When Christians from around the globe gather on intercontinental bases, they seek the specific gifts of Asian Christianity. This has been the case ever since the modern ecumenical movement was born at the missionary conference in Edinburgh, Scotland, in 1910. Mergers of church bodies in India, for example, have brought them into the central sphere of church unity movements.

Similarly, especially at and after the Second Vatican Council in the 1960s, worldwide Roman Catholicism has been attentive to the voices of Indian, Vietnamese, Philippine, and other Asian Catholic leaders. A road map of visits by Pope John Paul II at the end of the twentieth century suggests how intense the bonds among the billion Catholics across the continents have become.

We have traced the story of Christianity across the map and then around the globe in a series of episodes. The first Asian and African episodes were key to the development of early Christianity, but long before 1500 these had virtually ended. It is hard to picture any surviving but disappointed Christians in eighth-century Africa or fifteenth-century Asia who could have envisioned second episodes in either place, episodes which have seen the development of Christian communities that now number in the hundreds of millions. Similarly, while there has been continuity in the Christian presence in Europe, the first episode dominated by Western Catholicism or Protestantism came to an end. On its soil, as numerous Protestant movements came to prominence in much of northwest Europe, there to cooperate with strong Catholic witnesses, few observers in 1500 or often thereafter could have pictured the drastic decline in the Christian community in the old places by 2000. Will future demographers and analysts speak of that second Christian episode as having come to a virtual end?

Those who make attempts to count Christians suggest that one-third of the people around the globe are identified with Christianity, as they have been for a century, despite all the restrictions and liberations, declines and resurgences. Where they gather and what kind of influence they assert in various places shift. On every continent believers struggle with appropriate ways to witness to "the human Jesus the Jew as the exalted Lord." Some among them will be haunted and others impelled to action when they look into the future, read the gospels, and rehear the question Jesus posed among the first disciples. In the nature of the case it has to remain unanswered, but remains tantalizing: "When the Son of Man comes, will he find faith on the earth?"

# GLOSSARY

**agnosticism** An outlook on life which contends that humans do not know and probably cannot know answers to ultimate questions, such as about the existence of God.

**Albigensians** Members of a strict religious group which dissented from Catholicism in the Middle Ages; it was dualistic, which means that it conceived of a god of light and a god of darkness; Catholics regarded them as subversive and persecuted them.

**Anabaptists** Members of a group which opposed the baptism of infants, insisting that baptism was for people old enough to make their own decisions about faith. Other sixteenth-century Protestants persecuted them.

**Anchoritism** A form of monastic life in which devotees shunned company and lived as hermits, pursuing self-punishing ways of life.

**Anglican** The adjective describing what it means to be a member of the Church of England; its constituents regard themselves as "Catholic" in many senses, but are often seen as participants in Protestantism.

**Antioch** A city twenty miles from the Mediterranean in northwest Syria that may have been the third most populated city in the Roman Empire. Christians from Jerusalem fled to Antioch, and were there first called Christian. Bishops from Antioch were major figures in early Christian councils.

**Arianism** A movement devoted to the teachings of a presbyter in Alexandria, Egypt, which had great influence on early Christian debates, chiefly because its adherents denied that Jesus Christ was the Son of

God from eternity. It was condemned as early as in the Council of Nicaea in 325, and persisted to plague the orthodox.

**Arminianism** Named after Dutch theologian Jacobus Arminius (1560–1609), it was a critique of Calvinism in that it held that salvation belongs to all who believe in Christ, that he died for everyone, that the Holy Spirit enables believers to do good works and be holy, and that those who have been saved are able to lose the faith.

**Ascension** Might be called "Act II" of Jesus Christ's Resurrection; in the Book of Acts (or "Acts") (1:4–11), the story has Jesus being lifted from the sight of the disciples, taken to reign as the divine Son of God.

**Asia Minor** A western Asian territory whose boundaries roughly match those of modern Turkey; there Paul the apostle made early missionary trips, and in the fourth century and after it was a major site of Christian debates over doctrine.

**Axum** An ancient name for Ethiopia, a kingdom to which Frumentius (c. 325) brought Christianity, but in which Islam came to dominate in the seventh century.

**Baptist** A major Protestant emphasis which often produces church bodies in which infants are not baptized, local churches are quite independent of each other, and the believers have historically promoted religious freedom.

**Benedictine** A form of monasticism founded by Saint Benedict of Nursia after 529; it became a worldwide expression. Its members are known for the quality of their communal life and their ability to inspire reform of monasteries of all sorts.

**Cainites** A radical Gnostic sect which disdained worship of the Creator, whom they regarded as evil, and which celebrated Judas, the betrayer of Jesus.

**Calvinism** Derives from the teaching and practice of reformer John Calvin (1509–64) of Geneva, and which came to have great influence in Puritan England and New England, in the Netherlands, and elsewhere, whence it spread to all continents. Most notable in church history are teachings concerning divine foreknowledge and predestination, which holds that God is sovereign, in control, and serious. Opposed to and by Arminians.

**Carthage** North African coastal city, a major center of early Christianity in Africa and site of several African councils of bishops.

**cenobitic** The form of monastic life which stressed communal, not isolated, living and prayer.

**Chalcedon** Site of a major council in 451 at which bishops debated how the divine and human natures were present in Christ; they professed that the two natures met in him "unconfusedly, unchangeably, individually, and inseparably." This definition prevailed and remains influential into the present.

**chaplain** A cleric usually assigned to specific locations, among them military, in charitable institutions, and the like.

**Cistercians** One of the more strict and most influential of Benedictine orders of monks, founded in 1098 in France.

**Conciliarism** A movement based on the argument that councils of bishops share authority and may even have authority superior to that of the pope. It inspired arguments between popes and councils for two centuries before the fifteenth, but was reborn at the Second Vatican Council (1962–65), though not in forms of militant opposition between popes and the council of bishops.

**Confirmation** A Christian practice—a sacrament, in Roman Catholicism—from early Christian days, usually associated with infant baptism "reaffirmed," some say. It implies serious education and commitment.

**Congregationalist** A form of church government traced back to arguments within the Church of England in the Puritan era, living on where Protestants stress local control of churches.

**Corinth** An ancient Greek seaport, noted as a city of turmoil and experienced as such by the apostle Paul, who found tumult there and wrote two preserved letters which are rich in exposition of the faith but also interest in the details of church life.

**covenant** May refer to the "Old" and "New" Testaments, but can also be associated with any solemn agreement between God and humans or among humans.

**crucifixion** Believed to be the most savage form of punishment in ancient Rome. In it the condemned person was nailed or tied to a tree. It was reserved for uncommon and often revolutionary Christians—as well as Jesus Christ.

**Cyrene** A city founded by Greeks, the most important northern African port between Alexandria and Carthage, mentioned in the New Testament, home of numerous bishops.

**Deism** A philosophy popular in late-seventeenth- and early-eighteenth-century England and of some influence among the founding fathers in America; Deists held that an impersonal God created the world but does not take part in affairs of humans.

**denomination** While the term existed in England, it came to be of use in the United States to designate church bodies as voluntary agencies, independent of the state.

**Diatessaron** Around the year 150 a scholar named Tatian set out to "harmonize" the four gospels so they could be read as a continuous narrative.

**diet** An assembly convoked by princes or other authorities to deliberate imperial matters, especially on the European continent at the time of the birth of Protestantism.

**disciple** Any follower who tries to adhere to and propound the teachings of a leader; in Christian history it refers particularly to the first twelve people whom Jesus chose, according to the gospels.

**Divine Trinity** The classic Christian doctrine which witnesses to God the Father, Son, and Holy Spirit. A philosophical term not mentioned in the Bible, it set the stage for innumerable controversies in Christian history.

**Docetists** Believed that Jesus only "seemed" to be God in the form of a human; they believed that matter was evil, so God could not be part of matter, as bodies are.

**dogma** Refers to a formal doctrine of the church, one that possesses authority and is not lightly to be questioned, since it helps define the faith.

**Donatists** Made up a northern African movement in the fourth century; they vehemently disciplined those who had compromised to stay alive in persecutions. These Africans also used the movement to oppose the power of Rome in their areas.

**ecumenical/ecumenism** Comes from the word *oikoumene*, "the whole inhabited world," and signals the effort by Christians, mainly in the twentieth century, to overcome the differences that led them to be in separate and often conflicting church bodies.

**Edessa** The city in which Christians who spoke Syriac gathered in ancient times; it is the site of what is believed to be the oldest Christian worship structure.

**end-time** Signals the attempts of Christians to witness to the understanding that just as there had been a beginning at Creation, there would be some sort of end-time, perhaps through a violent apocalypse.

**Enlightenment** In Western Europe and then in the American colonies refers to thinkers who put a premium on reason over revelation, and devoted themselves to advancing science and promoting progress in human affairs.

**Ephesus** A city in Asia Minor which had been a center of devotion to the goddess Diana, but became newly famous because of the apostle Paul's visit and ministry there; it was also the location of a major church council in 431.

*episkopoi* "Overseers"—that is what the word means; it came to refer to bishops, who had oversight of clusters of believers in a general area.

**Essenes** A community of extremely pious and disciplined Jewish believers at the time of Jesus Christ. Some gathered near the Dead Sea and many scholars associate them with the famed Dead Sea Scrolls discovered in the middle of the twentieth century.

**Eucharist** Simply means "thanksgiving" and is one of the names Christians give to the sacred meal that is their central act of worship. For many it is interchangeable with terms like "Mass," "Lord's Supper," or "Holy Communion."

**evangelism** The name given to efforts made by Christians to spread their "evangel," gospel, or "good news" and to gain converts to the faith.

**excursus** A digression, a term useful in this book when it was necessary to deal with Christian moves that may well be taken up in both Eastern and Western Christianity but do not quite fit the plot of developments in either.

**Friesians** A Germanic people listed among barbarians in the Roman Empire and by Christian missionaries who converted them.

**Gaul** Another name for France, a part of the Roman Empire which was the scene of much early Christian activity in Europe.

**Gentiles** In biblical contexts were non-Jews, of interest in the writings of Paul and others among the first Christians who dealt with conflict between Jews and others.

**Gnosticism** Refers to secret "knowledge," and was chosen by numerous groups which surrounded and challenged orthodox Christianity, which accented "faith." For centuries Christians struggled to define themselves over against Gnostic movements.

**Hellenists** Greek-speaking Jews who represented one of the factions in first- and second-generation Christianity, and defined themselves over against temple worship.

**Hessians** Like the Friesians were Germanic peoples listed by Romans as barbarians, many of whom were converted by missionaries.

**Holy Communion** Refers to the Lord's Supper, which remembers the Last Supper before Jesus died, and which remains a sacrament into the present, sometimes under other names such as "The Lord's Supper" and "the Eucharist."

**Holy Spirit** Refers to "the Third Person of the Divine Trinity," along with the Father and the Son (Jesus Christ); Jesus promised that this Spirit would comfort and lead the disciples after his death, and the Holy Spirit is seen as remaining active by orthodox Christians everywhere.

**humanism** The name given to a movement of scholars in Western Europe who recovered ancient languages (Greek and Latin) and literature, and contributed to critical reforms in the church.

**Huns** "Barbarians" who plagued and attacked Rome and the Roman Empire, and were subjects of conversion by Christian missionaries.

**intercursus** A term invented here to represent an interruption of the plot, made necessary to introduce features that would inform the plot.

**Jacobites** Syrian Christians who, after the Council of Chalcedon in 451, rejected that council's definition of "two natures," divine and human in Christ, and were condemned at a council in 787.

**Jesuits** Members of the Society of Jesus founded in the 1530s by Ignatius of Loyola. One of the more aggressive and effective of Catholic religious orders, active in education and missionary work especially.

**Keraits** Belonged to Mongol tribes, and are interesting in Christian history because many of them upheld a Nestorian version of the doctrines.

**Kingdom of God** The common term Jesus in the gospels gave to the sovereign saving activity of God as embodied in and proclaimed by him.

**Logos** Means "word" in Greek and is applied in the Gospel of John to Jesus as the Word of God; it was a convenient term in discussions with philosophers in Greek contexts.

**Lombards** A Germanic people who ruled in a region of Italy and who gave trouble to Pope Gregory the Great and other popes and Holy Roman Emperors.

**Lutheran** A movement and a church that relates to the reformer Martin Luther (1483–1546); it is central to the development of Protestantism.

**Magyars** Migrated from Asia to Hungary in the ninth century, and represent a family of languages distinctive among Romance, Germanic, and other European tongues.

**Manichaeism** Derives from the teachings of Mani (216–276 or 277), who had great influence among Persians, but also had a bearing on many Christian developments. Light versus Dark and God and Matter are eternal; Jesus is an example of Light, which for a time is held in prison by Dark matter.

**Mass** Another word for the Lord's Supper, Holy Communion, or the Eucharist; it is the sacred meal observed by most Christians. The term comes from *missio*, referring to the "dismissal" of worshippers who were not eligible to receive the sacrament.

**memory-impression** A term used by some modern New Testament scholars to refer to the fact that behind the writing of the gospels were profound impressions left by Jesus on those who followed him.

**Mennonites,** who are Anabaptists, founded in Switzerland and the Low Countries; named after Menno Simons, one of the leaders of the group, which was persecuted by Catholics and Protestants alike. Mennonites stress simple and disciplined living.

*messias*/**Messiah**  Hebrew and Aramaic word for "anointed," and is applied in the gospels to Jesus and in some instances by Jesus to affirm that he was chosen by God for his specific mission. Most Jews looked for an Anointed One to lead them from oppression by conquerors and rulers.

**Methodism**  Began as a reform movement in the Church of England, particularly under the impetus of John Wesley (1703–91), who stressed Christian experience and holy living. It became a worldwide movement which accented missionary work.

**modernism**  In Catholicism, a movement to adapt Catholic teaching to the "enlightened" modern world; it was condemned by the papacy. In Protestantism it has been longer-lived, again as an effort to relate positively to science and modern philosophy.

**Monophysites**  Made up a party in the Eastern Church, people who rejected the teaching of the Council of Chalcedon: they held that in Jesus there was only a divine nature, not a dual divine-human nature.

**monotheism**  The belief in one God, over against pan- or poly- or other theisms, which held that all nature was "god" or that there were many gods. Jews and Muslims share monotheistic witness with Christians.

**Montanism**  Developed in Phrygia in the second century and spread beyond thanks to the missionary energies of some of its adherents; Montanists believed that the Holy Spirit worked among them in immediate ways, including through prophecy.

**Moravians**  Spiritual descendants of Jan Hus, a reformer who was condemned at the Council of Constance in 1415; in 1722 they were welcomed to the estate of Count Ludwig von Zinzendorf, from where they felt called to do missionary work in the United States and eventually in many places around the world.

**Mormon**  Another name for the Church of Jesus Christ of Latter-day Saints, founded in the 1830s by Joseph Smith, who claimed direct divine revelation of a new covenant, one which most other Christians regard as a new tradition far from orthodox Christianity. It grows rapidly in many parts of the world.

**Nestorians**  Did not agree with church councils which professed that Jesus Christ was a single Person, God and man. Instead, he was seen as two separate Persons, one divine and the other human. Followers of

Nestorius (?–451) rejected the council reference to the Virgin Mary as *theotokos,* the bearer of God. They remained a strong presence in Asia for a number of centuries.

**Novatianism** Developed after a persecution in 249–250, and joined with other parties in refusing to welcome back to the church those who had run from persecution. They were orthodox, but were nevertheless excommunicated.

**Numidia** Was a kingdom of Berbers which by the time of early Christian development had come under Roman rule.

*oikoumene* See "ecumenical/ecumenism"; *oikoumene* is a Greek term referring to the whole inhabited world.

**Old Testament** The name given to thirty-nine books of the Hebrew Scriptures, which became part of the Christian canon.

**pagan** Meant someone who came from a rural district, but in religion and especially in Christianity it came to represent those who had no religion or who had religions vastly different from Christianity, Judaism, Islam, and the like.

**parable** Can refer to all kinds of sayings and stories, but in Christianity it is usually associated with the teachings of Jesus, remembered and reproduced as stories designed to make a single point about the Kingdom of God.

**parish** A local congregation of Christians; in some church bodies, the boundaries within which adherents live are set by authority.

**Passion** In Christian language, refers to the suffering and death of Jesus Christ.

**patriarchate** Originally referred to the five bases for Christian "patriarch" bishops: Rome, Alexandria, Antioch, Constantinople, and Jerusalem, but in the modern Eastern Christian Church additional governing centers have been added.

*patronato* A right of "patronage" given by the pope to conquering regimes such as the Spanish in Latin America; it subjected the people within realms governed by such regimes to church and state regulations.

**Pentecost** The fiftieth day after the Resurrection of Jesus Christ; it had been a harvest festival in ancient Israel, but in the New Testament accounts it came to be associated by Christians with an event in which the Holy Spirit came to the disciples.

**Pentecostalism** Founded in the United States between 1900 and 1906 and has since spread to number hundreds of millions of followers, especially in Africa and Latin America. It witnesses to special gifts of the Holy Spirit, including healing.

**peregrinators** Monks who were not cloistered, which means not confined to one enclosed monastery, but were free to peregrinate, to wander, to lead pilgrimages, and the like.

**Pharisees** Strict followers of Jewish law, admired by many for their rigor and holiness, but in the gospels are usually poised over against Jesus, who accused them of hypocrisy and holding to false standards.

**Phoenicia** An ancient empire, but in the time of Jesus part of a Syrian province in the Roman Empire; it was north of Palestine.

**Presbyterian** A church body, a movement, or a form of government which stresses the rule of presbyters or elders; it is part of the Reformed or Calvinist family of churches, founded in Scotland by John Knox.

**profane/*profano*** Refers to that which does not belong in the sanctuary.

**Punic** Refers to northern African people whom the Romans fought and Christians regarded as barbarians whom they must convert.

**purgatory** In Roman Catholic teaching is a place (some would say "state") in which Catholics who have received grace are still punished for their sins after death, when and where they are purged before entering heaven.

**Quakers** A radical Christian movement founded by George Fox in the middle of the seventeenth century; they believe in the direct witness and revelation of the Holy Spirit.

**sacrament** The term for specific sacred rites in Christianity, beginning with baptism and the Lord's Supper or Eucharist. Most Protestants number only those two, while Catholicism lists seven.

**Sadducees** Opposed the Pharisees among the Jewish movements in Jesus' time; they tended to be aristocratic and wealthy as well as involved in politics.

**Samaritans** People who lived in Samaria, north of Judea and south of Galilee (Jesus' two main areas of operation). Jews conventionally disdained them, while the gospels show Jesus having more generous relations to them.

**Sassanids** The rulers in the last dynasty in Persia before the conquest by Muslims.

**sect** A faction, usually well defined, within a larger generic Christian body.

**secular** Can mean something as simple as not being under churchly control. It can also refer to an outlook on life which has no interest in and may be opposed to Christian explanations or rule.

**Separatist** A party of Puritans or Congregationalists in England and New England which would have nothing to do with the Church of England or other churches beyond the local or not associated with their movement.

*sobornost* A term favored by Eastern Orthodox Christian philosophers to suggest organic relatedness, "togetherness," things having an integral relation to each other; it was used to oppose Christian individualism, and has deep roots in Russian thought.

**Social Gospel** Refers to efforts by liberal Protestants in America early in the twentieth century to relate Christian teaching and action to social causes and reforms.

**synod** A churchly assembly, perhaps of bishops (as in Catholicism) or presbyteries and congregations; it can also be part of the name of a church body.

*theanthropos* Eastern Orthodox Christians like to use this word, which combines the Greek for "God" and "Man" to witness to the fact that Jesus is both divine and human.

**Tours** The home of Saint Martin, known as a stop for pilgrims in the Loire Valley.

**transubstantiation** A term that reflects Greek and Latin influences on biblical stories about the "substance" of bread and wine in the Lord's Supper; Catholics believe that the "substance" of bread and wine, despite appearances, turns into the body and blood of Jesus in the sacrament.

**Unitarians** Became a movement in the time of the Reformation (sixteenth century), and remain today in the United States and parts of Europe, to reject the Trinity.

**Vandals** Successful "barbarian" invaders of Spain and Italy early in the fifth century.

**Visigoths** Like the Vandals, invaded southern Europe, especially Spain and Italy; they sacked Rome in 455.

**witness** A word for "testimony"—a strong concept in Christianity, whether within the New Testament among people who had "seen" Jesus or their successors who carried out the personal word of their faith.

**Zealots** A radical revolutionary party in Israel around 66–70; they resisted Roman rule.

**Zoroastrianism** Prominent, even dominant, in the Persian Empire for a thousand years before Muslims invaded in 636. It is an ethical religion, posed over against the popular religions of Iran.

**Zwinglians** Reformers who helped shape Protestantism in sixteenth-century Switzerland, in the path of Huldreich Zwingli.

# Acknowledgments

In a work of this scope an author welcomes critiques by scholars in a variety of fields, along with suggestions from a sampling of general readers. I am indebted to the following readers of this manuscript, and I thank them: Albert Buelow, Mark Edwards, Paul Elbert, Paul Goetting, Stanley Grabarek, Dean Lueking, Joseph Price, Stephen Rowe, and Gertrude Stoffregen. Harriet Julia Marty heard and read the manuscript and assisted with proofreading, and I am grateful to her for her participation and encouragement, as always.

Authors also profit from the efforts of usually nameless personnel in the publishing house. In this instance, I want to name David Ebershoff, Diana Fox, and Vincent La Scala, who were especially attentive in matters editorial.

# INDEX

MARTIN MARTY is the Fairfax M. Cone Distinguished Service Professor Emeritus at the University of Chicago, where for thirty-five years he taught in the Divinity School, the history department, and on the Committee on the History of Culture. His focus is on American religious history, but since 1988 he has enlarged his specialty to include global concerns. Typical of these is the five-volume work *The Fundamentalism Project* for the American Academy of Arts and Sciences, which he co-edited. He was subsequently awarded the Academy's medal. He also received the National Humanities Medal and the National Book Award.

Author of over fifty books, he wrote the three-volume *Modern American Religion,* which is considered to be a landmark in its field. An ordained Lutheran minister, he has been engaged in ecumenical and inter-religious work for decades, and is past president of the American Catholic Historical Association, the American Society of Church History, and the American Academy of Religion.

He and his wife, Harriet, a musician, live in Chicago.